SEXUAL ORIENTATION, GENDER IDENTITY, AND THE LAW

IN A NUTSHELL®

FOURTH EDITION

RUTH COLKER
Distinguished University Professor Emerita
Heck-Faust Memorial Chair in
Constitutional Law Emerita
Michael E. Moritz College of Law,
The Ohio State University

WEST ACADEMIC

860 Blue Gentian Road, Suite 350
Eagan, MN 55121
1-877-888-1330

Published in the United States of America

ISBN: 979-8-89545-459-6

PREFACE

The objective of this book is to help law students, lawyers and others recognize and understand the federal and state laws protecting the lesbian, gay, bisexual and transgender community from discrimination. Students taking courses related to sexual orientation, sexuality, and gender are among the intended beneficiaries. The book will also benefit other students as well, such as those taking courses on civil rights issues. In addition, the book will assist lawyers, educators, employers, members of the LGBTQ+ community and others who have direct or indirect interests in these significant federal and state laws, either on their own behalf or on behalf of those they represent or with whom they work.

As with all Nutshells, a word of caution is required. This book presents an *overview* of the relevant federal and state laws and major legal decisions pertaining to discrimination against the LGBTQ+ community. It is not intended to provide a comprehensive analysis of those laws. Case citations are provided but the citations are not exhaustive as might occur with a Treatise. With a few exceptions, there is little discussion of policy issues, although the relevant statutes, regulations and case law are often placed in historical perspective for clarity.

This *Nutshell* reflects updates as of July 2025 in a rapidly changing area of the law. Where appropriate, this *Nutshell* notes areas of uncertainty but the last decade of legal developments should highlight the enormous uncertainty nearly always present in this area of the law.

This edition of the *Nutshell* was made possible by a generous research grant from the Michael E. Moritz College of Law at The Ohio State University, and the research assistance of Moritz Reference Librarian Stephanie Ziegler.

RUTH COLKER

July 2025

OUTLINE

TABLE OF CASES

References are to Pages

SEXUAL ORIENTATION, GENDER IDENTITY, AND THE LAW

IN A NUTSHELL®

FOURTH EDITION

CHAPTER 1
INTRODUCTION AND OVERVIEW

§ 1.1 HISTORICAL BACKGROUND

The topic of this *Nutshell*—sexual orientation, gender identity and the law—is one that has rapidly evolved in the last several decades.

Until 1961, when Illinois repealed its sodomy statute, every state in the United States had a sodomy statute. These statutes frequently banned non-procreative sexual activity by heterosexuals or homosexuals. It was not until the American Law Institute promulgated the Model Penal Code in 1955 and recommended that legislatures decriminalize consensual sexual relations conducted in private that state legislatures began updating their criminal law to eliminate such legislation. *See* Model Penal Code § 213.2, cmt. 2, at 372 (Am. Law Inst. 1980). Nonetheless, it was not until 2003 that the United States Supreme Court overturned the remaining sodomy laws in *Lawrence v. Texas*, 539 U.S. 558 (2003).

When Bill Clinton ran for President of the United States in 1992, he pledged to lift the ban on gay men and lesbians serving openly in the military. *See* Dan Belz, *A Promise That Held Inevitable Collision*, WASH. POST, Jan. 28, 1993 at A6. At that time, Department of Defense regulations stated: "Homosexuality is incompatible with military service." 32 C.F.R. pt. 41, app. A (1992). Despite that campaign pledge, Congress adopted a statute often described as "Don't Ask, Don't Tell," ("DADT"), which maintained the policy that "[t]he presence in the armed forces of persons who demonstrate a propensity or intent to engage in homosexual acts would create an unacceptable risk to the high standards of morale, good order and discipline, and unit cohesion that are the essence of military capability." 10 U.S.C. § 654(a)(15) (2006) (repealed 2010). Congress enacted legislation to repeal DADT in December 2010 and the policy formally ended on September 20, 2011. Don't Ask, Don't Tell Act of 2010, Pub. L. No. 111–321, § 2(f)(1)(A), 124 Stat. 3515, 3516.

Until 1993, marriage between same-sex couples was not possible in any state in the United States. For a brief period following the Hawaii Supreme Court's decision in *Baehr v. Lewin*, 852 P.2d 44, 74 (1993) that excluding same-sex couples from marriage was presumptively invalid, it appeared that same-sex couples would be able to marry in Hawaii. Following action by both the Hawaii state legislature and the voters of Hawaii to amend the state constitution, same-sex marriage did not become possible in Hawaii at that time. Nationally, Congress responded to the possibility of same-sex marriage by enacting the Defense of Marriage Act, ("DOMA"), Pub. L. No. 104–199, 110 Stat. 2419 (1996) by a veto-proof margin in 1996. Following the adoption of DOMA, more than half of the states amended their state constitutions to prohibit the recognition of same-sex marriage. It was not until 2004, as a result of a legal decision, that one state—Massachusetts—

began to permit same-sex marriages. *See Goodridge v. Dep't of Pub. Health*, 798 N.E.2d 941 (Mass. 2003).

And, then, in 2014 and 2015, the United States Supreme Court concluded that § 2 and § 3 of DOMA were unconstitutional and that, additionally, it was unconstitutional for states to ban same-sex marriage. *See Obergefell v. Hodges*, 576 U.S. 644 (2015) (discussed in *Nutshell* § 5.6). In the span of 20 years, same-sex marriage went from being a legal non-entity to a right in every state in the United States.

The legal developments, for those who identify broadly as "trans," have been less dramatic but have also been evolving in a more protective manner. When the gay rights community first proposed the "Employment Nondiscrimination Act," which was a federal law to prohibit discrimination against gay men, lesbians, and bisexuals, that bill explicitly did not seek to extend protections to people on the basis of "trans" identity or expression. *See, e.g.*, S. 2056, 104th Cong. (1996). Nonetheless, the most recently proposed "Equality Act" seeks to ban discrimination on the basis of one's "gender identity" which is defined as the "gender-related identity, appearance, mannerisms, or other gender-related characteristics of an individual, regardless of the individual's designated sex at birth." *See* H.R. 5, 116th Cong. (2019). Further, in 2020, the Supreme Court interpreted Title VII to ban discrimination both on the basis of sexual orientation and transgender status. *See Bostock v. Clayton County*, 590 U.S. 644 (2020). Nonetheless, as we will see in Ch. 3, there have also been significant attempts at the state and local government level to impose discrimination on transgender people.

This Fourth Edition is being published as many areas of LGBTQ+ protection are coming under steady attack. The courts have begun to backtrack on some victories in this area. The claims for religious protection from enforcement of LGBTQ+ rights is also ongoing and often receiving a receptive ear by the courts. Thus, it is important that the reader update any discussions in this *Nutshell* with an assessment of further developments.

§ 1.2 OVERVIEW

The topic of the rights of the LGBTQ+ community is very broad and could include a nearly endless list of topics. This *Nutshell* has tried to focus on the topics that are unique to the LGBTQ+ community rather than focus on the topic of "gender" broadly as it applies to these communities and others. In other words, this is not a *Nutshell* on the broad topics of sex or gender discrimination. The topics included in this *Nutshell* include: regulation of sexuality, regulation of gender/appearance, regulation of marriage and family, the United States military, federal state and local nondiscrimination statutes and ordinances, First Amendment case law, and religious freedom. But these topics are only covered as they relate to the LGBTQ+ community.

This topic is very dynamic as reflected in the abrupt reversal of abortion protection in 2022 with a potential impact on LGBTQ+ rights. This *Nutshell* is not intended to serve as a substitute for thorough analysis and examination of the very complex legal rules at issue. It should be used as guidance only, for a very broad background of the subject matter. Readers are encouraged to supplement this *Nutshell* with research on the current legal rules.

CHAPTER 2
REGULATION OF SEXUALITY

§ 2.1 EARLY SODOMY CASES

Historically, state sodomy statutes often proscribed "crimes against nature" that prohibited non-procreative sexual practices of both heterosexuals and homosexuals, although gay men typically faced the brunt of the enforcement of such statutes. The United States Supreme Court ruled in a *per curiam* opinion in *Rose v. Locke*, 423 U.S. 48 (1975) that such statutes were not unconstitutionally vague.

The legal profession sought to decriminalize sodomy in the 1960s. The Model Penal Code of 1955 endorsed such decriminalization. *See* Model Penal Code § 213.2, cmt. 2, at 372 (Am. Law Inst. 1980). Similarly, the British *Wolfenden Report* of 1957 recommended the decriminalization of sodomy. Committee on Homosexual Offenses and Prostitution, *The Wolfenden Report*, 33 BRIT. J. VENER. DIS. 205 (1957), available at http://www.ncbi.nlm.nih.gov/pmc/articles/PMC1054166/pdf/brjvendis00142-0001.pdf. Great Britain repealed the prohibition against private consensual sodomy in 1967. Sexual Offences Act 1967, ch. 60, § 1. State law in the United States largely governs such matters. The first state to repeal its sodomy law was Connecticut in 1969. Not all states moved in that direction; Texas adopted a sodomy law limited to criminalizing same-sex sexual activity in 1973. *See generally* WILLIAM ESKRIDGE, JR., GAYLAW: CHALLENGING THE APARTHEID OF THE CLOSET (1999).

State law was not the only arena in which the LGBTQ+ community faced adverse treatment due to their sexual activities. The 1952 Immigration and Nationality Act, for example, barred entry of immigrants "afflicted with psychopathic personality," which the Immigration and Naturalization Service interpreted to include all "homosexuals and sex perverts." *See* Jorge L. Carro, *From Constitutional Psychopathic Inferiority to AIDS: What Is in the Future for Homosexual Aliens?*, 7 YALE L. & POL. REV. 201, 209–11. (1989). That statute was used to deport Clive Michael Boutilier to Canada who was characterized as having a "psychopathic personality" due to his "sexual deviation." Boutilier challenged his deportation on the grounds that Congress did not intend the statute to exclude homosexuals. The Supreme Court ruled that "Congress used the phrase 'psychopathic personality' not in the clinical sense, but to effectuate its purpose to exclude from entry all homosexuals and other sex perverts." *Boutilier v. Immigration and Naturalization Serv.*, 387 U.S. 118, 122 (1967). Boutilier also argued the statute was unconstitutionally vague, but the Court ruled that the "fair warning" rule has no applicability to the admission of aliens. *Id.* at 124. Thus, it affirmed the ruling of the court below. Justices Douglas and Fortas dissented. While they considered the homosexual to be "one, who by some freak, is the product of an arrested development," they concluded that he should not be considered someone who is "afflicted" with a psychopathic personality. *Id.* at 127, 133. Congress repealed the exclusion of homosexuals in 1990. Immigration Act of 1990, Pub. L. No. 101–649, § 601, 104 Stat. 4978.

Following the Supreme Court's ruling in *Griswold v. Connecticut*, 381 U.S. 479 (1965) that the Due Process Clause of the Fourteenth Amendment could be interpreted to protect a woman's right to use contraceptives, the LGBTQ+ legal community thought that it might be time for the Court to similarly conclude that the Fourteenth Amendment's Due Process Clause also protected the right of the LGBTQ+ community to engage in consensual sexual activity. Citing Justice Goldberg's concurrence in *Griswold* in which he emphasized that "adultery, homosexuality and the like are sexual intimacies which the State forbids," a three-judge district court in Virginia rejected that argument in *Doe v. Commonwealth's Attorney for Richmond*, 403 F. Supp. 1199, 1201 (E.D. Va. 1975). The United States Supreme Court summarily affirmed that decision. *See Doe v. Commonwealth's Att'y for Richmond*, 425 U.S. 901 (1976) (Justices Brennan, Marshall and Stevens stating that they would have noted probable jurisdiction and set the case for oral argument).

§ 2.2 BOWERS V. HARDWICK

Despite the loss in *Doe v. Commonwealth's Attorney*, the LGBTQ+ community thought that the Court's abortion jurisprudence would lead it to provide similar due process protections to the sexual activity of gay men and lesbians. Thus, the American

Civil Liberties Union ("ACLU") and other organizations continued to look for the appropriate case to challenge state sodomy laws. After Michael Hardwick was arrested in 1982 for violating the state of Georgia's sodomy laws, the ACLU brought such a case. The Georgia sodomy statute, on its face, applied to both heterosexual and homosexual conduct, making it a criminal offense when a person "performs or submits to any sexual act involving the sex organs of one person and the mouth or anus of another." Ga. Code Ann. § 16–6–2(a) (1984). It also proscribed a significant penalty: "A person convicted of the offense of sodomy shall be punished by imprisonment for not less than one nor more than 20 years." *Id.* at § 16–6–2(b).

In the original complaint, Michael Hardwick was joined in challenging the state sodomy statute by John and Mary Doe, a married, heterosexual couple who claimed that they desired to engage in sexual activity proscribed by the statute, but they had been "chilled and deterred" by the existence of the statute and the recent arrest of their acquaintance, Michael Hardwick. *Hardwick v. Bowers*, 760 F.2d 1202 (11th Cir. 1985), *rev'd*, 478 U.S. 186 (1986). The district court ruled that the Does did not have standing to bring suit and that Hardwick's legal claim was foreclosed by the earlier *Doe* decision. *Id.* at 1204. The Eleventh Circuit affirmed the dismissal of the Does from the lawsuit but remanded the case back to the district court to consider the argument that Hardwick's constitutional right to personal autonomy regarding "decisions [that] are essentially private and beyond the legitimate reach of a civilized society" had been violated. *Id.* at 1211. It remanded the case for trial "at which time the State must prove in order to prevail that it has a compelling interest in regulating this behavior and that this statute is the most narrowly drawn means of safeguarding that interest." *Id.* at 1213. That legal standard is what is often called the "strict scrutiny" standard—requiring proof of compelling state interest for the "ends" and narrowly drawn rules for the "means" to serve those ends. Judge Kravitch dissented, concluding that the Eleventh Circuit was bound by the *Doe* decision.

The state appealed the Eleventh Circuit's decision to the Supreme Court, which accepted certiorari. Justice White delivered the 5–4 opinion for the Court, reversing the Eleventh Circuit decision on the merits. *Bowers v. Hardwick,* 478 U.S. 186 (1986). Chief Justice Burger and Justices Powell, Rehnquist, and O'Connor joined the majority opinion. Justices Burger and Powell filed concurring opinions. Justices Blackmun and Stevens filed dissenting opinions. Reportedly, Justice Powell initially voted to affirm the Eleventh Circuit decision but changed his mind before the final decision was issued. *See* Bruce C. Hafen, *Individualism and Autonomy in Family Law: The Waning of Belonging,* 1991 BYU L. REV. 1, 10.

In reversing the Eleventh Circuit, the Supreme Court did not merely rely on its summary affirmance in *Doe.* Instead, it chose to give "plenary consideration to the merits" of the case. *Id.* at 190 n.4. Unlike the Eleventh Circuit, it concluded that strict scrutiny was not appropriate because Hardwick had not alleged the deprivation of a fundamental right.

First, the Court concluded that its prior cases should not be construed "to confer a right of privacy that extends to homosexual sodomy." *Id.* at 190. It found that those cases were limited to matters involving family, marriage or procreation; they did not "stand for the proposition that any kind of private sexual conduct between consenting adults is constitutionally insulated from state proscription." *Id.* at 191.

Having established that prior precedent did not create a right to "homosexual sodomy," the court then asked if it would be appropriate for it to "announce" such a right. *Id.* at 191. The applicable standard, the Court said, to determine if such a new right should be identified is whether the new right is one that is " 'implicit in the concept of ordered liberty' such that 'neither liberty nor justice would exist if [they] were sacrificed.' " *Id.* at 191–92 (quoting *Palko v. Conn.*, 302 U.S. 319 (1937)). The right to "homosexual sodomy" did not meet that legal standard because the Court concluded that "[p]roscriptions against that conduct have ancient roots." *Id.* at 192. Further, the Court concluded that it would be inappropriate for it to take an "expansive view" of its authority to "discover new fundamental rights," because the "Court is most vulnerable and comes nearest to illegitimacy when it deals with judge-made constitutional law having little or no cognizable roots in the language or design of the Constitution." *Id.* at 194.

Concluding that there was no basis to use strict scrutiny to consider the violation of a fundamental right, the Court asked if the state statute could be invalidated under the traditional rational basis test. Under that test, one asks if the state statute furthered a "legitimate" state interest and if the means chosen were "rationally related" to that legitimate state interest. Hardwick argued that the only basis to support this law was the view of the Georgia electorate that homosexual sodomy is immoral, and such a view is not enough to sustain a statute under the rational basis test. The Court disagreed, concluding that it would be inappropriate to invalidate the sodomy laws of twenty-five states on the basis that their moral choice is constitutionally invalid. *Id.* at 196.

Justice Burger concurred separately to emphasize that proscriptions against sodomy have "very ancient roots." *Id.* at 196. Justice Powell's concurrence noted that he might have been inclined to conclude that the statute violated the Eighth Amendment, but that issue was not presented in this case, in part because the state had chosen not to present a charge to a grand jury. Further, he was persuaded by the fact that there has been a history of nonenforcement of such statutes, making them of a "moribund character." *Id.* at 198 n.2. He also explained that he joined the majority opinion because he could not "say that conduct condemned for hundreds of years has now become a fundamental right." *Id.* at 198 n.2. Justice Powell's emphasis on the "moribund" character of sodomy laws caused the LGBTQ+ legal community to emphasize in future cases the impact these laws have on the lives of the LGBTQ+ community, even if prosecutions are unlikely.

Justice Blackmun's dissent, which was joined by Justices Brennan, Marshall and Stevens, took issue with the majority's assumption that the case involved the right to engage in "homosexual sodomy," especially because the Georgia statute applied to both heterosexual and homosexual sexual activity. *Id.* at 199. Instead, he characterized the case as being about the "right to be left alone." *Id.* at 199 (citing *Olmstead v. United States*, 277 U.S. 438, 478 (1928)). Justice Blackmun concluded that the issue raised in the case was protected by the Court's prior privacy jurisprudence because it included both the "decisional and spatial aspects of the right to privacy." *Id.* at 204. The case involved a right to make important decisions about one's intimate associations and the alleged conduct occurred in the privacy of Hardwick's home. *Id.* at 206.

Justice Blackmun also took issue with the concept that religious doctrine, alone, can justify state legislation. "The legitimacy of secular legislation depends instead on whether the State can advance some justification for its law beyond its conformity to religious doctrine." *Id.* at 211. He ended his opinion with the prediction that the Court would someday see the error of its decision in this case.

> I can only hope that . . . . the Court soon will reconsider its analysis and conclude that depriving individuals of the right to choose for themselves how to conduct their intimate relationships poses a far greater threat to the values most deeply rooted in our Nation's

> history than tolerance of non-conformity could ever do.

Id. at 214.

Justice Stevens also authored a dissent, which was joined by Justices Brennan and Marshall (but not Blackmun). He focused on the fact that the state chose to enforce the sodomy statute only against homosexuals. He concluded that such selective enforcement could not be constitutionally justified. Although the majority concluded that the statute could be justified by the "presumed belief of a majority of the electorate in Georgia that homosexual sodomy is immoral and unacceptable," he argued that the Georgia legislature did not "single out homosexuals as a separate class meriting special disfavored treatment." *Id.* at 219. His dissenting opinion is the first hint of an equal protection approach to considering issues involving unfavorable treatment of gay men and lesbians. (It would be some time before any members of the Court showed concern about discrimination against members of the transgender community.)

§ 2.3 STATE INVALIDATION OR REPEAL OF SODOMY STATUTES

Despite the defeat in *Bowers v. Hardwick*, the LGBTQ+ legal community sought to use state constitutional law as a basis to overturn state sodomy statutes. Before *Bowers* was decided, those efforts were successful in New York and Pennsylvania. *See People v. Onofre*, 415 N.E.2d 936 (N.Y. 1980); *see also Commonwealth v. Bonadio*, 415

A.2d 47 (Pa. 1980). Following *Bowers*, those efforts were successful in Georgia, Kentucky, Montana, and Tennessee. *See Jegley v. Picado*, 80 S.W.3d 332 (Ark. 2002); *Powell v. State*, 510 S.E.2d 18 (Ga. 1998); *Commonwealth v. Wasson*, 842 S.W.2d 487 (Ky. 1992); *Gryczan v. State*, 942 P.2d 112 (Mont. 1997); *Campbell v. Sundquist*, 926 S.W.2d 250 (Tenn. Ct. App. 1996). These courts typically concluded that the state sodomy statute violated both the liberty and equality interests of the gay men who brought these challenges. While resting its decision on state law grounds, the Kentucky Court was quite critical of the United States Supreme Court, saying "We view the United States Supreme Court decision in *Bowers v. Hardwick, supra*, as a misdirected application of the theory of original intent." *Kentucky v. Wasson*, 842 S.W.2d at 497.

Not all state courts, however, concluded that sodomy statutes should be overturned on state constitutional grounds. *See, e.g., State v. Walsh*, 713 S.W.2d 508 (Mo. 1986); *Sawatzky v. Oklahoma City*, 906 P.2d 785 (Okla. Crim. App. 1995).

Some states also repealed their state sodomy statutes. Arizona, the District of Columbia, Nevada and Rhode Island did so. *See* Ariz. Rev. Stat. Ann. ch. 14, § 13–1411 (2010) *repealed by* Equity Act of 2001, ch. 382, § 1; D.C. Code § 22–3502 (2010) (repealed 1995); Nev. Rev. Stat. Ann. § 201.193 (LexisNexis 2012) *repealed by* Acts 1993, ch. 236, § 5, 518; 11 R.I. Gen. Laws § 11–10–1 (2002) (repealed 1998). *See also* Melinda D. Kane, *Timing Matters: Shifts in the Casual Determinations of Sodomy Law*

Decriminalization, 1961–1998, 54 SOC. PROBLEMS 211, 214 tbl.1 (2007), available at https://academic.oup.com/socpro/article-abstract/54/2/211/1676064.

§ 2.4 LAWRENCE V. TEXAS

When the Supreme Court refused to extend the *Griswold* line of cases to the *Bowers* decision, some members of the legal community thought the Court was foreshadowing that it was willing to overturn *Roe v. Wade*. In 1992, however, the Court re-affirmed *Roe* in *Planned Parenthood of Southeastern Pennsylvania v. Casey*, 505 U.S. 833 (1992), giving new hope to the LGBTQ+ legal community that the Supreme Court might still invalidate state sodomy statutes. Further, because some of the sodomy statutes that had been in effect when *Bowers* was decided were either repealed or invalidated, the LGBTQ+ legal community hoped that the political climate would make it easier for the Court to move in that direction.

Despite the uncertainties about the Court's abortion jurisprudence, and how that jurisprudence might continue to support sodomy statutes, the Supreme Court signaled in *Romer v. Evans*, 517 U.S. 620 (1996) that it was willing to invalidate anti-LGBTQ+ measures. Colorado voters had enacted a state-wide initiative that precluded Colorado municipalities from enacting LGBTQ+ nondiscrimination ordinances. In a 6–3 opinion, authored by Justice Kennedy, the Supreme Court invalidated the initiative. The opinion purported to use mere rational basis legal analysis but was quite sharp in its condemnation of the state measure. For example, the Court said: "A law declaring that in general it shall be more difficult for one group of citizens than for all others to seek aid from the government is itself a denial of equal protection of the laws in the most literal sense." *Id.* at 633. It also concluded that the initiative imposed a disadvantage that is born of animosity toward the class of persons affected." *Id.* at 634. As noted by Justice Scalia's dissent, the Court's holding implicitly contradicted *Bowers v. Hardwick*, 478 U.S. 186 (1986). *Id.* at 636 (Scalia, J., dissenting). If a state could not preclude local government from enacting nondiscrimination ordinances on behalf of the LGBTQ+ community, it seemed unlikely that a state could impose a criminal sentence on an individual for engaging in private, consensual, sexual behavior. The Court soon resolved this issue in *Lawrence v. Texas*, 539 U.S. 558 (2003), when it finally ruled that a state sodomy statute was unconstitutional.

John Geddes Lawrence and Tyron Garner were arrested on September 17, 1998, for allegedly engaging in homosexual conduct in violation of Texas' sodomy law. The Texas sodomy statute stated that "deviate sexual intercourse" means: "(A) any contact between any part of the genitals of one person and the mouth or anus of another person; or (B) the penetration of the genitals or the anus of another person with an object." Tex. Penal Code Ann. § 21.06 (2003). Although the statute could, in theory, apply to heterosexuals, the state conceded that it only enforced the statute against homosexuals.

Lawrence and Garner were held overnight in jail and each fined $200 and assessed court costs of $141.25. They then challenged the constitutionality of the underlying state statute. In an *en banc* decision, the Texas Court of Appeals held that the statute under which they were convicted did not violate the Due Process or Equal Protection clauses of the Fourteenth Amendment and did not violate the Texas Equal Rights Amendment. *Lawrence v. Texas*, 41 S.W.3d 349 (Tex. App. 2001). Justice Anderson was joined by Justice Murphy in dissenting. They argued that the Texas statute violated the Equal Protection Clause of the Fourteenth Amendment as well as the Texas Constitution because it applied only to homosexuals but not to heterosexuals who also might engage in "deviate sexual intercourse." *Id.* at 367. Nonetheless, they recognized that *Bowers* foreclosed ruling for the plaintiff on due process grounds.

In *Lawrence v. Texas*, 539 U.S. 558 (2003), the Supreme Court accepted certiorari on three questions: (1) whether the state statute violated the Equal Protection Clause of the Fourteenth Amendment, (2) whether the state statute violated the Due Process Clause of the Fourteenth Amendment, and (3) whether *Bowers* should be overruled. *Id.* at 564. In a 5–4 decision, authored by Justice Kennedy and joined by Justices Stevens, Souter, Ginsburg and Breyer, the Court answered the second and third questions in the affirmative.

Justice O'Connor concurred in the judgment but wrote separately to indicate that she would resolve the case entirely on the basis of the first issue. Thus, there were six votes for the Court's judgment, invalidating the state sodomy statute. While recognizing the Equal Protection argument might have merit, the Court majority concluded it was more appropriate to decide the case on Due Process grounds. "Were we to hold the statute invalid under the Equal Protection Clause some might question whether a prohibition would be valid if drawn differently, say, to prohibit the conduct both between same-sex and different-sex participants." *Id.* at 575. The court did note, however, that equality and due process rights are linked, "a decision on the latter point [i.e., due process] advances both interests." *Id.* at 575.

In overruling *Bowers*, the Court was highly critical of every step of the Court's prior analysis. First, the Court held that the *Bowers* Court "misapprehended the claim of liberty there presented to it." *Id.* at 567. Rather than consider the challenged laws to merely infringe the "fundamental right upon homosexuals to engage in sodomy," the Court found that the "penalties and purposes .... have more far-reaching consequences, touching upon the most private human conduct, sexual behavior, and in the most private of places, the home." *Id.* at 567.

Second, the Court found that it is historically inaccurate to conclude that proscriptions against homosexual sodomy "have ancient roots." *Id.* at 567. Instead, the Court found there was a history of banning non-procreative sexual activity, irrespective of the gender of the participants. Further, the Court found there was no history of prosecuting consensual acts committed in private and by adults. *Id.* at 569. In contrast to *Bowers*, the Court stated that the majority may not use "the power of the State to enforce [their] views on the whole society through operation of the criminal law." *Id.* at 571.

Third, citing legal developments in the European Union and the United States, the Court concluded that the "deficiencies" in *Bowers* have become "even more apparent in the years following its announcement." *Id.* at 573.

While recognizing it could invalidate the Texas statute by relying on Equal Protection grounds, the Court emphasized it was important to decide it on Due Process grounds to directly overrule *Bowers* because its "continuance as precedent demeans the lives of homosexual persons." *Id.* at 575. The *Lawrence* Court cited Justice Stevens' dissent in *Bowers* with approval, agreeing with his conclusion that the right of adults to engage in sexual intimacy without state interference is a form of liberty protected by the Due Process Clause of the Fourteenth Amendment. *Id.* at 578. In overruling *Bowers*, the Court found that it "was not correct when it was decided, and it is not correct today." *Id.* at 578.

Despite the sweeping language in the *Lawrence* opinion overturning *Bowers*, the Court was careful to state explicitly that the case did not involve the issue of same-sex marriage. The case "does not involve whether the government must give formal recognition to any relationship that homosexual persons seek to enter." *Id.* at 578.

Further, despite emphasizing the importance of the plaintiffs' liberty interest, the Court did not purport to apply strict scrutiny to the legal issue at stake. Using the language of rational basis scrutiny, the Court said: "The Texas statute furthers no legitimate state interest which can justify its intrusion into the personal and private life of the individual." *Id.* at 578.

Justice O'Connor, who had joined the majority opinion in *Bowers*, concurred separately. She stated that the Court should not have overruled *Bowers*; instead, it should have rested its decision on the Equal Protection Clause of the Fourteenth Amendment. *Id.* at 579. She concluded that:

> Moral disapproval of [homosexuals], like a bare desire to harm the group, is an interest that is insufficient to satisfy rational basis review under the Equal Protection Clause. . . . Indeed, we have never held that moral disapproval, without any other asserted state interest, is a sufficient rationale under the Equal Protection Clause to justify a law that discriminates among groups of persons.

Id. at 582. Thus, like the majority opinion, she concluded that the statute could not survive rational basis scrutiny. Also, like the majority opinion, she was careful to suggest that her reasoning did not invalidate the limitation of marriage to opposite-sex couples because she concluded that the state had a legitimate interest in "preserving the traditional institution of marriage." *Id.* at 585.

Justice Scalia dissented, joined by Chief Justice Rehnquist and Justice Thomas. Justice Scalia's opinion strongly criticized the Court for overturning *Bowers*; he especially considered its consideration of the principle of stare decisis to be in contrast to the views expressed by Justices O'Connor, Kennedy and Souter in their plurality opinion in *Casey* (although Justice O'Connor had not joined that part of the *Lawrence* opinion that overruled *Bowers*). Justice Scalia accused the three members of the Court who joined the *Casey* joint opinion of exposing their "extraordinary deference to precedent [in *Casey*] for the result-oriented expedient that it is." *Id.* at 592. He also criticized the majority for its "aspersions" on the *Bowers* conclusion that homosexual sodomy is not a "fundamental right" while also noting that the *Lawrence* Court (through its use of rational basis scrutiny) did not actually determine that homosexual sodomy is a "fundamental right." *Id.* at 594. Finally, he sharply criticized Justice O'Connor for concluding that plaintiffs had a valid Equal Protection claim. He argued that her "reasoning leaves on pretty shaky grounds state laws limiting marriage to opposite-sex couples" because those laws, he argued, really rested on the state's "*moral disapproval* of same-sex couples." *Id.* at 601 (emphasis in original). In an often-quoted passage, Justice Scalia said:

> Today's opinion is the product of a Court, which is the product of a law-profession culture, that has largely signed on to the so-called homosexual agenda, by which I mean the agenda promoted by some homosexual activists directed at eliminating the moral opprobrium

that has traditionally attached to homosexual conduct.

Id. at 602.

Justice Thomas dissented to emphasize that he considered the Texas statute to be "uncommonly silly" (quoting *Griswold v. Conn.*, 381 U.S. 479, 527 (1965) (Stewart, J., dissenting)) and that he would vote to repeal it as a member of the legislature. But he concluded that, as a judge, he was "not empowered to help petitioners and others similarly situated." *Id.* at 605.

§ 2.5 LAWRENCE V. TEXAS AFTERMATH

The application of the *Lawrence* decision has been highly contested. In the criminal law area, a Virginia state court concluded that *Lawrence* did not invalidate a state sodomy statute where the criminal defendant solicited oral sodomy in a public place. *See Singson v. Va.*, 621 S.E.2d 682 (Va. Ct. App. 2005). The Hawaii Supreme Court concluded that *Lawrence* did not invalidate its state's prostitution statute. *State v. Romano*, 155 P.3d 1102 (Haw. 2007). Similarly, the Texas Court of Appeals concluded that *Lawrence* did not invalidate a criminal statute providing for a charge of aggravated sexual assault when an adult has sex with a child younger than fourteen years of age. *Fleming v. State*, 323 S.W.3d 540 (Tex. App. 2010), *vacated on other grounds*, 341 S.W.3d 415 (Tex. Crim. App. 2011). Finally, the California Court of Appeal concluded that *Lawrence* did not invalidate the state incest statute. *People v. McEvoy*, 215 Cal. App. 4th 431 (Cal. Ct. App. 2013).

Outside the criminal law area, the Eleventh Circuit concluded in *Lofton v. Secretary of Department of Children and Family Services*, 358 F.3d 804 (11th Cir. 2004) that *Lawrence* did not invalidate a statute prohibiting adoptions by homosexuals. In 2008, a state trial court issued a 53-page judgment declaring the Florida law unconstitutional under the Florida Constitution. That decision was affirmed by the state Court of Appeal. *See Florida Department of Children and Families v. In re Matter of Adoption of X.X.G. and N.R.G.*, 45 So.3d 79 (Fla. Dist. Ct. Appeal 2010). Although the state did seek to enforce the statute in both the trial and appellate courts, it argued the case under a stipulation by the Florida Department of Children and Families "that gay people and heterosexuals make equally good parents." *See* Joanna L. Grossman, *Will Gays and Lesbians in Florida Finally Gain the Right to Adopt Children?*, FindLaw.com, October 26, 2010, https://supreme.findlaw.com/legal-commentary/will-gays-and-lesbians-in-florida-finally-gain-the-right-to-adopt-children.html. The state did not appeal the court of appeals decision to its Supreme Court and stopped enforcing the law in 2010. The state legislature repealed the abortion ban in 2015 when it engaged in comprehensive adoption reform.

The Tenth Circuit concluded that *Lawrence* did not provide a police officer with a fundamental liberty interest to engage in private sexual conduct, when that conduct arguably negatively impacted her work as a police officer. *Seegmiller v. LaVerkin City*, 528 F.3d 762 (10th Cir. 2008) (married police officer, who was separated from her husband, had a sexual encounter with an officer from another department while attending a police department funded conference). Thus, under rational basis scrutiny, the department could constitutionally require her to act in a manner "that does not bring discredit to [the officer] or [the] agency." *Id.* at 772.

The Eleventh Circuit also concluded in *Williams v. Attorney General of Alabama*, 378 F.3d 1232 (11th Cir. 2004) that the right to sexual privacy did not include the right to purchase "sex toys." Alabama law prohibited the commercial distribution of "any device designed or marketed as useful primarily for the stimulation of human genital organs for any thing of pecuniary value," but did not prohibit the use or possession of such devices. Ala. Code § 13A–12–200.2 (2015). Such laws have been struck down by state supreme courts (in pre-*Lawrence* cases), *see People v. Seven Thirty-Five East Colfax, Inc.*, 697 P.2d 348 (Colo. 1985) (en banc); *State v. Hughes*, 792 P.2d 1023 (Kan. 1990); *State v. Brenan*, 772 So. 2d 64 (La. 2000), but are still on the books in four states other than Alabama. *See* Ga. Code Ann. § 16–12–80 (2011); Miss. Code Ann. § 97–29–105 (2011); Tex. Penal Code Ann. §§ 43.21, 43.23 (West 2011); Va. Code Ann. § 18.2–373 (2014).

In an unpublished opinion, the Texas Court of Appeals upheld the constitutionality of the Texas statute banning the sale of sex toys. *See State v. Acosta*, No. 08–04–00312–CR, 2005 WL 2095290 (Tex. App. Aug. 31, 2005). But the Fifth Circuit invalidated that statute in 2008, concluding that it violated the Fourteenth Amendment. *See Reliable Consultants, Inc. v. Earle,* 517 F.3d 738 (5th Cir. 2008). Relying on *Lawrence,* the Fifth Circuit found that the statute "burdens the substantive due process right to engage in private intimate conduct of his or her choosing." *Id.* at 744. Thus, the Fifth and Eleventh Circuits are split on the constitutionality of statutes banning the sale of sex toys.

The Courts have consistently not applied the *Lawrence* holding to any sexual activities that could be considered "public." In *Fleck and Associates, Inc. v. Phoenix,* 356 F. Supp. 2d 1034 (D. Ariz. 2005), *rev'd on other grounds,* 471 F.3d 1100 (9th Cir. 2006), the district court refused to enter an injunction to prevent the enforcement of a city ordinance that prohibited "the operation of a business for purposes of providing the opportunity to engage in . . . . or view . . . . live sex acts." Similarly, adult movie theatres and nightclubs cannot use *Lawrence* to protect the right of their patrons to engage in sexual conduct at the commercial establishment. *See 832 Corp. v. Gloucester Twp.,* 404 F. Supp. 2d 614 (D.N.J. 2005); *Commonwealth v. Can-Port Amusement Corp.,* 19 Mass. L. Rptr. 562 (Mass. Super. Ct. 2005).

Despite those narrow interpretations of *Lawrence,* the Supreme Court did cite it extensively in 2015 when it found that states may not limit marriage to opposite-sex couples. *See Obergefell v. Hodges,* 576 U.S. 644 (2015) (discussed in *Nutshell* § 5.6).

The current status of *Lawrence* is in legal jeopardy because of the Supreme Court's decision to overturn *Roe* in *Dobbs v. Jackson Women's Health*

Organization, 597 U.S. 215 (2022) (discussed in *Nutshell* § 2.8). The majority opinion in *Dobbs* deflects that possibility by repeating the assertion that "nothing in this opinion should be understood to cast doubt on precedents that do not concern abortion." *Id.* at 290. By contrast, Justice Thomas's concurrence states that the Court "should reconsider all of this Court's substantive due process precedents, including *Griswold, Lawrence, and Obergefell.*" *Id.* at 332. In 2022, Texas Attorney General Ken Paxton stated that he would defend a state sodomy law. *See* Timothy Bella, *Texas AG says he'd defend sodomy law if Supreme Court revisits ruling,* WASH. POST. (June 29, 2022).

Twelve states in the United States (Florida, Georgia, Kansas, Kentucky, Louisiana, Massachusetts, Michigan, Mississippi, North Carolina, Oklahoma, South Carolina and Texas) still have sodomy laws on their books. *See Sodomy Laws Remain in 12 States. Race to Avoid Roe v. Wade Repeat Begins,* NEWSWEEK (Jan. 24, 2025). Any one of those states could seek to enforce their sodomy laws to challenge the current validity of *Lawrence.*

§ 2.6 STATE REGULATION OF SEX FOR COMPENSATION

The *Lawrence* decision broadened the right of adults to make consensual decisions about their private, sexual behavior. Yet, it remains constitutional in the United States for states to make it illegal for two adults to engage in consensual sexual relations if an exchange of compensation has taken place, i.e., prostitution. At this time, the *Lawrence* decision has had no impact on the laws that criminalize prostitution, although, from a historical perspective, laws against prostitution and sodomy have often been linked.

The famous *Wolfenden Report*, (i.e., THE REPORT OF THE COMMITTEE ON HOMOSEXUAL OFFENCES AND PROSTITUTION) which recommended the decriminalization of homosexuality in England in 1957, also recommended much *stiffer* penalties for prostitution. As one commentator reflected in 1957, "on prostitution, the Committee's views and recommendations will receive wide endorsement. The main object of the Committee is to remove from the streets the affront to public decency presented by the presence of prostitutes looking for customers." Committee on Homosexual Offenses and Prostitution, *The Wolfenden Report*, 33 BRIT. J. VENER. DIS. 205 (1957).

At the federal level, United States law has a history of quite rigid restrictions on prostitution. The immigration laws have been one source of such restrictions. Through the Act of March 3, 1875, relating to immigration, it was a felony to "knowingly and willfully import, or cause any importation of, women into the United States for the purposes of 'prostitution.' " Act of March 3, 1975, 43d Cong., ch. 141, 18 Stat. § 477. On February 20, 1907, Congress passed a more comprehensive immigration law that also banned the importation of "any alien woman or girl for the purpose of prostitution, or for any other immoral purpose." Act of February 20, 1907, 59th

Cong., ch. 1134, 34 Stat. § 898. The Supreme Court interpreted "or for any other immoral purpose" to include importation to be a "concubine" rather than merely a prostitute. *See United States v. Bitty*, 208 U.S. 393 (1908).

Congress also tried to deal with the problem of prostitution in the early twentieth century by enacting the White Slavery Traffic Act of 1910 (also called the "Mann Act"), 18 U.S.C. § 2421 (2012). Rather than merely limit the importation of women or girls for the purpose of prostitution, this statute banned the transportation of prostitutes across state lines. Like the 1907 immigration statute, it also banned such interstate travel for "immoral purposes," raising the question of what that term meant. The Supreme Court ruled that the statute should be interpreted to include a woman who is a "concubine" despite the title of the statute, impliedly limiting its reach to prostitutes. *See Caminetti v. United States*, 242 U.S. 470 (1917).

Until 1986, when the Mann Act was amended, it could be used to prosecute anyone who transported a woman across state lines to engage in noncommercial sexual activity outside of marriage. The 1986 version of the Mann Act limits criminalization of "any individual . . . . with intent that such individual engage in prostitution, or in any sexual activity for which any person can be charged with a criminal offense." Child Sexual Abuse and Pornography Act of 1986, Pub. L. No. 99–628, 100 Stat. 3510, § 5(b)(1) (codified at 18 U.S.C. § 2421). Because the *Lawrence* decision appears to protect consensual, noncommercial sexual acts from criminal prosecution, it would appear that the Mann Act today is limited to prosecuting interstate travel for the purpose of prostitution.

The proper role of the law in dealing with prostitution is an issue that divides the feminist community. At one end of the pole are Catharine MacKinnon and Kathleen Barry who believe that it is not possible for women to "consent" to prostitution. These feminists tend to favor a ban on prostitution with the legal system criminalizing the work of "pimps, brothel owners and managers, clients, and any third parties who assist women to travel and work in the sex industry." Janie A. Chuang, *Rescuing Trafficking from Ideological Capture: Prostitution Reform and ANTI-Trafficking Law and Policy*, 158 U. PA. L. REV. 1655, 1669 (2010). From a critical race perspective, Cheryl Nelson Butler, building on the work of Catharine MacKinnon, has argued that "economic coercion too often is misconstrued as consent." Cheryl Nelson Butler, *A Critical Race Feminist Perspective on Prostitution & Sex Trafficking in America*, 27 YALE J.L. & FEMINISM 95, 138 (2015). Butler argues that feminists must continue to explore the "role of the State in supporting laws and policies that coerce people of color into prostitution and otherwise make them vulnerable to sexual abuse and exploitation." *Id.* at 139. At the other end of the spectrum are sex-positive feminists who believe that prostitution should be decriminalized or legalized. For an excellent discussion of the range of views on prostitution, *see* Lindsey H. Jemison, *Feminist Theory and Sex Work*

Regulation: Comparing Regulatory Models and Implementation of Theoretical Policy, 21 J. L. SOCIETY 163 (2021).

The legal system has not been a strong tool for prostitution advocates to overturn laws that ban or limit prostitution in the United States. *See generally* Paul M. Coltoff, *Prostitution and Related Offenses,* 73 C.J.S. PROSTITUTION AND RELATED OFFENSES § 3, (March 2021 Update). In Canada, however, laws that restricted prostitution were found to violate the Canadian Charter of Rights and Freedoms. *See Att'y Gen. v. Bedford,* 3 R.C.R. 1101 (S.C.C. 2013). Prostitution, itself, was not illegal in Canada, but federal law outlawed public communication for the purposes of prostitution and made it illegal to operate a bawdy house or live off of the avails of prostitution. Three sex workers challenged these rules as depriving them of their right to security by forcing them to work secretly. In a unanimous ruling, the Canadian Supreme Court struck down each of these provisions, overturning a 1990 decision that had upheld these provisions. The Court, however, suspended the declaration of invalidity for a year, to give the Canadian Parliament time to create constitutional regulations. Chuang, *supra* at 1165.

§ 2.7 STATE REGULATION OF POLYGAMY AND BIGAMY

The *Lawrence* decision has had no impact on the longstanding ban against polygamy and bigamy. One of the earliest cases involving the ban on polygamy and bigamy was *Murphy v. Ramsey,* 114 U.S. 15

(1885). Pursuant to an Act of Congress, approved on March 22, 1882, the petitioners in this case were deprived of the right to vote due to their alleged bigamy or polygamy. The petitioners challenged Congress' power to enact such legislation. The Supreme Court resoundingly found that the law came within Congress' powers:

> For, certainly, no legislation can be supposed more wholesome and necessary in the founding of a free, self-governing commonwealth, fit to take rank as one of the co-ordinate states of the Union, than that which seeks to establish it on the basis of the idea of the family, as consisting in and springing from the union for life of one man and one woman in the holy estate of matrimony; the sure foundation of all that is stable and noble in our civilization; the best guaranty of that reverent morality which is the source of all beneficent progress in social and political improvement. And to this end no means are more directly and immediately suitable than those provided by this act, which endeavors to withdraw all political influence from those who are practically hostile to its attainment.

Id. at 45.

After a fifty-year hiatus, the state of Utah brought criminal charges against Tom Green for bigamy and first-degree felony rape of a child. Green had boasted of his familial arrangement in a 1999 episode of *Dateline NBC,* causing the local prosecutor to initiate charges. *See* Alyssa Rower, *The Legality of Polygamy: Using the Due Process Clause of the Fourteenth*

Amendment, 38 Fam. L. Q. 711, 719–20 (2004). The Utah Supreme Court upheld his conviction for plural marriage, finding that the law "serves the State's interest in protecting vulnerable individuals from exploitation and abuse." *State v. Green*, 99 P.3d 820, 830 (2004).

In 2013, a polygamist family brought an action against the county attorney challenging the constitutionality of Utah's statute banning plural marriage. *See Brown v. Buhman*, 947 F. Supp. 2d 1170 (D. Utah 2013). The Utah statute did not merely ban multiple marriages but also banned "cohabitation" under which a married person "purports to marry another person or cohabits with another person." Utah Code Ann. § 76–7–101 (LexisNexis 2012). The district court struck the "or cohabits with another person" language as unconstitutional under the Free Exercise Clause of the First Amendment and the Due Process Clause of the Fourteenth Amendment. *Id.* at 1176. That decision was vacated on mootness grounds in *Brown v. Buhman*, 822 F.3d 1151 (10th Cir. 2016), because there was no credible threat of prosecution. While the *Lawrence* opinion could, in theory, be used to attack the morality-based justifications for statutes banning plural marriage, such efforts have not been successful at this time. Bans on plural marriage are often cited with approval in family law cases in which one party may have failed to dissolve a prior marriage before entering into a new one. *See, e.g., In re the Matter of: Michael E. Hammett Sr. v. Ann Pearly Joy Cuizon Hammett,* 247 Ariz. 556 (Ct. Appeals Ariz. 2019); *In the Matter of the Estate of*

Bobby Joe Brown, Jr. v. Ami Alley, 384 P.3d 496 (Okl. S. Ct. 2016).

§ 2.8 REPRODUCTIVE FREEDOM CASE LAW

While a complete discussion of the Court's reproductive freedom jurisprudence is beyond the scope of this *Nutshell*, a brief survey of that case law can help show the interplay between that area of the law and the sodomy case law, discussed above. In both areas, the Court has wrestled with the question of whether it should broadly define the meaning of the term "Due Process" to encompass personal liberty-based decisions.

In *Poe v. Ullman*, 367 U.S. 497 (1961), the Supreme Court found that a case involving the state's contraceptive law was not ripe for adjudication but Justice Harlan wrote a strong dissent that later became the foundation for the invalidation of the state's law in *Griswold v. Connecticut*, 381 U.S. 479 (1965). His opinion also foreshadowed the tension between the reproductive freedom case law and the gay rights case law when he said:

> Adultery, homosexuality and the like are sexual intimacies which the State forbids altogether, but the intimacy of husband and wife is necessarily an essential and accepted feature of the institution of marriage, an institution which the State not only must allow, but which always and in every age it has fostered and protected.

Poe, 367 U.S. at 553. Four years later, the Court did strike down the Connecticut statute prohibiting the sale or use of contraceptives in *Griswold*. Although the Court offered many rationales for its decision, seven members of the Court joined the holding. Justice Stewart's dissent, which was joined by Justice Black, made the well-known statement that the statute was "an uncommonly silly law" but not one that violated the United States Constitution. *Id.* at 527.

Using the Fourteenth Amendment's Equal Protection Clause, the Supreme Court extended the right to use contraceptives to unmarried couples in *Eisenstadt v. Baird*, 405 U.S. 438 (1972). The Court used the "rational relation" test to conclude that the statute unconstitutionally discriminated against individuals who were not married and sought to use contraceptives. *Id.* at 447.

A year later, in *Roe v. Wade*, 410 U.S. 113 (1973), the Court ruled in a 7–2 decision that the right of privacy "is broad enough to encompass a woman's decision whether or not to terminate her pregnancy." *Id.* at 153. Further, it found that this right was a "fundamental right" whose infringement must be justified by a state's articulation of a "compelling state interest." *Id.* at 155. The compelling state interests that it found could justify abortion regulations were maternal health and fetal viability. *Id.* at 164–65. Justices White and Rehnquist dissented.

The broad ruling in *Roe v. Wade* was reaffirmed in *Akron v. Akron Center for Reproductive Health, Inc.*,

462 U.S. 416 (1983) in a 6–3 decision and in *Thornburgh v. American College of Obstetricians & Gynecologists*, 476 U.S. 747 (1986) in a 5–4 decision. The Court seemed to signal that it was willing to reconsider *Roe* in 1989 when it upheld a requirement that doctors test for viability before performing an abortion after the twentieth week of pregnancy. *Webster v. Reprod. Health Servs.*, 492 U.S. 490 (1989). Chief Justice Rehnquist wrote a plurality opinion, which was joined by Justices White and Kennedy, in which he disagreed with the trimester framework of *Roe* but declined to determine whether *Roe* should be overturned because "[t]he facts of the present case . . . . differ from those at issue in *Roe*." *Id.* at 521. Similarly, Justice O'Connor voted to uphold the state law but declined to determine whether *Roe* should be overturned. She indicated that "there will be time enough to reexamine *Roe*. And to do so carefully." *Id.* at 526. In his concurrence, Justice Scalia made it clear that he was ready to overrule *Roe*. *Id.* at 532. In light of the slender thread on which *Roe* rested, it was, therefore, not surprising that the Court declined to extend the right to privacy in *Bowers* in 1986.

With the replacement of Justices Brennan and Marshall with Republican-appointed Justices Souter and Thomas, it was thought that *Roe* would be overturned. In a somewhat surprising decision, the Court in *Planned Parenthood of Southeastern Pennsylvania v. Casey*, 505 U.S. 833 (1992) declined to overturn *Roe*. Justices O'Connor, Kennedy and Souter authored a joint opinion in which they concluded that principles of stare decisis required reaffirmation of *Roe*, but that several of the state law requirements could nonetheless be upheld under the appropriate constitutional standard. Justices Rehnquist, White, Scalia and Thomas expressed their willingness to overturn *Roe*.

As we saw in the Court's opinion in *Lawrence*, the joint opinion in *Casey* offered arguments for affirming and for overruling *Bowers*. The lengthy discussion of the importance of stare decisis made it difficult for the Court to overturn *Bowers*. But the reaffirmation of the right to privacy as a fundamental right provided fodder for that right to be extended to the gay rights area.

The Supreme Court's 2016 decision in *Whole Woman's Health v. Hellerstedt*, 579 U.S. 582 (2016), re-affirmed the heightened scrutiny that existed in the area of reproductive freedom. For the first time since *Casey*, a majority of the Court struck down state regulations as inconsistent with the "undue burden" standard. These state laws imposed admission privileges and surgical center requirements that the Court found were unduly burdensome on women's right to seek a pre-viability abortion, because they created obstacles without providing any benefits to women's health. Justice Thomas' dissenting opinion criticized the *Lawrence* decision as inappropriately reflecting what he called a "made-up test" for tiers of scrutiny. *Id.* at 2327 (Thomas, J., dissenting). Justice Alito's dissent, which was joined by Chief Justice Roberts and Justice Thomas, did not challenge the validity of the *Casey* framework but argued, instead, that the undue burden standard could not be met in this case. *See Id.* at 2330–53 (Alito, J., dissenting).

Nonetheless, the status of *Roe* was soon again in play with the Court having changed significantly since the *Whole Women's Health* decision. The *Whole Women's Health* five-vote majority included Justices Kennedy and Ginsburg, who were replaced by Justice Kavanaugh and Justice Coney Barrett. Justice Scalia had passed away when that case was decided and was subsequently replaced by Justice Gorsuch.

The first significant hint that the Court was not likely to attach much precedential weight to *Roe* arose in the series of cases involving enforcement of Texas's "bounty hunter" law, which allowed private citizens to sue those who perform or assist with abortions if the physician detected a fetal heartbeat. *See* Tex. Health & Safety Code Ann. §§ 171.204(a), 171.207(a), 171.208(a)(2), (3). The Supreme Court allowed this law to go into effect with Justice Gorsuch fully supported by Justices Thomas, Alito, Kavanaugh and Barrett. *See Whole Women's Health v. Jackson*, 595 U.S. 30 (2021). Justice Roberts, joined by Justices Breyer, Sotomayor, and Kagan wrote a separate opinion dissenting in part, in which he emphasized that the "clear purpose and actual effect of S.B. 8 has been to nullify this Court's rulings. It is, however, a basic principle that the Constitution is the 'fundamental and paramount law of the nation,' and '[i]t is emphatically the province and duty of the judicial department to say what the law is.' " *Id.* at 61–62.

Unsurprisingly, the Court did overturn *Roe* in *Dobbs v. Jackson Women's Health Organization,* 597 U.S. 215 (2022) on June 24, 2022. Justice Alito delivered the opinion of the Court, joined by Justices Thomas, Gorsuch, Kavanaugh and Barrett. Justice Roberts voted to uphold the state's 15-week ban on abortions but declined to overturn *Roe*. But his vote was the fifth for overturning the Mississippi statute, leaving states free to enact any abortion statutes so long as they could meet the most lenient "rational basis" test. Under this test, "[i]t follows that the States may regulate abortion for legitimate reasons, and when such regulations are challenged under the Constitution, courts cannot 'substitute their social and economic beliefs for the judgment of legislative bodies'. . . . A law regulating abortion, like other health and welfare laws, is entitled to a 'strong presumption of validity.' It must be sustained if there is a rational basis on which the legislature could have thought that it would serve legitimate state interests. These legitimate interests include respect for and preservation of prenatal life at all stages of development; the protection of maternal health and safety; the elimination of particularly gruesome or barbaric medical procedures; the preservation of the integrity of the medical profession; the mitigation of fetal pain; and the prevention of discrimination on the basis of race, sex, or disability." *Id.* at 300–01 (citations omitted).

The Court listed no countervailing interests that a state must respect (like the life or health of the pregnant person) as a backstop against any of these reasons for restricting abortion access. In Justice

Kavanaugh's concurrence, he made passing reference in a footnote that it is possible that an exception to a State's restriction on abortion would be constitutionally required "when an abortion is necessary to save the life of the [pregnant person]." *Id.* at 339 n. 2

The scope of the medical exception rule is not clear at this time. Texas law prohibits abortions unless the pregnancy "places the female at risk of death or poses a serious risk of substantial impairment of a major bodily function." Tex. Health & Safety Code § 170A.002(b)(2). Two weeks after the Supreme Court decided *Dobbs*, the Biden administration issued guidance and a supporting letter to state healthcare-agency directors saying that the Emergency Medical Treatment and Active Labor Act of 1986 (EMTALA) required hospitals to provide abortions when a pregnant person is experiencing a medical condition for which abortion is the appropriate stabilizing treatment. Texas v. Becerra, 89 F.4th 529, 535–36 (5th Cir. 2024). The Fifth Circuit affirmed a lower court's injunction against enforcement of the Biden policy, relying on administrative law considerations. It found that HHS was required to subject the Guidance to notice and comment. *Id.* at 546. The Supreme Court denied cert. *Becerra v. Texas,* 145 S. Ct. 139 (2024).

A similar case proceeded in Idaho. When it became clear that there was a factual dispute about Idaho's policy, the Supreme Court dismissed a writ of certiorari as having been improvidently granted. *See Moyle v. United States,* 144 S. Ct. 2015 (mem) (2024).

The case was remanded to the lower courts for factual development. In March 2025, Idaho's Attorney General announced that the Trump administration agreed to dismiss any further action under EMTALA against the state of Idaho. *See* https://www.ag.idaho.gov/newsroom/ag-labrador-announces-dismissal-of-emtala-challenge-to-idaho-defense-of-life-act/. *See also United States v. Idaho,* 131 F.4th 798 (mem) (9th Cir. 2025).

For the purpose of this *Nutshell*, it is hard to know the implications of the *Dobbs* decision on issues like enforcement of sodomy statutes or marriage equality. The majority (with Justice Thomas disagreeing) emphasized that this case was only about abortion which implicates the issue of the protection of fetal life. Because *Lawrence* (discussed in *Nutshell* § 2.4) and *Obergefell* (discussed in *Nutshell* § 5.6) rest on the assumption that *Roe* was correctly decided, it is hard to know if the Court's reasoning will be limited to abortion rights.

§ 2.9 WASHINGTON V. GLUCKSBERG: LIBERTY FRAMEWORK

Another case that deserves brief mention because it is frequently cited when courts consider whether to expand the liberty interests protected by the Fourteenth Amendment is *Washington v. Glucksberg*, 521 U.S. 702 (1997). The plaintiffs in *Glucksberg* were terminally ill patients, physicians and a nonprofit organization that opposed a statute banning assisted suicide. They argued that the right to assisted suicide was a fundamental liberty interest protected by the Due Process Clause. Chief Justice Rehnquist delivered the opinion of the Court, which was joined by Justices O'Connor, Scalia, Kennedy, and Thomas. The entire Court agreed that the Washington statute was constitutional, although the liberal members of the Court would have given greater protection to the plaintiffs' asserted constitutional liberty interest.

The majority opinion recognized that the Due Process Clause "guarantees more than fair process, and the 'liberty' it protects includes more than the absence of physical restraint." *Id.* at 719. It said that the right also includes "heightened protection against the government interference with certain fundamental rights and liberty interests" which include "the rights to marry . . . . to have children . . . . to direct the education and upbringing of one's children . . . . to marital privacy . . . . to use contraception . . . . to bodily integrity . . . . and to abortion . . . . [and] the traditional right to refuse unwanted lifesaving medical treatment." *Id.* at 720.

The framework recognized by *Glucksberg* to determine whether to extend liberty interests included a two-step process. "First, we have regularly observed that the Due Process Clause specifically protects those fundamental rights and liberties which are, objectively, deeply rooted in this Nation's history and tradition." *Id.* at 720–21. "Second, we have required in substantive-due-process cases a 'careful description' of the asserted fundamental liberty interest." *Id.* at 721. Applying these principles, the Court found that there "the law's treatment of assisted suicide in this country has been and continues to be one of the rejection of nearly all efforts to permit it." *Id.* at 728. Further, applying rational basis scrutiny, the Court found that the state's ban on assisted suicide was "rationally related to legitimate government interests." *Id.* at 728. Justice Souter concurred in the judgment, although, he would have recognized a stronger right by individuals to make personal decisions regarding their own bodies and medical care. Nonetheless, he also concluded the legislature should be permitted to determine appropriate legislation in this area.

The majority opinion in *Glucksberg* did not cite either *Roe* or *Bowers*. The majority opinion in *Lawrence* did not cite *Glucksberg*, but Justice Scalia cited it in his dissent. He said that *Glucksberg* "eroded" both *Roe* and *Casey*. *Lawrence*, 539 U.S. at 588. Because the majority opinion in *Lawrence* did not cite *Glucksberg*, it is hard to evaluate its continued constitutional vitality. Lower courts tend to cite both *Lawrence* and *Glucksberg* when asked to consider arguments for further protection of an individual's liberty interest.

CHAPTER 3

REGULATION OF GENDER IDENTITY AND EXPRESSION

§ 3.1 A NOTE ON TERMINOLOGY

The terms used to describe people who do not conform to traditional gender identities have changed in the last several decades and continues to evolve. Terms like "transvestite" and "transsexual" have been used to describe individuals who, today, often identify as "transgendered" or "trans."

The National Center for Transgender Equality publishes resources on the various terminologies that have been used over time, noting that "transsexual" is a somewhat older term that has grown in disfavor "because it is thought to sound overly clinical." *See* The Nat'l Ctr. for Transgender Equal., *Transgender Terminology* (Jan. 2014), available at https://www.nawj.org/uploads/files/annual_conference/session_materials/transgender/transgender_terminology-ncte.pdf. Some people prefer to use terms such as "genderqueer" to connote that they do not identify as male or female. Alternatively, some people use the label "bi-gendered" to indicate that they identify as both male and female. In the legal arena, one typically sees references to terms such as "transgender" rather than these newer labels that suggest a lack of conformity to a single gender identity. The term "trans" is sometimes used as shorthand for "transgender." *Id.* The term "transsexual" also persists in legal decisions. This chapter will typically use the term "transgender" except when quoting material that uses other terms.

Another term that sometimes appears in the LGBTQ+ legal literature is "gender identity." Some states or cities have laws that protect against "gender identity" discrimination. GLAAD offers a helpful definition of gender identity:

> A person's internal, deeply held sense of their gender. For transgender people, their own internal gender identity does not match the sex they were assigned at birth. Most people have a gender identity of man or woman (or boy or girl). For some people, their gender identity does not fit neatly into one of those two choices. . . . Unlike gender expression . . . . gender identity is not visible to others.

Gay & Lesbian Alliance Against Defamation, *GLAAD Media Reference Guide—Transgender,* available at https://www.glaad.org/reference/transgender.

Although the transgender movement is primarily concerned with issues of gender identity, rather than sexual orientation, it is currently aligned politically with the gay rights movement, now typically called the "LGBT" movement or the "LGBTQ+" movement. As discussed in *Nutshell* § 7.16, the alignment of the transgender movement within the gay rights movement has been a source of political tension but, at this time, the two movements are politically aligned.

In addition to the "transgender" movement, a related movement involves individuals who are described as "intersex." They are typically born with characteristics that do not perfectly align with traditional notions of being "male" or "female." Such persons used to be called "hermaphrodites." There is a range of individuals who are considered to be intersex. A person can be born with XX chromosomes and ovaries but have genitalia that are not traditionally associated with males or females. Other persons are born with XY chromosomes and undescended testes. They appear female at birth but, at puberty, develop high levels of testosterone, a deeper voice, an elongated clitoris and increased muscle mass. Finally, other persons have XY chromosomes and internal testes but appear female throughout their lives due to insensitivity to testosterone. Unless they compete in sports at a high level, and are subject to gender testing, or have infertility problems that result in gender testing, some individuals never realize they are "intersex." As we will see below, in recent years, there have been increased efforts to regulate whether people who are "intersex" or transgender can compete in sports consistently with their gender identity.

An emerging issue is whether faculty can refuse to identify students by their chosen pronoun. That issue is discussed in *Nutshell* § 8.3. The Sixth Circuit has ruled in favor of a professor who claimed a freedom of speech and religious free exercise right not to comply with a university policy that required him to address a student by the student's preferred pronoun. *See Meriwether v. Hartop*, 992 F.3d 492 (6th Cir. 2021) (professor's refusal to use student's preferred gender-identity pronouns during political philosophy class involved constitutionally protected speech on a matter of public concern that outweighed state's interest in administering its gender-pronoun policy).

The Trump Administration weighed in on this issue when it issued Executive Order 14168 on January 20, 2025, entitled "Defending Women From Gender Ideology Extremism and Restoring Biological Truth to the Federal Government," https://www.whitehouse.gov/presidential-actions/2025/01/defending-women-from-gender-ideology-extremism-and-restoring-biological-truth-to-the-federal-government/. This Executive Order essentially dismisses the concept of a person identifying with a sex other than the one assigned at birth. It says that "gender identity . . . does not provide a meaningful basis for identification and cannot be recognized as a replacement for sex." *Id.* at Sec. 2 (g). Further, this Executive Order requires all government-issued identity documents to reflect the Executive Order's definition of sex. It is conceivable that such a policy could be interpreted to require universities and other entities (that receive federal funds) to identify people's sex as the one assigned at birth. Another provision of the Executive Order states that "federal funds should not be used to promote gender ideology." *Id.* at Sec. 3 (g). "Gender ideology" is defined as ideology that permits "the false claim that males can identify as and thus become women and vice versa and requiring all institutions of society to regard this false claim as true." *Id.* at Sec. 2(f). One could imagine that the Trump administration would require that a recipient of federal funding *not* allow students to identify their gender identity. As will be discussed in *Nutshell* § 3.7, below, it also is not clear if Title IX even protects students from transgender discrimination.

§ 3.2 EARLY ORDINANCES REGULATING APPEARANCE AND CLOTHING

The legal system has regulated gender expression for a long time, often citing biblical references in support of such regulation. For example, a 1974 New York Criminal Law Court cited a Deuteronomy passage in support of its enforcement of clothing regulations: "The woman shall not wear that which pertaineth unto a man, neither shall a man put on a woman's garment: for all that do so are abomination until the Lord, thy God." *See People v. Simmons*, 79 Misc. 2d 249, 252–53 (N.Y. Crim. Ct. 1974) (quoting *Deuteronomy* 22:5).

Local ordinances have historically banned dressing in clothing that did not "belong[ ] to his or her sex." *See, e.g.*, St. Louis, Mo., Ordinance No. 5421, art. II, § 2 (1861). Further, cities have used "disguise" laws to arrest people who did not follow the norms for their gender. For example, until 1967, New York had a law that prohibited "[a] person, who, having his face painted discolored, covered or concealed, or being otherwise disguised, in a manner calculated to prevent his being identified." N.Y. Crim. Proc. Law § 887 (repealed by New York Criminal Procedure Law 1967, ch. 681). Lesbians who frequented gay bars were thought to have been arrested for cross-dressing.

> An urban myth soon emerged in lesbian communities that had little basis in legal reality: [t]he police could not arrest a woman for masquerading if she was wearing three articles of women's clothing . . . . Gay women held on to the "three articles" myth as though it were a talisman. But it did little to help them avoid capricious arrests.

LILLIAN FADERMAN & STUART TIMMONS, GAY L.A.: A HISTORY OF SEXUAL OUTLAWS, POWER POLITICS, AND LIPSTICK LESBIANS, 96 (2006). Thus, appearance ordinances were often a way to enforce gender norms for people who, for a variety of reasons, might not choose to conform to social norms for their gender.

An Ohio judge refused to find an ordinance unconstitutional in 1970 which provided: "No person shall appear upon any public street or other public place in a state of nudity or in a dress not belonging to his or her sex or in an indecent or lewd dress." *See City of Columbus v. Zanders*, 266 N.E.2d 602, 604 (Franklin Cty. Mun. Ct., Ohio 1970) (upholding the ordinance because it "has a real and substantial relation to the public safety").

By contrast, a St. Louis ordinance, which prohibited any person from appearing "in any public place in a state of nudity or in a dress not belonging to his or her sex or in an indecent or lewd dress," was found to be unconstitutionally vague, because of the vagueness of the term "indecent or lewd dress." *See D.C. v. City of St. Louis*, 795 F.2d 652 (8th Cir. 1986); *see also City of Columbus v. Rogers*, 324 N.E.2d 563 (Ohio 1975) (invaliding ordinance as unconstitutionally void for vagueness). The Illinois Supreme Court found such laws to be a violation of an individual's liberty interest. *See City of Chicago v. Wilson*, 389 N.E.2d 522 (Ill. 1978). Rejecting a public safety defense, it found "the city has offered no evidence to substantiate its reasons for infringing on the defendants' choice of dress" and, therefore, concluded the ordinances constituted an "unconstitutional infringement of their liberty interest" as applied to the defendants. *Id.* at 534.

When New York repealed its disguise law in 1967, it replaced it with a provision that defined a "loiterer" as a person who "being masked or in any manner disguised by unusual or unnatural attire or facial alteration, loiters, remains or congregates in a public place with other persons so masked or disguised." *See People v. Simmons*, 79 Misc. 2d 249, 253 (N.Y. Crim. Ct. 1974) (citing N.Y. Penal Law § 240.35(4)). The Penal Code also provided it was illegal for a person to "falsely personate" another. *Id.* at 253 (citing N.Y. Penal Law § 190.25(1)). The New York court ruled that the phrase "falsely personate" could not be used to convict a man for dressing as a woman; the statute required one to be a particular person, not merely the opposite sex. *Id.* at 255. In discussing the legislative history of the New York Penal Law, the court noted that the legislature may have recognized "that women are wearing their hair shorter and men's hair is now being worn longer, that men are using facial makeup and hair dyes and that men's and women's clothing styles are becoming increasingly similar." *Id.* at 253. Thus, both legislative and judicial changes were becoming somewhat more permissive in the

1970s and 1980s about the clothing worn by men and women in public, although, the disguise ordinances stayed on the books.

§ 3.3 TITLE VII APPLICATION TO SEXUAL STEREOTYPING

Although the modern gender expression case law often applies to cases involving individuals who identify as a member of the lesbian, gay, bisexual, transgender, and queer ("LGBTQ+") community, the leading case in this area involved a woman who allegedly faced discrimination merely because she wasn't sufficiently "feminine." *See Price Waterhouse v. Hopkins*, 490 U.S. 228 (1989).

Title VII of the Civil Rights Act of 1964, 42 U.S.C. § 2000e to 2000e–17 (2012), makes it an unlawful employment practice for an employer "to fail or refuse to hire or to discharge any individual, or otherwise to discriminate against any individual with respect to his compensation, terms, conditions, or privileges of employment, because of such individual's . . . . sex." 42 U.S.C. § 2000e–2(a)(1). This *Nutshell* only discusses Title VII as it relates to issues involving the LGBTQ+ community. For a general consideration of Title VII, the reader should consult other sources.

Ann Hopkins filed suit under Title VII after she was denied a partnership in her accounting firm. *Price Waterhouse*, 490 U.S. at 232. While she was seeking promotion to partner, she had been advised that she should "walk more femininely, talk more femininely, dress more femininely, wear make-up, have her hair styled, and wear jewelry." *Id.* at 235 (quoting *Hopkins v. Price Waterhouse*, 618 F. Supp. 1109, 1117 (D.D.C. 1985)). Social psychologist Dr. Susan Fiske testified at the trial that Price Waterhouse was likely influenced by "sex stereotyping" when it made its partnership decision. *Id.* at 235.

The Supreme Court found that "sex stereotyping" has legal relevance to a claim under Title VII:

> [W]e are beyond the day when an employer could evaluate employees by assuming or insisting that they matched the stereotype associated with their group . . . . An employer who objects to aggressiveness in women but whose positions require this trait places women in an intolerable and impermissible catch 22: out of a job if they behave aggressively and out of a job if they do not. Title VII lifts women out of this bind.

Id. at 251. Thus, a sexual stereotyping theory has been available under Title VII since 1989.

§ 3.4 TITLE VII POST-PRICE WATERHOUSE

While the *Price Waterhouse* case did not involve a plaintiff who considered herself to be a member of the LGBTQ+ community, the decision in that case has been very useful to many cases involving such plaintiffs. It has sometimes been useful for individuals who identify as transgender or for individuals who are gay men or lesbians and do not subscribe to traditional notions of masculinity or femininity.

Before *Price Waterhouse* was decided, the federal courts had uniformly concluded that Title VII could not be used to protect people from transgender discrimination. *See, e.g., Ulane v. E. Airlines, Inc.*, 742 F.2d 1081 (7th Cir. 1984); *Holloway v. Arthur Andersen & Co.*, 566 F.2d 659 (9th Cir. 1977); *Sommers v. Budget Mktg., Inc.*, 667 F.2d 748 (8th Cir. 1982). The rationale behind these cases was that Title VII merely barred discrimination on the basis of "sex" but not "gender." *See, e.g., Ulane*, 742 F.2d at 1084.

Following the *Price Waterhouse* decision, many federal courts began to re-think the sex/gender distinction with respect to Title VII coverage. The Ninth Circuit reconsidered its own decision in *Holloway* and concluded that federal law can bar discrimination against someone because he or she identifies as transgender. *See Schwenk v. Hartford*, 204 F.3d 1187 (9th Cir. 2000) (finding that the Gender Motivated Violence Act parallels Title VII and thereby protects transgendered prisoners from gender-based, as well as sex-based, discrimination).

Title VII was found to provide a cause of action for: a man whose co-workers and supervisors repeatedly referred to him as "she" and "her" and mocked him for walking and carrying his serving tray "like a woman," *Nichols v. Azteca Restaurant Enters, Inc.*, 256 F.3d 864 (9th Cir. 2001); a man who did not meet stereotyped expectations of masculinity, *Higgins v. New Balance Athletic Shoe, Inc.*, 194 F.3d 252 (1st Cir. 1999); a man who was treated "like a woman," *Rene v. MGM Grand Hotel, Inc.*, 305 F.3d 1061 (9th

Cir. 2002); a man who was treated adversely when he began to express less masculine and more feminine mannerisms and appearance, *Smith v. City of Salem*, 378 F.3d 566, 572 (6th Cir. 2004); and a transgendered woman who wore women's clothing at work, *Glenn v. Brumby*, 663 F.3d 1312 (11th Cir. 2011).

The *Price Waterhouse* theory has also been applied to the Gender Motivated Violence Act and the Equal Credit Opportunity Act. *See Schwenk v. Hartford*, 204 F.3d 1187 (9th Cir. 2000); *Rosa v. Park W. Bank & Trust Co.*, 214 F.3d 213 (1st Cir. 2000).

In 2012, The Equal Employment Opportunity Commission ("EEOC") began using the *Price Waterhouse* theory to pursue claims of discrimination against individuals who are transgendered as part of its federal sector enforcement authority on behalf of a transgender individual. *See Macy v. Holder*, EEOC Appeal No. 0120120821, 2012 WL 1435995 (April 20, 2012). Mia Macy alleged that she was denied a position with the Bureau of Alcohol, Tobacco, Firearms and Explosives because she was transitioning from male to female. The Bureau had refused to process her entire complaint, finding that Title VII did not cover her transgender allegations. The EEOC reversed the Bureau's decision and remanded the case to the Bureau for corrective action. The EEOC explained:

> When an employer discriminates against someone because the person is transgender, the employer has engaged in disparate treatment "related to the sex of the victim." . . . . This is

> true regardless of whether an employer discriminates against an employee because the individual has expressed his or her gender in a non-stereotypical fashion, because the employer is uncomfortable with the fact that the person has transitioned or is in the process of transitioning from one gender to another, or because the employer simply does not like that the person is identifying as a transgender person. In each of these circumstances, the employer is making a gender-based evaluation, thus violating the Supreme Court's admonition that "an employer may not take gender into account in making employment decision."

Id. at *7.

Similarly, in *Lusardi v. McHugh*, EEOC Appeal No. 0120133395, 2015 WL 1607756 (April 2, 2015), the EEOC reversed the final decision of the Department of the Army, finding that Lusardi was subjected to disparate treatment and harassment based on sex when the Agency restricted her from using the common female restroom and a team leader intentionally and repeatedly referred to her by male pronouns and made hostile remarks.

The EEOC also found that it may be unlawful to intentionally misuse a transgender employee's preferred name and pronoun, *see Jameson*, Appeal No. 0120130992, 2013 WL 2368729 (E.E.O.C. May 21, 2013); and that it may be unlawful to intentionally refuse to revise a transgendered employee's records to reflect the employee's gender identity, *see Complainant v. Shinseki*, Appeal No.

0120133123, 2014 WL 1653484 (E.E.O.C. April 16, 2014).

On July 15, 2015, the Commission took the position that claims of sexual orientation discrimination necessarily constitute sex discrimination under Title VII. *See Baldwin v. Foxx*, Appeal No. 0120133080, 2015 WL 4397641 (E.E.O.C. July 15, 2015). David Baldwin alleged that he was not selected for a permanent Front Line Manager position because he was gay. He alleged that his supervisor had made several negative comments about his sexual orientation. Baldwin filed a claim of discrimination with the Federal Aviation Administration ("Agency"). The Agency did not find in Baldwin's favor, and he appealed their determination to the EEOC.

One issue raised in Baldwin's complaint was whether his claim of sexual orientation discrimination was cognizable under Title VII. Rather than limit its jurisdiction to certain types of sexual orientation claims, the Commission found that "sexual orientation is inherently a 'sex-based consideration,' and an allegation of discrimination based on sexual orientation is necessarily an allegation of sex discrimination under Title VII." *Id.* at *5.

The Commission offered several explanations for why that conclusion was legally correct. First, it observed that "sexual orientation discrimination is sex discrimination because it necessarily entails treating an employee less favorably because of the employee's sex." *Id.* at *5. A female employee who is treated adversely because her partner is a woman is treated differently, on the basis of sex, if a male employee would not be treated adversely because his partner was a woman. This interpretation of Title VII is consistent with the district court decision in *Hall v. BNSF Railway Company*, No. C13–2160 RSM, 2014 WL 4719007 (W.D. Wash. Sept. 22, 2014) (finding that Title VII covered a claim by a man who alleged he was treated differently than a woman who was married to a man).

Second, it found that sexual orientation discrimination is "sex discrimination because it is associational discrimination on the basis of sex." *Baldwin* at *6. A person is treated differently because of the sex of the person with whom the person associates. Relying on cases in which courts held that it was illegal to treat someone differently because they associated with a person of a particular *race*, the Commission found that that analysis "is not limited to the context of race discrimination." *Id.* at *7.

Third, it found that sexual orientation discrimination is sex discrimination "because it necessarily involves discrimination based on gender stereotypes." *Id.* at *7. Further, these stereotypes involve "far more than assumptions about overt masculine or feminine behavior." *Id.* at *7. They are often "motivated by a desire to enforce heterosexuality defined gender norms." *Id.* at *8 (quoting *Centola v. Potter*, 183 F. Supp. 2d 403, 410 (D. Mass. 2002)).

The Commission then deflected the argument that Title VII could not be interpreted to prohibit sexual orientation discrimination because the 1964 Congress did not intend Title VII to have that interpretation. Citing the Supreme Court's unanimous opinion in *Oncale v. Sundowner Offshore Services, Inc.*, 523 U.S. 75 (1998), the Commission found that statutory prohibitions are often interpreted to cover "reasonably comparable evils" and that "it is ultimately the provisions of our laws rather than the principal concerns of our legislators by which we are governed." *Id.* at *9. Citing a district court, the Commission noted that nothing in the text of Title VII "suggests that Congress intended to confine the benefits of [the] statute to heterosexual employees alone." *Id.* at *9 (quoting *Heller v. Columbia Edgewater Country Club*, 195 F. Supp. 2d 1212, 1222 (D. Or. 2002)). The Commission concluded that its role is to "apply the words of the statute Congress has charged us with enforcing" irrespective of whether Congress has specifically decided to amend the statute to clarify such a meaning. *Id.* at *9–10. Therefore, it concluded that federal agencies should process claims of sexual orientation discrimination "as complaints of sex discrimination." *Id.* at *10. The case was remanded to the Agency for further processing for a determination on the merits.

These cases were resolved through the EEOC's internal mechanism where the EEOC is the final arbiter of the complaint because the complaining party works for the federal government. The EEOC also began to file complaints using similar legal theories against private employers where a federal court would ultimately decide the case if the parties did not settle. For example, on January 21, 2016, the

EEOC settled a suit against Deluxe Financial Services Corporation for $115,000. *See* Press Release, U.S. Equal Emp't Opportunity Comm'n, Deluxe Financial to Settle Sex Discrimination Suit on Behalf of Transgender Employee (Jan. 21, 2016), available at https://www.eeoc.gov/newsroom/deluxe-financial-settle-sex-discrimination-suit-behalf-transgender-employee. The company had refused to let Britney Austin use the women's restroom after she began to present as female at work and subjected her to a hostile work environment with epithets and deliberate use of the wrong gender pronouns. It had previously settled a lawsuit against a Florida eye clinic and a Detroit area funeral home regarding employees who faced discrimination when they were transitioning from male to female. *See* Press Release, U.S. Equal Emp't Opportunity Comm'n, EEOC Sues Detroit Funeral Home Chain for Sex Discrimination against Transgender Employee, (Sept. 25, 2014), available at https://www.eeoc.gov/newsroom/eeoc-sues-detroit-funeral-home-chain-sex-discrimination-against-transgender-employee.

The EEOC was also active in filing amicus briefs in cases filed against private sector defendants who have allegedly engaged in discrimination on the basis of transgendered status. Some of these suits settled. *See, e.g., Dawson v. H & H Electric, Inc.*, No. 4:14CV00583 SWW, 2015 WL 5437101 (E.D. Ark. Sept. 15, 2015) (court denying defendant's summary judgment in case where plaintiff fired after she began transitioning and her boss said she was being fired because "you're too much of a distraction").

§ 3.5 BOSTOCK V. CLAYTON COUNTY

The Supreme Court resolved the status of the coverage of transgender and sexual orientation discrimination issues under Title VII Court on June 15, 2020 when it decided *Bostock v. Clayton County, Georgia,* 590 U.S. 644 (2020) in a 6–3 decision. *Bostock* was a consolidated consideration of several cases, one of which involved a transgender woman who was terminated from her employment at a funeral home when she was in the process of transitioning from male to female. Justice Gorsuch wrote the opinion for the Court which was joined by Chief Justice Roberts and Justices Ginsburg, Breyer, Sotomayor, and Kagan. The dissenters included Justices Alito, Thomas and Kavanaugh. *Bostock* also resolved the issue of whether Title VII covered sexual orientation discrimination. Thus, that issue will be discussed here as well.

In deciding this case, Justice Gorsuch first resolved the kind of intent that is required in a Title VII case. Citing the *Price Waterhouse* decision, the Court said:

> If the employer intentionally relies in part on an individual employee's sex when deciding to discharge the employee—put differently, if changing the employee's sex would have yielded a different choice by the employer—a statutory violation has occurred.

Id. 659–60.

The Court then applied this intent standard to the transgender plaintiff who was fired after she informed her employer that she would be gender transitioning. The Court said:

> Or take an employer who fires a transgender person who was identified as a male at birth but who now identifies as a female. If the employer retains an otherwise identical employee who was identified as female at birth, the employer intentionally penalizes a person identified as male at birth for traits or actions that it tolerates in an employee identified as female at birth. Again, the individual employee's sex plays an unmistakable and impermissible role in the discharge decision.

Id. at 660.

After resolving what the Court considered to be a straightforward application of the but-for causation test to the cases before them, the Court also considered what issues were *not* before them in these cases and might be present in the future.

First, the Court mentioned cases that might involve sex-segregated bathrooms, locker rooms, and dress codes, and merely said that those issues are not before the Court and "have not had the benefit of adversarial testing." *Id.* at 681.

Second, the Court mentioned the possibility of these cases involving free exercise of religion issues. Here, the Court used stronger language suggesting that Title VII might have to yield to free exercise protection. It noted that Congress has passed the Religious Freedom Restoration Act ["RFRA"], which provides even greater religious liberty protection than the First Amendment:

> That statute prohibits the federal government from substantially burdening a person's exercise of religion unless it demonstrates that doing so both furthers a compelling governmental interest and represents the least restrictive means of further than interest. § 2000bb–1. Because RFRA operates as a kind of super statute, displacing the normal operation of other federal laws, it might supersede Title VII's commands in appropriate cases.

Id. at 682.

Further, the Court noted that the defendant-funeral home did unsuccessfully pursue a RFRA-based defense in the lower courts but declined to raise this issue in the certiorari petition. "So while other employers in other cases may raise free exercise arguments that merit careful consideration, none of the employers before us today represent in this Court that compliance with Title VII will infringe their own religious liberties in any way." *Id.* at 682.

With respect to the sexual orientation complaint that was part of the *Bostock* case, the majority concluded that a textual interpretation of Title VII causes one to conclude that it bans discrimination on the basis of sexual orientation. This is the key language in the majority opinion on that issue:

> The statute's message for our cases is equally simple and momentous: An individual's

homosexuality or transgender status is not relevant to employment decisions. That's because it is impossible to discriminate against a person for being homosexual or transgender without discriminating against that individual based on sex. Consider, for example, an employer with two employees, both of whom are attracted to men. The two individuals are, to the employer's mind, materially identical in all respects, except that one is a man and the other is a woman. If the employer fires the male employee for no reason other than the fact he is attracted to men, the employer discriminates against him for traits or actions it tolerates in his female colleague. Put differently, the employer intentionally singles out an employee to fire based on part on the employee's sex, and the affected employee's sex is a but-for-cause of his discharge. . . .

Imagine an employer who has a policy of firing any employee known to be homosexual. The employer hosts an office holiday party and invites employees to bring their spouses. A model employee arrives and introduces a manager to Susan, the employee's wife. Will that employee be fired? If the policy works as the employer intends, the answer depends entirely on whether the model employee is a man or a woman. To be sure, that employer's ultimate goal might be to discriminate on the basis of sexual orientation. But to achieve that purpose the employer must, along the way, intentionally

> treat an employee worse based in part on that individual's sex.

Id. at 661–62.

Justice Alito dissented in an opinion joined by Justice Thomas. He accused the majority of enacting legislation rather than interpreting it, noting that Congress has considered but not enacted legislation amending Title VII to ban discrimination on the basis of sexual orientation and gender identity. They insist that the proper textual question is how Americans in 1964 would have understood the term "sex discrimination." They argue that Americans in 1964 would have been "shocked" to learn that Congress was banning sexual orientation discrimination and "bewildered" to hear that Congress was banning a category that was not even widely understood to exist in 1964. *Id.* at 714–15.

Alito's dissenting opinion also lays out the potential consequences of the majority's opinion, including discussion of *"bathrooms, locker rooms, [and other things] of [that] kind."* (*Id.* at 725; italics in original) Justice Alito then explains at length the consequences of the majority decision:

> The Court may wish to avoid the subject, but it is a matter of concern to many people who are reticent about disrobing or using toilet facilities in the presence of individuals whom they regard as members of the opposite sex. . . . For women who have been victimized by sexual assault or abuse, the experience of seeing an unclothed person with the anatomy of a male in a confined

> and sensitive location such as a bathroom or locker room can cause serious psychological harm. . . . Thus, a person who has not undertaken any physical transitioning may claim the right to use the bathroom or locker room assigned to the sex with which the individual identifies at that particular time. The Court provides no clue why a transgender person's claim to such bathroom or locker room access might not succeed.

Id. at 726.

Alito's dissent also listed other issues that are potentially implicated by the majority decision, including women's sports, housing, employment by religious organizations, health care, freedom of speech, and constitutional claims to heightened scrutiny. He predicts that the "entire Federal Judiciary will be mired for years in disputes about the reach of the Court's reasoning." *Id.* at 734. He then included a lengthy appendix which listed the relevant dictionary definitions and a list of all the laws that have "because of sex" language which are potentially affected by the Court's decision.

Justice Kavanaugh wrote a separate dissent in which he re-iterated the point about the importance of the judiciary interpreting rather than updating laws. But rather than emphasize the tragic consequences for bathrooms, locker rooms and the like, he ended his opinion with an acknowledgement of the victory the majority decision entailed for the gay and lesbian community (but, interestingly, does not mention the transgender community).

While certainly serving as a victory for the transgender community, the *Bostock* opinion raises as many issues as it answers. Only four members of the *Bostock* majority (Gorsuch, Roberts, Sotomayor and Kagan) are still on the Court. Justice Jackson usually votes with the liberal wing of the Court so she can be expected to follow that ruling, creating a five-vote majority in favor of the opinion. With five members of the Court likely supporting *Bostock's* holding, there is little reason to think that the Court will repudiate the basic statutory question of Title VII coverage. While Justice Alito may be wrong that courts will be "mired for years" in cases involving bathrooms, locker rooms, and similar issues, we can certainly expect some of those issues to arise in the lower courts under other statutes such as Title IX, as will be discussed below. The *Bostock* opinion offers little guidance for resolving these other issues except to suggest that RFRA defenses may be applicable. The decision in *United States v. Skrmetti*, 145 S. Ct. 1816 (2025) (discussed in *Nutshell* § 3.6) also offers little guidance except to say: "We have not yet considered whether *Bostock's* reasoning reaches beyond the Title VII context, and we need not do so here." *Id.* at 1834.

It is also important to recognize that, at this time, the Trump administration appears to be interpreting *Bostock* narrowly with regard to Title VII. For example, Treasury Secretary Scott Bessent indicated that he planned to remove sexual orientation and gender identity as bases for sex discrimination in several EEOC forms. *See* Christopher Kane, *House Democrats oppose Bessent's removal of SOGI from discrimination complaint forms,* WASH. BLADE, July 1, 2025, https://www.washingtonblade.com/2025/07/01/house-democrats-oppose-bessents-removal-of-sogi-from-discrimination-complaint-forms/. The removal of that language from the form does not overturn *Bostock* but certainly reflects a disinterest in enforcing this area of the law by the Trump administration. On July 1, 2025, the EEOC sent a memo from its Office of Field Programs to EEOC staff which said:

> For those charges that fall squarely under *Bostock*, e.g., hiring, discharge or promotion, you are clear to continue processing these charges. If the evidence indicates that a cause determination will be issues, send a copy of the charge, IM [Investigation Memo], LOD [Letter of Determination] and cause memo (if prepared by legal) to [name redacted], Senior Attorney Advisor, OFP prior to the LOD being issued. After [name redacted] reviews, we will discuss with OCH [Office of the Chair] and circle back with you for the issuance of the LOD.

See https://static1.squarespace.com/static/67f14b136c5a8838cca88ae0/t/687d867215f8a2128c6e9c2a/1753056882929/EEO+Leadership+Group+Statement+on+EEOC%27s+Processing+of+LGBTQ%2B+Charges+07.21.25.pdf?fbclid=IwY2xjawLrjvFleHRuA2FlbQIxMQABHiHlpEJngHc8r8pBlwOg8E998Ne1IV_QDaZt5JBNmzOvQv2ROruotYWfgQST_aem_QkjuQNEosDIoPQMrQ1AZ-Q.

One could imagine that a field office might be reluctant to go through all those additional steps to do their job and might even worry about retaliation for trying to pursue such a complaint.

Given this narrow interpretation of Title VII, as discussed in *Nutshell* Chapter 4 one might want to consider suing under a state nondiscrimination statute, especially if it explicitly bans sexual orientation or gender identity discrimination.

Another consequence of *Bostock* may be cases by heterosexuals who claim that lesbians or gay men received preferential treatment in comparison to them. The Supreme Court recently made it easier for such cases to move forward in *Ames v. Ohio Department of Youth Services,* 605 U.S. 303 (2025). Plaintiff Marlean Ames alleged that she was denied a management position and demoted because of her heterosexual sexual orientation. The candidates who attained those positions were a lesbian and a gay man. Prior Title VII case law had established that "a plaintiff who is a member of a majority group must also show background circumstances to support the suspicion that the defendant is that unusual employer who discriminates against the majority." *Id.* at 305 In a unanimous opinion authored by Justice Jackson, the Court overturned that precedent, vacated the judgment below, and remanded for application of the proper prima facie standard. This decision applies to all Title VII cases, not just ones that allege sexual orientation discrimination.

Finally, it is not clear if the EEOC will be permitted to broadly interpret *Bostock.* District Court Judge Matthew Kacsmaryk found the EEOC's

2024 Enforcement Guidance to be unlawful. *See* 88 Fed. Reg. 67750 (Oct. 2, 2023) (notice and comment period). He especially singled out language in the enforcement guidance that says that sexual harassment includes "repeated and intentional use of a name or pronoun inconsistent with the individual's known gender identity (misgendering)" and "denial of access to a bathroom or other sex-segregated facility consistent with the individual's gender identity." *Texas v. EEOC,* 2025 WL 1414332, *2 (N.D. Tex. May 15, 2025). When Judge Kacsmaryk issued this opinion, the EEOC lacked a quorum to seek to rescind that guidance (which was also inconsistent with Trump's Executive Order 14168). Because the Trump administration is unlikely to seek to enforce this guidance, the decision has no immediate impact. But it could limit future administrations that seek to interpret *Bostock* more broadly.

§ 3.6 UNITED STATES V. SKRMETTI

While *Bostock* was certainly a highly significant case under Title VII, *United States v. Skrmetti,* 145 S. Ct. 1816 (2025), may prove to be even more transformative. This section will describe the analytical framework used by the Court in *Skrmetti* to determine that a state can ban gender-affirming care for minors. That framework may have application outside the healthcare setting and may, in some instances, narrow the application of *Bostock.* Its possible application to health care issues, outside the context of gender-affirming care for minors, will be discussed in *Nutshell* § 3.11, below.

Skrmetti involved the constitutionality of a 2023 Tennessee law (SB1) that banned various kinds of gender-affirming care for transgender minors. The law prohibited a healthcare provider from:

> "[s]urgically removing, modifying, altering, or entering into tissues, cavities, or organs of a human being," or "[p]rescribing, administering, or dispensing any puberty blocker or hormone, § 68–33–102(5), for the purpose of (1) "[e]nabling a minor to identify with, or live as, a purported identity inconsistent with the minor's sex," or (2) "[t]reating purported discomfort or distress from a discordance between the minor's sex and asserted identity," § 68–33–103(a)(1).

Id. at 1826.

Three transgender minors, their parents, and a doctor brought a pre-enforcement challenge to SB1. They argued that SB1 violated the Equal Protection Clause of the Fourteenth Amendment. The district court partially enjoined enforcement of SB1; the Sixth Circuit reversed. The Supreme Court affirmed the Sixth Circuit.

The plaintiffs' main arguments rested on sex equality and transgender equality claims. First, they argued that SB1 constituted sex discrimination (and therefore heightened scrutiny) because "SB1 prohibits certain treatments for minors of one sex while allowing those same treatments for minors of the opposite sex." *Id.* at 1829. In other words, an adolescent whose biological sex is female can receive estrogen treatment but an adolescent whose biological sex is male cannot.

The Court rejected the claim that SB1 could be understood as sex discrimination. The Court concluded that SB1:

> does not prohibit conduct for one sex that it permits for the other. Under SB1, *no* minor may be administered puberty blockers or hormones to treat gender dysphoria, gender identity disorder, or gender incongruence; minors of *any* sex may be administered puberty blockers or hormones for other purposes.

Id. at 1831.

The dissent responded to this argument by emphasizing that SB1 promotes sex stereotypes by including statutory findings that its purpose is to "encourage[e] minors to appreciate their sex." *Id.* at 1832. While acknowledging that the Fourteenth Amendment does invalidate sex stereotyping, the Court found that "statutory findings to which the plaintiffs point do not themselves evince sex-based stereotyping." *Id.* at 1832. Further, the Court noted that sex stereotyping argument must demonstrate that the law was "motivated by an invidious discriminatory purpose." In rejecting the sex stereotyping theory, the Court said: "Tennessee's stated interests in 'encouraging minors to appreciate their sex' and in prohibiting medical care 'that might encourage minors to become disdainful of their sex, § 68–33–101(m), simply reflect the State's concerns regarding the use of puberty blockers and hormones to treat gender dysphoria, gender identity disorder, and gender incongruence." *Id.* at 1832. The Court then discussed the possibility that a minor could regret their decision or become disdainful of their sex. *Id.* at 1832. In other words, the Court accepted the argument from the Sixth Circuit that: "A concern about potentially irreversible medical procedures for a child is not a form of stereotyping." *Id.* at 1832.

An important take-away is that neither the Sixth Circuit, nor the Supreme Court, in upholding SB1 questioned whether a sex-role stereotyping theory is still available to challenge a legislative classification. The reader should watch the developments in this area to see if the courts find other examples of discrimination against transgender individuals to be based on sex-role stereotyping.

Plaintiffs' second legal theory was that "SB1 warrants heightened scrutiny because it discriminates against transgender individuals who the plaintiffs assert constitute a quasi-suspect class." *Id.* at 1832. The Court does not reach that issue because the statute "does not classify on the basis of transgender status." *Id.* at 1833. They found that SB1 classifies on the basis of age and "gender dysphoria, gender identity disorder or gender incongruence" and not on the basis of transgender status. *Id.* at 1833. The Court explained:

> SB1 does not exclude any individual from medical treatments on the basis of transgender status but rather removes one set of diagnoses—gender dysphoria, gender identity disorder, and gender incongruence—from the range of

> treatable conditions. SB1 divides minors into two groups: those who might seek puberty blockers or hormones to treat the excluded diagnoses, and those who might seek puberty blockers or hormones to treat other conditions. *See* Tenn. Code Ann. § 68–33–103. Because only transgender individuals seek puberty blockers and hormones for the excluded diagnoses, the first group includes only transgender individuals; the second group, in contrast, encompasses both transgender and nontransgender individuals. Thus, although only transgender individuals seek treatment for gender dysphoria, gender identity disorder, and gender incongruence—just as only biological women can become pregnant—there is a "lack of identity" between transgender status and the excluded medical diagnoses. The plaintiffs, moreover, have not argued that SB1's prohibitions are mere pretexts designed to effect an invidious discrimination against transgender individuals. Under these circumstances, we decline to find that SB1's prohibitions on the use of puberty blockers and hormones exclude any individuals on the basis of transgender status.
>
> *Id.* at 1833–34.

Having concluded that heightened scrutiny was not required, the Court then analyzed the case under rational basis scrutiny. The Court then recited Tennessee's arguments for banning puberty blockers and hormonal therapy for minors. It said:

> We also decline the plaintiffs' invitation to second-guess the lines that SB1 draws. It may be true, as the plaintiffs contend, that puberty blockers and hormones carry comparable risks for minors no matter the purposes for which they are administered. But it may also be true, as Tennessee determined, that those drugs carry greater risks when administered to treat gender dysphoria, gender identity disorder, and gender incongruence. We afford States "wide discretion to pass legislation in areas where there is medical and scientific uncertainty." . . . . The fact that the line may have been drawn differently at some points is a matter for legislative, rather than judicial, consideration.

Id. at 1836.

While this holding makes clear that states can ban gender-affirming care for minors, it is hard to know how far its holding extends to other areas. Following the *Skrmetti* decision, the Supreme Court sent four cases back to the courts of appeals to be reconsidered in light of *Skrmetti*. Two involved Medicaid exclusions for gender-affirming medical care, one involved public teachers' health insurance plans, and one involved birth certificate policies. *See Crouch v. Anderson*, 100 F.4th 122 (4th Cir. April 2024), *cert. granted & judgment vacated*, 2025 WL 1787687 (June 30, 2025); *Kadel v. Folwell*, 100 F.4th 122 (4th Cir. 2024), *cert. granted & judgment vacated by Folwell v. Kadel*, 2025 WL 1787687 (June 30, 2025); *Stitt v. Fowler*, 104 F.4th 770 (10th Cir. 2024), *cert. granted & judgment vacated*, 2025 WL 1787695

(June 30, 2025); *Hamso v. M.H.*, 2024 WL 4100235 (9th Cir. Sept. 6, 2024), *cert. granted & judgment vacated,* 2025 WL 1787693 (June 30, 2025).

The two Fourth Circuit cases involved health plans that denied gender-affirming care for transgender individuals. One case was from North Carolina's state-operated insurance plan for teachers and state employees. The other case was from West Virginia's Medicaid program. The district court found for the plaintiffs and both cases, and the Fourth Circuit affirmed those decisions. Similarly, the Ninth Circuit case involved Medicaid coverage (in Idaho). The case involved a qualified immunity issue but the underlying legal issue involved an equal protection challenge to a denial of Medicaid coverage. The Ninth Circuit ruled against the defendant's qualified immunity argument.

Unlike *Skrmetti,* these cases involved the coverage of adults. But, unlike *Skrmetti*, the state did not ban the medical coverage; it merely made it unavailable through a health care plan. These health care issues will be discussed further in § 3.11, below.

The Tenth Circuit case involved the state of Oklahoma's refusal to issue sex-designation amendments to birth certificates. The Tenth Circuit found that the policy constituted sex-based discrimination and subjected it to heightened scrutiny. Identity document legal issues will be discussed in *Nutshell* § 3.9, below. The decision to vacate and remand this case, however, suggests that the Court may be willing to allow states to refuse to change gender designations on birth certificates for transgender individuals.

In ending this discussion, however, it is important to emphasize three points. *Skrmetti* did not resolve the question of whether discrimination against transgender individuals can ever be considered under heightened scrutiny, whether discrimination against transgender individuals can be overturned as reflecting animus towards the class, and whether the deferential consideration of medical arguments about minors would apply to cases involving transgender adults. These are issues to watch as the courts consider more cases in this area.

§ 3.7 TITLE IX APPLICATION TO GENDER IDENTITY AND EXPRESSION

A. GENERAL CONSIDERATIONS

Title IX of the Education Amendments of 1972 prohibits educational entities that receive federal financial assistance from discriminating on the basis of sex. 20 U.S.C. § 1681 et seq (2006).

The coverage of transgender issues under Title IX is one of the rapidly evolving areas of the law. This *Nutshell* can only offer a snapshot of court decisions as of summer 2025. The *Bostock* decision suggests that courts could conclude that the "because of sex" language under Title IX will be interpreted to cover discrimination on the basis of transgender status. Thus, one might expect that it would be unlawful for a school or university to treat a student adversely because of their transgender status.

There are two countervailing developments that question that result: Trump administration executive actions and the Supreme Court's decision in *Skrmetti*. On January 20, 2025, President Trump issued Executive Order 14168 entitled "Defending Women From Gender Ideology Extremism and Restoring Biological Truth to the Federal Government." This Executive Order defines the terms "male" and "female" based on their reproductive cells "at conception." *Id.* at Sec. 2 (d) & (e). The E.O. also criticizes the Biden administration's application of *Bostock* to Title IX in the context of "access to single-sex spaces." *Id.* at Sec. 2(f). The E.O. orders the Attorney General to issue guidance to assist "agencies in protecting sex-based distinctions." *Id.* In compliance with that E.O., the Acting Assistant Secretary for Civil Rights, U.S. Dept. of Education, authored a letter stating that the Office for Civil Rights (OCR) at the U.S. Dept. of Education (ED) would enforce the 2020 Title IX Rule rather than the 2024 Title IX Rule regarding "the procedural protections owed to complainants and respondents, the provision of supportive measures to complainants, and school-level reporting processes." *See* Letter from Craig Trainor, Acting Assistant Secretary for Civil Rights, U.S. Dept. of Educ., Feb. 4, 2025. https://www.ed.gov/media/document/title-ix-enforcement-directive-dcl-109477.pdf The repudiated 2024 regulations did seek to protect transgender students from adverse treatment at school, including harassment because it defined discrimination on the basis of sex to include discrimination on the basis of gender identity. 34

C.F.R. § 106.10. They have been enjoined by a number of courts including the granting of a nationwide injunction in one court. *See Tennessee v. Cardona,* 762 F. Supp.3d 615 (E.D. Ky. 2025). That case is on appeal to the Sixth Circuit but one would expect that the Trump administration would not defend the Biden regulations. So, the nationwide injunction may stand even without the February OCR letter.

This regulatory back and forth relates to how the federal government will choose to enforce Title IX. The Trump administration has made it clear that it will not consider transgender complaints brought under Title IX. But that does not resolve the question of how *courts* might interpret Title IX if a student filed a complaint against a university as a private right of action. The Supreme Court has ruled that students have a private right of action under Title IX. *See Cannon v. University of Chicago,* 441 U.S. 677 (1979). In more recent years, the Court has said it is bound by *Cannon's* holding, but the decision's "language" no longer controls the issue of whether a federal statute provides an implied right of action. *See Alexander v. Sandoval,* 532 U.S. 275, 282 (2001). So, it is possible that a transgender student could seek to enforce Title IX by arguing that it bars transgender discrimination, relying on *Bostock's* statutory analysis of Title VII.

The second countervailing issue is that the *Skrmetti* Court explicitly stated that: "We have not yet considered whether *Bostock's* reasoning reaches beyond the Title VII context, and we need not do so here." *Skrmetti,* at 1834. *See Nutshell* § 3.6, above, for further discussion of *Skrmetti.*

B. BATHROOMS AND LOCKER ROOMS

Coverage under Title IX raises questions about bathrooms, locker rooms, and sports that were not resolved by *Bostock*. This section will discuss the Title IX cases that were brought during the Obama, Biden and Trump administrations concerning access to bathrooms and locker rooms. Athletics will be discussed in *Nutshell* § 3.1, below.

In 2015, the Occupational Safety and Health Administration ("OSHA") issued a four-page booklet detailing the best practices for providing restroom access to transgender workers. Those guidelines specify that workers should be allowed to use restroom facilities that correspond with their gender identity. Single-occupancy gender-neutral (unisex) facilities or multiple-occupant, gender-neutral facilities with lockable single occupant stalls may be offered as an option that all employees may choose but may not be required to use. It is not clear that OSHA itself would bring an action against an employer for violating that best practice policy, but the guidance notes that legal actions for violating that policy may be brought under Title VII or state nondiscrimination statutes. *See* OCCUPATIONAL SAFETY AND HEALTH ADMINISTRATION, OSHA3795–2015, BEST PRACTICES: A GUIDE TO RESTROOM ACCESS FOR TRANSGENDER WORKERS (2015). OSHA has taken down the link to this guide. Other organizations have summarized these guidelines although the OSHA link is no longer available. *See, e.g.*, BEST PRACTICES: A GUIDE TO RESTROOM ACCESS FOR TRANSGENDER WORKERS, https://assets2.hrc.org/files/assets/resources/OSHA_Guidelines_Transgender_Bathroom_Access_Best_Practices.pdf. Most of the cases involving bathroom access have involved the U.S. Constitution or Title IX, not OSHA policy. The fact that OSHA has taken down the link suggests that it is no longer enforcing those policies. Thus, this section will discuss other avenues that have been used to challenge restrictive bathroom policies.

On October 10, 2011, the National Center for Lesbian Rights filed a complaint on behalf of a student who had transitioned from female to male. The school refused to allow him to change in the boy's gym or use the boy's locker room. On a school overnight trip, he was not allowed to room with the other boys. On July 24, 2013, the Department of Education and the Department of Justice announced that they had resolved the complaint. *See* Letter from Anurima Bhargava, United States Department of Justice and Arthur Zeidman, United States Department of Education to Asaf Orr, National Center for Lesbian Right (July 24, 2013), available at The Resolution Agreement required the school district to "permit the Student to use male-designated facilities at school and on school-sponsored trips and to otherwise treat the Student as a boy in all respects." *See* Mark Walsh, *District Settles Federal Complaint by Transgender Student,* EDUCATION WEEK, July 24, 2013, available at https://

www.edweek.org/education/district-settles-federal-complaint-by-transgender-student/2013/07.

On April 29, 2014, the United States Department of Education issued Guidance on "Responsibilities of Schools to Address Sexual Violence, Other Forms of Sex Discrimination." *See* Press Release, U.S. Dep't of Educ., Guidance Issued on Responsibilities of Schools to Address Sexual Violence, Other Forms of Sex Discrimination (April 29, 2014), available at https://www2.ed.gov/about/offices/list/ocr/docs/qa-201404-title-ix.pdf. The Guidance clarified that Title IX provides protections for transgender students.

On December 1, 2014, the Department of Education issued one paragraph in a thirty-four-page memo in which it stated:

> All students, including transgender students and students who do not conform to sex stereotypes, are protected from sex-based discrimination under Title IX. Under Title IX, a recipient generally must treat transgender students consistent with their gender identity in all aspects of the planning, implementation, enrollment, operation, and evaluation of single-sex classes.

See Office for Civil Rights, United States Department of Education, Questions and Answers on Title IX and Single-Sex Elementary and Secondary Classes and Extracurricular Activities (Dec. 1, 2014) at 25, available at https://www2.ed.gov/about/offices/list/ocr/docs/faqs-title-ix-single-sex-201412.pdf.

The United States Department of Justice also initially took the position that Title IX protects the rights of transgender students to use the restroom that matches their gender identity. They filed an amicus brief on behalf of the plaintiff in a case involving Gloucester County School Board's decision to adopt a policy that requires transgendered students to use "alternative private" facilities rather than a public restroom. Gavin Grimm, a transgender male student at Gloucester High School, had notified school administrators during his sophomore year that he would like to socially transition to being male in all aspects of his life, including use of the boys' restroom. *See* American Civil Liberties Union, *Grimm v. Gloucester County School Board* (Aug. 3, 2016), available at https://www.aclu.org/cases/grimm-v-gloucester-county-school-board?redirect=cases/gg-v-gloucester-county-school-board.

After two months of Grimm's using the boys' restroom, the School Board adopted a resolution stating that "It shall be the practice of the GCPS to provide male and female restroom and locker room facilities in its schools, and the use of said facilities shall be limited to the corresponding biological genders, and students with gender identity issues shall be provided an alternative appropriate private facility." *G.G. v. Gloucester County School Board*, 822 F.3d 709 (4th Cir. 2016). The day after this resolution was adopted, the school principal notified Grimm "that he could no longer use the boys' restroom and would be disciplined if he did." *G.G. v. Gloucester County School Board*, 132 F. Supp.3d 736, 741 (E.D. Va. 2015). He was permitted to use one of three unisex restrooms or the restroom in the nurse's office, as well as the female restrooms and locker rooms. *Id.* at 749.

The district court ruled for the school district on September 4, 2015, finding that the Department of Education's regulations that authorized sex-segregated restrooms precluded relief on the plaintiff's behalf. *Id.* Department of Education regulations provide: "A recipient may provide separate toilet, locker room, and shower facilities on the basis of sex, but such facilities provided for students of one sex shall be comparable to such facilities provided for students of the other sex." 34 C.F.R. § 106.33.

The district court judge recognized that the Department of Education had also issued a letter and guidance document providing that transgender students must be treated consistently with their gender identity. *G.G.*, 132 F. Supp.3d at 745. The district court, however, refused to give "controlling weight" to that guidance because it "is plainly erroneous and inconsistent with the regulation." *Id.* at 746.

Grimm appealed the case to the Fourth Circuit. The Department of Justice filed an amicus brief on behalf of the plaintiff on October 28, 2015. The Fourth Circuit concluded that the district court used the wrong evidentiary standard in assessing plaintiff's motion for a preliminary injunction, vacated the denial of a preliminary injunction and remanded for consideration under the correct standard. *G.G. v. Gloucester Cty. Sch. Bd.*, 822 F.3d 709 (4th Cir. 2016).

The Fourth Circuit and district court disagreed about how to interpret the Title IX regulation that allows schools to have separate restrooms on the basis of sex so long as there are comparable facilities. The district court concluded that that regulation precluded the relief that Grimm was seeking. The School Board had argued that it assigned Grimm to a restroom based on their belief that he was "biologically female." *G.G.*, 132 F. Supp. at 744. While it was true that the Department of Education had issued a guidance document in 2015 stating that a school must treat transgender students consistent with their gender identity, the district court concluded that that guidance letter conflicted with the restroom regulation that had been subjected to notice and comment and was subject to *Chevron* deference. The district court concluded that the regulation unambiguously provided authority to school districts to assign students to restrooms on the basis on the school district's understanding of the student's biological sex. Because they considered the regulation to be clear on that issue, they found no reason to defer to the later issued guidance by the Department of Education.

The Fourth Circuit, by contrast, found the restroom regulation ambiguous because it did not specify how one would determine which individuals are male or female in setting restroom policies. *Id.* at 719. It also found that the subsequent transgender guidance was the result of "fair and considered judgment." *Id.* at 719. Because the Department of Education had been enforcing its current position on bathroom access for transgender students since 2014, the Fourth Circuit also found that it was not merely "a convenient litigating position" or a "post hoc rationalization." *Id.* at 719. Therefore, based on principles of administrative law, it concluded that the Department of Education's interpretation of its own restroom regulations should be "accorded controlling weight in this case." *Id.* at 723.

Further, the Fourth Circuit found that the district court judge used the wrong evidentiary standard in considering the plaintiff's request for a preliminary injunction (to be allowed to use the boys' restroom). The Fourth Circuit vacated the district court's denial of plaintiff's motion for a preliminary injunction and remanded the case to consider the request for a preliminary injunction under the appropriate legal standard. Circuit court Judge Paul Neimeyer issued a strong dissent, stating, "This unprecedented holding overrules custom, culture, and the very demands inherent in human nature for privacy and safety." *Id.* at 731 (Neimeyer, J., dissenting).

On remand, on June 23, 2016, the trial court judge issued an injunction prohibiting the school board from implementing its policy limiting restroom use to students' "biological sex." *See G.G. v. Gloucester County School Board*, 2016 WL 3581852 (E.D. Va. June 23, 2016). But then, in a 5–3 vote, on August 3, 2016, the United States Supreme Court stayed the entry of the injunction while it considered an application for a writ of certiorari on the underlying

Fourth Circuit decision. In his concurrence, Justice Breyer explained that he voted to grant the stay as a matter of courtesy. *See Gloucester County School Board v. G.G.*, 579 U.S. 961 (2016). On March 6, 2017, the Supreme Court vacated and remanded the Fourth Circuit's decision for further consideration in light of a guidance document issued by the U.S. Department of Education and Department of Justice on February 22, 2017. *Gloucester County School Board v. G.G.*, 580 U.S. 1168 (2017).

The guidance document mentioned by the Supreme Court was a "Dear Colleague" letter issued jointly by the U.S. Department of Justice and the U.S. Department of Education on February 22, 2017. This "Dear Colleague" letter rescinded the "Dear Colleague" letters that had been issued on January 7, 2015 and May 13, 2016, which took the position that Title IX requires "access to sex-segregated facilities based on gender identity," available at https://www2.ed.gov/about/offices/list/ocr/letters/colleague-201702-title-ix.pdf. The 2017 guidance document said that those earlier guidance documents did not "contain extensive legal analysis or explain how the position is consistent with the express language of Title IX, nor did they undergo any formal public process." The 2017 document therefore concluded that "the Departments thus will not rely on the views expressed within them."

Because the Fourth Circuit's decision had been based on its understanding of the government's interpretation of Title IX and guidance documents, the withdrawal of that position removed the heart of the Fourth Circuit's analysis. After two years of litigation, the plaintiffs found themselves needing to argue the meaning of Title IX, without reference to government guidance documents, or presenting other arguments such as a constitutional challenge.

In light of the Supreme Court remand, the plaintiffs amended their complaint and argued that Grimm had a gender stereotyping claim under Title IX and an equal protection claim under intermediate scrutiny. The district court judge denied the school district's motion to dismiss for failure to state a claim. *Grimm v. Gloucester County School Board,* 302 F. Supp.3d 730 (E.D. Va. 2018). The district court then ruled that the Board's policy violated Grimm's rights under the Fourteenth Amendment and Title IX. , *Grimm v. Gloucester County School Board,* 400 F. Supp.3d 444 (E.D. Va. 2019). The Fourth Circuit affirmed that decision. *See Grimm v. Gloucester County School Board,* 972 F.3d 586 (4th Cir. 2020). A cert. petition was filed in the U.S. Supreme Court on Feb. 19. 2021. On June 28, 2021, the Supreme Court announced that it would not accept certiorari with Justices Thomas and Alito saying they would have preferred to hear the case. The Fourth Circuit decision is therefore controlling in its jurisdiction.

Before the Supreme Court decided *Skrmetti*, the courts of appeals were divided on the bathroom issue. The Seventh Circuit had ruled for a transgender boy who sought to use the boys' restroom. *See Whitaker by Whitaker v. Kenosha Unified School District No. 1 Board of Education,* 858 F.3d 1034 (7th Cir. 2017) (granting preliminary injunction for transgender boy to use boys' restroom). The Eleventh Circuit upheld a school board's decision to separate bathrooms based on biological sex while maintaining single-stall bathrooms for transgender students. *See Adams by and through Kasper v. School Board of St. Johns County,* 57 F.4th 791 (11th Cir. 2022). It relied on the logic that the Court accepted in *Skrmetti*—that the policy does not unlawfully discriminate on the basis of transgender status because it merely constituted discrimination on the basis of biological sex. *Id.* at 809. District courts had typically ruled for transgender students. *See, e.g., Evancho v. Pine-Richland School District,* 237 F. Supp.3d 267 (W.D. Pa. 2017) (granting injunction to transgender students under intermediate scrutiny under Equal Protection Clause but denying injunction on Title IX grounds; court found that school's policy was not saved by availability of single-stall facilities); *M.A.B. v. Board of Education of Talbot County,* 286 F. Supp.3d 704 (D. Md. 2018) (rejecting defendant's motion to dismiss case concerning access to male locker room for transgender boy; access to single-stall restroom to change his clothes not considered adequate); *A.H. v. Minersville Area School District,* 408 F. Supp.3d 536 (M.D. Pa. 2019) (largely ruling in favor of female transgender student's right to use female restroom while leaving some issues involving fieldtrips and other issues for further factual development).

After the Supreme Court issued the *Skrmetti* decision, however, the Seventh Circuit *sua sponte* vacated its opinion dated June 12, 2025, in a case involving bathroom access, saying that the panel should rehear the case and consider overruling *Whitaker*. *See D.P. by A.B. v. Mukwonago*, 140 F.4th 826 (7th Cir. June 12, 2025), vacating and remanding, 2025 WL 1794428 (7th Cir. June 30, 2025).

Although attempts to limit bathroom use by transgender people seem to be increasingly successful, there are some interesting counterexamples. Three are discussed below.

First, a North Carolina law, which was passed in March 2016, was particularly sweeping in banning bathroom use by transgender people. It was passed in response to the approval of an ordinance on February 22, 2016, by the Charlotte City Council that amended its existing public accommodations protections by barring discrimination in public accommodations based on "gender identity, gender expression" and "sexual orientation." Before the ordinance could go into effect, the state of North Carolina held a special session on March 23, 2016, to pass a law that provides that "local boards of education shall require every multiple occupancy bathroom or changing facility that is designated for student use to be designated for and used only by students based on their biological sex." It also precludes individuals from using restrooms in public facilities that do not correspond to the sex indicated on their birth certificate. "Biological sex" is defined as "the physical condition of being male or female, which is stated on a person's birth certificate." H.R. 2, 152d Sess., 2d Extra Sess., at Section 115C–521.2 (N.C. 2016). The bill passed unanimously less than ten hours after it was introduced and was signed into law by Governor McCrory on that same night.

Passage of the law (called "House Bill 2") generated enormous backlash with Bruce Springsteen cancelling a concert and PayPal deciding against expanding its business operations to North Carolina. Both the ACLU and Lambda Legal Defense Fund filed legal challenges against the law, on behalf of individuals who are transgender, and their gender identification does not correspond to the sex denoted on their birth certificate. Plaintiffs argued that House Bill 2 violated both the Equal Protection and Due Process Clauses of the Fourteenth Amendment as well as Title IX. *See* Complaint for Declaratory and Injunctive Relief, *Carcaño v. McCrory*, No. 1:16–cv–236 (M.D.N.C. March 28, 2016).

One argument made in the complaint was that the law required individuals who are transgender to undergo "sex reassignment surgery" to use an appropriate restroom. Such surgery is not always medically necessary or appropriate for individuals who are transgender; it is also very expensive and not always covered by health insurance. Plaintiffs argued that the requirement, therefore, violated their liberty and autonomy to refuse unwanted medical treatment in violation of the Fourteenth Amendment's Due Process Clause. They also argued that the law violated the Equal Protection Clause of the Fourteenth Amendment by constituting sex discrimination and sexual orientation discrimination. Further, they argued the law violated the right to privacy as protected by the Due Process

Clause of the Fourteenth Amendment by forcing them to disclose personal information to people who see them using a restroom, or other facility, inconsistent with their gender identity or gender expression.

On August 26, 2016, the district court granted a preliminary injunction to prevent enforcement of the law finding that it likely violated Title IX but did not likely violate the equal protection clause. *See Carcaño v. McCrory*, 203 F. Supp.3d 615 (N.C. 2016). Litigation in North Carolina continued and was complicated by new bills that were adopted in the state as part of a partial repeal of HB 2. For discussion of these various changes in state law and their constitutionality, *see Carcaño v. Cooper*, 350 F. Supp.3d 388 (M.D. N.C. 2018). Thus, a combination of public outcry and litigation stalled implementation of these restrictions.

Second, a free speech case on the bathroom issue emerged in Tennessee. A preliminary injunction was granted on July 9, 2021, involving one of these bathroom laws. Curb Records and the Mike Curb Foundation, Nashville-based companies that seek to operate inclusive businesses, challenged the bathroom sign law in federal court. *See Bongo Productions v. Lawrence,* 548 F. Supp.3d 666 (M.D. Tenn. 2021). If a facility allows transgender people to use a restroom that conforms to their gender identity, Tennessee law requires a facility to post a sign that is at least eight inches high, six inches tall, has a red background with the word "notice" in yellow text at the top of the sign. The bottom two-thirds of the sign must contain in boldface, black letter the following statement centered on that portion of the sign:

> **THIS FACILITY MAINTAINS A POLICY OF ALLOWING THE USE OF RESTROOMS BY EITHER BIOLOGICAL SEX, REGARDLESS OF THE DESIGNATION OF THE RESTROOM**

The Tennessee district court issued a preliminary injunction against enforcement of the statute finding that it was a content-based restriction that was "presumptively unconstitutional." *Id.* at 680. "On its face, the Act unambiguously mandates that the plaintiffs and other regulated parties speak a particular message, in public, that they have shown, with evidence, that they earnestly consider to be anathema to their beliefs and values. It even tells them what colors to use: red and yellow, like a hazard sign. That the First Amendment would look askance at such a practice, therefore, should surprise no one." *Id.* at 680. Applying First Amendment principles that are discussed in *Nutshell* § 17.1, the court applied strict scrutiny and found that the state was not likely to meet that standard of scrutiny. Even if a lower standard of scrutiny applied, however, the court found that the plaintiffs had a meaningful likelihood of success on the merits because "there is no rational basis for adopting a color scheme that any reasonably, contemporary American viewer will know to convey a sense of warning and alarm." *Id.* at 685. A motion for summary judgment was granted about a year later. *See Bongo Productions v. Lawrence,* 603 F. Supp.3d 584 (N.D. Tenn. 2022).

Third, high school students have unsuccessfully sought to prevent a school district from allowing students to use the restroom that conformed to their gender identity. *See Parents for Privacy v. Barr,* 949 F.3d 1210 (9th Cir. 2020) (affirming dismissal); *Doe v. Boyertown Area School District,* 897 F.3d 518 (3rd Cir. 2018) (affirming district court decision; finding plaintiffs not likely to succeed on merits of their due process, Title IX or state law claims); *Parents for Privacy v. Dallas School District No. 2,* 326 F. Supp.3d 1075 (D. Oregon 2018) (granting motion to dismiss in favor of defendant school board). In light of the Supreme Court's decision in *Mahmoud v. Taylor,* 145 S. Ct. 2332 (U.S. June 27, 2025), nonetheless, one could imagine parents refiling some of these claims as religious freedom arguments, or the Court ruling that high school students can bring these kinds of claims under Title IX.

The reader should follow these and other cases to see how the courts implement *Skrmetti* in the bathroom context. Will they require students to have access to a gender-neutral single-stall toilet if states are allowed to ban access for transgender students? How will school districts enforce these bans? Will the courts interpret Title IX to *require* a transgender ban on the use of restrooms that align with a transgender student's gender identity? Will schools be allowed to enforce dress codes that require students to dress or wear their hair in a way that conforms to their sex assigned at birth? Does the sex stereotyping theory that the Court recognized in *Skrmetti* provide any legal protection for students who do not wish to conform to traditional gender norms? As discussed in

Nutshell § 3.8, below, it is possible that coverage of transgender students under the Americans with Disabilities Act would result in a single-occupancy facility being a required accommodation for students with gender dysphoria.

§ 3.8 COVERAGE OF TRANSGENDER PEOPLE UNDER DISABILITY LAW

The Americans with Disabilities Act ("ADA") makes it illegal for a covered entity to discriminate on the basis of "disability." 42 U.S.C. § 12112 (2006). 42 U.S.C. § 12208 (2006) states: "For the purposes of this Act, the term "disabled" or "disability" shall not apply to an individual solely because that individual is a transvestite." 42 U.S.C. § 12211(b)(1) (2006) further states that the term "disability" shall not include "transvestism, transsexualism, pedophilia, exhibitionism, voyeurism, gender identity disorders not resulting from physical impairments, or other sexual behavior disorders."

This legislative exclusion occurred in reaction to a federal court decision, *Blackwell v. United States Department of Treasury*, 639 F. Supp. 289 (D.D.C. 1986), in which a federal court rejected defendant's motion to dismiss on a claim under § 504 of the Rehabilitation Act. William Blackwell argued that the Treasury Department eliminated his position because he was regarded as handicapped due to his "transvestitism." *Id.* at 290. At the time, the American Psychiatric Association considered "transvestitism" to be a mental disorder. *Id.* at 290. Even though Blackwell was not successful in his legal action, it received a lot of Congressional attention. *See generally* RUTH COLKER, THE DISABILITY PENDULUM 24–26 (2005).

Although the *Blackwell* court found that "transvestitism" could be a disability under § 504 of the Rehabilitation Act, state courts have interpreted similar language *not* to include those who are transgendered. For example, Andria Adams filed suit under Title VII and Pennsylvania state disability law arguing that she faced unlawful discrimination as a "transsexual." The court found that "transsexualism" was not a handicap as that term was used under the Pennsylvania statute. *Dobre v. Nat'l R.R. Passenger Corp.*, 850 F. Supp. 284, 289 (E.D. Pa. 1993). *See also Sommers v. Iowa Civil Rights Comm'n*, 337 N.W.2d 470 (Iowa 1083) (finding "transsexualism" not to be a covered handicap).

The question of whether the ADA should exclude those who are transgendered from potential coverage is controversial, because many individuals who are transgendered do not consider themselves to be "disabled." Further, the disability label makes the condition seem overly medicalized. On the other hand, the ADA was amended in 2008 to broadly cover those regarded as disabled, even if they do not consider themselves to have a disabling condition. Therefore, transgendered individuals could, in theory, be covered under the "regarded as" statutory prong. *See generally* Kevin M. Barry, *Disabilityqueer: Federal Disability Rights Protection for Transgender People*, 16 YALE HUM. RTS. & DEV. L.J. 1 (2013). The American Psychiatric Association's Diagnostic and

Statistical Manual of Mental Disorders, Fifth Edition ("DSM-5") lists "gender dysphoria" as an impairment for those who "are at risk of experiencing, distress if they do not receive the right support, ranging from talk therapy to pharmacological and surgical interventions." *Id.* at 4. *See* AM. PSYCHIATRIC ASS'N, DIAGNOSTIC AND STATISTICAL MANUAL OF MENTAL DISORDERS (5th ed., 2013). *But see* Dean Spade, *Laws as Tactics,* 21 COLUM. J. GENDER & L. 40 (2012) (criticizing need to use medical evidence to make claims by trans people).

In *Blatt v. Cabela's Retail, Inc.*, No. 5:14–cv–04822 (E.D. Pa. Aug. 15, 2014) (Westlaw), Kate Lynn Blatt, a transgender woman, filed suit under Title VII and the ADA. She alleged that her employer initially refused to allow her to be known by her female name, refused to allow her to use the store's female restroom and refused to order a female uniform for her. She was also allegedly a victim of harassment. She was fired for conduct that Blatt denies happened. She brought her claim under the ADA, as well as Title VII, so that she could argue that she was denied reasonable accommodation.

Blatt argued that she was protected from disability discrimination under the ADA and that it would be unconstitutional for Congress to exclude individuals who are transgendered from ADA coverage. The United States Department of Justice filed a statement of interest in which they argued that the "transvestite" exclusion could be interpreted *not* to exclude people with gender identity disorders ("GID") "in light of the evolving scientific evidence suggesting that gender dysphoria may have a physical basis." *See* Second Statement of Interest of the United States of America at 5, *Blatt v. Cabela's Retail, Inc.*, No. 5:15–cv–04822 (E.D. Pa. filed Nov. 16, 2015), available at https://www.glad.org/cases/blatt-v-cabelas-retail-inc.

Blatt argued that she was covered under the ADA because she had gender dysphoria, which substantially limited her major life activities of interacting with others, reproducing, and social and occupational functioning. She also alleged that she had been subjected to "degrading and discriminatory comments on the basis of her disability, that she requested a female nametag and uniform and use of the female restroom as accommodations for her disability, and that as a result of requesting these accommodations she was subjected to a 'pattern of antagonism' prior to her termination." *Blatt v. Cabela's Retail*, 2017 WL 2178123, *4 (E.D. Pa. May 18, 2017). The defendant argued that she was excluded from ADA coverage and sought to have that cause of action dismissed. The district court denied the defendant's motion to dismiss finding that the ADA could be interpreted to cover people with gender dysphoria. *Id.* The case appears not to have been appealed.

In response to the *Blatt* decision, which they also helped litigate, Kevin Barry and Jennifer Levi have argued that the decision opens a "new path for transgender rights." *See* Kevin Barry & Jennifer Levi, *Blatt v. Cabela's Retail, Inc. and a New Path for Transgender Rights*, 127 YALE L.J. FORUM 373 (2017). They argue that the *Blatt* decision could be used to argue that states must change an individual's birth certificate to match gender confirmation surgery, that state prisons must provide appropriate medical care and facilities to prisoners with gender dysphoria and that schools must allow students like Grimm to use the restrooms that conform to their gender identity. Despite this assertion in 2017, there appear to be few cases proceeding under that legal theory. Others have suggested that a disability approach to transgender issues poses significant challenges. *See* Ali Szemanski, *When Trans Rights Are Disability Rights: The Promises and Perils of Seeking Gender Dysphoria Coverage Under the Americans with Disabilities Act,* 43 HARV. J. L. & GENDER 137 (2020).

There have been few cases pursuing transgender discrimination claims under the ADA. The courts are split on ADA coverage. *See Parker v. Strawser Construction, Inc.,* 307 F. Supp.3d 744 (S.D. Ohio 2018) (finding no ADA coverage); *Michaels v. Akal Sec., Inc.,* 2010 WL 2573988 (D. Col. June 24, 2010) (finding no ADA coverage); Doe v. Mass. Dep't of Correction, 2018 WL 2994403 (D. Mass. June 14, 2018) (denying defendant's motion to dismiss ADA claim); Tay v. Dennison, 2020 WL 2100761 (S.D. Ill. May 1, 2020) (denying defendant's motion to dismiss ADA claim).

Possibly, the Supreme Court's decision in *Skrmetti* furthers the argument that gender dysphoria is a covered disability under the ADA, even though the statute excludes coverage of gender identity disorder. Through the *Skrmetti* decision, the Court noted that the state had prohibited health care providers to administer puberty blockers or hormones to minors to treat certain conditions such as "gender dysphoria, gender identity disorder, or gender incongruence." *See, e.g., Skrmetti*, 145 S. Ct. at 1829. The Court distinguished gender dysphoria from gender identity disorder throughout its opinion, lending strength to the argument that these are not synonymous terms. On the other hand, the Court was merely quoting the state statute, not stating that it agreed that those terms are distinguishable from each other. In light of *Skrmetti*'s holding—that a ban on puberty blockers or hormone treatment for minors with gender dysphoria does not violate the Fourteenth Amendment—one could imagine that future litigation might seek to proceed under the ADA.

§ 3.9 IDENTITY DOCUMENTS

A. PASSPORTS

Another important legal issue is identity documents for those who identify as intersex or non-binary. This issue has been pursued under a variety of state and federal legal strategies because state and federal officials issue identity documents. Individuals who have brought these challenges may prefer not to use the label of male or female. Similarly, they often prefer the pronoun, "they," used in the singular form rather than the pronouns, "he" or "she." They have often sought to use the designation "X" rather than "M" or "F" on identification documents such as passports.

Until 2021, the United States Department of State only offered binary options for a passport, but it did have a policy in place for people transitioning from one gender to another. According to the State Department, the government can issue two different kinds of passports depending on the stage of the gender transition. U.S. Dep't of State, *Gender Transition Applicants*. If an individual is in the process of a gender transition, that person could be issued a temporary passport that was valid for two years. If the gender transition was completed, the person was issued a new permanent passport. However, there were several requirements that accompany this issuance. In addition to the normally required documents, until June 30, 2021, an individual had to provide an ID that resembled current appearance, a passport photo that resembled current appearance, proof of legal name change, and a physician statement that validated that the person had completed, or was in the process of treatment for, gender transition.

On June 30, 2021, the State Department announced that it would allow individuals to declare their self-identified gender on their passports without providing medical documents. This change in policy reflected a 2020 federal court decision in which a federal court had ruled an individual should not have to provide medical documentation to request a change in gender identification on a passport. *See Morris v. Pompeo*, 706 F. Supp.3d 1071 (D. Nev. 2020)(finding that medical documentation requirement could not survive heightened scrutiny). This change was also a first step toward creating a gender marker on U.S. passports and citizenship certificates for people who identify as nonbinary or intersex. The nonbinary option was not immediately effective, but the lack of medical documentation was immediately effective. In May 2021, the State Department had also stated that it would start granting U.S. citizenship to babies born abroad to married couples with at least one American parent—no matter which parent was biologically related to the child. That decision disproportionately benefited the LGBTQ+ community.

The refusal by the State Department to permit nonbinary designations on passports also spawned litigation. Dana Alix Zzyym brought one of those lawsuits. Zzyym was born "intersex" and does not want to be forced to make a false choice by picking "male" or "female" on government documents. *See* Salim Essaid, *Intersex Veteran Sues over Passport Denial*, CNN (July 23, 2016), available at https://www.cnn.com/2016/07/23/us/veteran-intersex-passport-lawsuit/index.html. Zzyym's attorney presents the issue as a catch-22, in which, "They have to either lie on their passport application about their gender identity and violate the law or not apply for a passport at all." *Id.*

Zzyym alleged that a refusal to issue a passport reflective of plaintiff's gender identity was 1) discrimination based on sex, 2) a violation of plaintiff's Due Process rights, 3) and an infringement on plaintiff's fundamental and liberty interests. The complaint further sets forth the process in which a child is sexed (by a visual assessment immediately after birth) but posits that, because of a number of other factors invisible to the eye, intersex characteristics are often ignored or misattributed. *See generally* Complaint, *Zzyym v. Kerry*, No. 1:15–CV–02362 (D. Colo. filed Oct. 25, 2015).

Currently, the gender on Zzyym's birth certificate is listed as "unknown." Essaid, *Intersex Veteran Sues over Passport Denial* at 7. When a passport is issued, it is required that every statement made on the application is "true," pursuant to 22 U.S.C. § 213 (2000), along with a birth certificate and question regarding binary gender identification. *Id.* Thus, plaintiff was placed in the position of either falsifying their passport application or leaving the gender box incomplete.

During oral arguments in federal district court on July 20, 2016, Judge Brooke Jackson urged the State Department to find a way to allow Zzyym to accurately reflect their gender identity, stating, "A lot of things are changing in our world." Debra Cassens Weiss, *Federal Judge Considers Suit Seeking Gender-Neutral Passport*, ABA J. (July 22, 2016), available at https://www.abajournal.com/news/article/federal_judge_considers_suit_seeking_gender_neutral_passport.

On November 22, 2016, the district court judge ruled that the Department acted arbitrarily in implementing its binary-only gender policy and remanded its decision for further consideration at the Department level. *See Zzyym v. Kerry,* 220 F. Supp.3d 1106 (D. Col. 2016). When the case returned to the district court in 2018, Zzyym prevailed. *See Zzyym v. Pompeo,* 341 F. Supp.3d 1248 (D. Col. 2018). The Tenth Circuit vacated and remanded that decision in 2020. *See Zzyym v. Pompeo,* 958 F.3d 1014 (10th Cir. 2020). The Tenth Circuit found that most of the reasons provided by the State Department for denying Zzyym's request were invalid and instructed the agency to reprocess Zzyym's application so that it did not use its authority in an arbitrary and capricious manner. But the court did not go so far as to dictate the outcome.

As mentioned above, the State Department under President Biden moved towards recognizing nonbinary designations on U.S. passports.

Those policies have changed dramatically under the Trump administration. Pursuant to Executive Order 14168, the State Department has issued new guidance on its website. Although current passports continue to be valid, the State Department says "If you submit a passport application requesting an X marker or requesting a sex marker that differs from the sex marker at birth, you may experience delays getting your passport . . . We will issue you a new passport that matches your biological sex at birth, based on your supporting documents and our records about your previous passports." https://travel.state.gov/content/travel/en/passports/passport-help/sex-marker.html. (last read on July 1, 2025).

On June 17, 2025, a district court judge entered a preliminary injunction barring enforcement of the new passport policy against six of the original seven plaintiffs and required the State Department to issue those plaintiffs passports consistent with their gender identities. *See Orr v. Trump,* 2025 WL 1695941, *1 (D. Mass. June 17, 2025). The plaintiffs subsequently amended their complaint to seek class certification, and the district court granted plaintiffs' motions to certify two classes. It also granted a preliminary injunction to a subset of each of those classes. *Id.* at *1. Those classes include:

1. a class of all people (1) whose gender identity is different from the sex assigned to them under the Passport Policy and/or who have been diagnosed with gender dysphoria, and (2) who have applied, or who, but for the Passport Policy, would apply, for a U.S. passport issued with an "M" or "F" sex designation that is different from the sex assigned to that individual under the Passport Policy ("M/F Designation Class");

2. A class of all people whose gender identity is different from the sex assigned to them under the Passport Policy and who have applied, or who, but for the Passport Policy, would apply, for a U.S. passport with an "X" designation ("X Designation Class").

Id. at *15–16.

After the Supreme Court decided *Skrmetti*, the Justice Department filed a motion asking the judge to dissolve the preliminary injunction. On July 10, 2025, the judge denied that request saying that executive order and passport policy "are based on unconstitutional animus toward transgender Americans," which is unconstitutional under any level of scrutiny. The judge also denied a request to stay the injunction pending appeal. An appeal is pending in the First Circuit.

It is impossible to predict how the Supreme Court will ultimately decide this case. The fact that it remanded a birth certificate case suggests that it may be open to government having the discretion to only recognize sex assigned at birth. On the other hand, the purpose of a passport is to provide a visual identification of an individual. A passport designation that is inconsistent with someone's visual identity would seem not to serve that purpose (even under a low level of scrutiny).

B. SOCIAL SECURITY RECORDS

On June 14, 2013, the Social Security Administration (SSA) announced a new policy that will allow individuals seeking to change their gender designation in their Social Security records "to submit either government-issued documentation that reflects a gender change, a court order directing legal recognition of the change, or a physician's statement confirming the transgender individual has received 'appropriate clinical treatment for gender transition.' " *See Recent Administrative Policy*, 127 HARV. L. REV. 1863 (2014). In 2022, SSA allowed people to self-select their gender without medical documentation.

As of January 31, 2025, SSA has issued new guidance prohibiting updates to the sex designation in a person's records. The Social Security does not list an individual's gender, but SSA maintains a person's sex in its database for verification and statistical purposes. SSA instituted this change as an "emergency" change that went into effect immediately. The SSA took down the page on how to change your sex identification even before this emergency order went into effect. Readers should watch for litigation about this change, which may have violated some requirements of the Administrative Procedures Act.

C. BIRTH CERTIFICATES

Two issues often arise in the birth certificate context. First, some individuals seek to choose a non-binary gender option on their birth certificate, often denoted by the letter X. Second, some individuals seek to amend their birth certificate in order for it to be consistent with their gender identity rather than their sex assigned at birth.

There is not much case law involving those who prefer a non-binary gender option on state-issued identity documents. Jamie Shupe received a court order in Oregon to have the designation on the birth certificate changed from female to "non-binary." *See In re Sex Change of Jamie Shupe*, No. 16CV13991 (Or. Cir. Ct. Multnomah Cty. June 10, 2016) (Cir. Ct. J. Amy Holmes Hehn). Pursuant to a court decision, Oregon now allows the birth certificate to be changed to gender nonbinary. *See In the Matter of Jones David Hollister,* 305 Or. App. 368 (Oregon Ct. Appeals 2020). As of July 2025, 16 states and the District Columbia allow nonbinary identification on driver's licenses or state IDs. *See Non-Binary Birth Certificates and State IDs: Fully Guide*, https://www.

usbirthcertificates.com/articles/gender-neutral-birth-certificates-states. In the last couple of years, some states have become more restrictive in allowing non-binary designations. Those states include Florida, Kansas, and Oklahoma.

Nonetheless, transgender individuals have successfully brought challenges to state laws or policies that categorically denied transgender individuals the right to change the sex on their birth certificates to match their gender identity. *See, e.g., F.V. v. Barron,* 286 F. Supp.3d 1131 (D. Idaho 2018) (finding policy lacked rational basis under equal protection clause); *Ray v. McCloud,* 507 F. Supp.3d 925 (S.D. Ohio 2020) (granting plaintiff's motion for summary judgment under equal protection and due process clauses).

But the *Skrmetti* decision vacated and remanded a case from the Tenth Circuit which had ruled that transgender people could correct their birth certificates in Oklahoma. *See Fowler v. Stitt,* 104 F.4th 770 (10th Cir. 2025), judgment vacated, 2025 WL 1787695 (June 30, 2025). The Tenth Circuit found that the state policy, which did not permit amending the sex designation on a birth certificate, could not even withstand rational basis review. On remand, the Tenth Circuit will need to reconsider that decision in light of *Skrmetti*. If it concludes that a state may constitutionally permit states to preclude amending the sex designation on a birth certificate, then one can imagine that more states will follow that practice. Because an individual must make such a request from the state that initially issued the birth certificate, a transgender individual cannot get around this problem by moving to another state. At this time, it is also unknown if states may try to rescind the validity of previously amended birth certificates.

§ 3.10 HOUSING

The Fair Housing Act, 42 U.S.C. § 3601 et seq (2006), prohibits housing discrimination based on race, color, national origin, religion, sex, disability, and familial status. In 2010, the United States Department of Housing and Urban Development ("HUD") issued guidance saying it would investigate complaints of housing discrimination against transgender people. *See HUD Issues Guidance on LGBT Housing Discrimination Complaints,* July 1, 2010, available at https://archives.hud.gov/news/2010/pr10-139.cfm.

On February 3, 2012, the Department of Housing and Urban Development issued regulations requiring equal access to housing in HUD programs regardless of sexual orientation or gender identity. *See* Equal Access to Housing in HD Programs Regardless of Sexual Orientation or Gender Identity, 77 Fed. Reg. 5661 (Feb. 3, 2012) (codified at 24 C.F.R. § 5.105). These regulations becamc effective on March 5, 2012. The language includes the following rule:

> (2) Equal access to HUD-assisted or insured housing.

(i) Eligibility for HUD-assisted or insured housing. A determination of eligibility for housing that is assisted by HUD or subject to a mortgage insured by the Federal Housing Administration shall be made in accordance with the eligibility requirements provided for such program by HUD, and such housing shall be made available without regard to actual or perceived sexual orientation, gender identity, or marital status.

(ii) Prohibition of inquiries on sexual orientation or gender identity. No owner or administrator of HUD-assisted or HUD-insured housing, approved lender in an FHA mortgage insurance program, nor any (or any other) recipient or subrecipient of HUD funds may inquire about the sexual orientation or gender identity of an applicant for, or occupant of, HUD-assisted housing or housing whose financing is insured by HUD, whether renter-or owner-occupied, for the purpose of determining eligibility for the housing or otherwise making such housing available. This prohibition on inquiries regarding sexual orientation or gender identity does not prohibit any individual from voluntarily self-identifying sexual orientation or gender identity. This prohibition on inquiries does not prohibit lawful inquiries of an applicant or occupant's sex where the housing provided or to be provided to the individual is temporary, emergency shelter that involves the sharing of sleeping areas or bathrooms, or inquiries

> made for the purpose of determining the number of bedrooms to which a household may be entitled.

Equal Access to Housing in HD Programs Regardless of Sexual Orientation or Gender Identity, 77 Fed. Reg. 5661 (Feb. 3, 2012) (codified at 24 C.F.R. § 5.105(a)(2)).

The 2012 regulation is broader than the 2010 directive but is limited to HUD-assisted or insured housing. In an August 20, 2014, interpretive document, HUD clarified that the protection against discrimination for HUD housing also included protection against sexual harassment that might occur after the person secured HUD housing. It provided an example of a gay man who was a tenant, was harassed by a maintenance worker, and received no remedy from the public housing authority when he filed a complaint. *See* U.S. Dep't of Hous. & Urban Dev. Office of Pub. & Indian Hous., Notice PIH 2014–20(HA) at 6–7.

There have not been a lot of cases interpreting HUD's regulations or the scope of its authority to ban discrimination on the basis of sexual orientation and gender identity. In *Thomas v. Osegueda*, No. 2:15–CV–0042–WMA, 2015 WL 3751994 (N.D. Ala. June 16, 2015), the district court found that the regulations were within HUD's authority but did not provide a cause of action under the 2010 directive for a man who claimed that he faced discrimination in housing because he was *not* gay. His *pro se* complaint was ambiguous about the issue of whether the housing was HUD housing and therefore covered under the 2012 regulation. Alleged violations of the 2012 regulations must be filed with the Office of Community Planning and Development, not with a federal court. The district court judge indicated that plaintiff's complaint had been forwarded to the appropriate administrative office for action.

On July 24, 2020, the Trump administration proposed a rule change that would have allowed HUD CPD-funded shelters to exclude transgender people from facilities that conformed to their gender identity. On April 27, 2021, the Biden administration withdrew that proposed rule. *See Making Admission or Placement Determinations Based on Sex in Facilities Under Community Planning and Development Housing Programs; Withdrawal; Regulatory Review,* 86 Fed. Reg. 22125 (April 27, 2021) (withdrawal of proposed rule).

In 2025, Housing Secretary Scott Turner announced that he was halting HUD's enforcement of its gender identity rule. He announced that he would ensure that "housing programs, shelters and other HUD-funded providers offer services to Americans based on their sex at birth: male or female." *See Secretary Scott Turner Halts Enforcement Actions of HUD's Gender Identity Rule,* https://www.hud.gov/news/hud-no-25-026#:~:text=The%20Equal%20Access%20Rule%20was,gender%20identity%20or%20marital%20status.

§ 3.11 HEALTH CARE ISSUES

Note: State bans on gender-affirming care for minors was discussed in *Nutshell* § 3.6, above.

A. MEDICAID

Individuals who are transgender often face problems with receiving coverage under Medicaid for medical treatment that they consider necessary as part of their gender transitioning. The courts have been mixed on this issue.

In 1976, the New York Court of Appeals concluded that it was not arbitrary and capricious for the state commissioner of social services to deny a request for medical assistance for sexual conversion surgery. *See In re Denise R. v. Lavine*, 39 N.Y.2d 279 (N.Y. 1976). The court concluded that the Department of Social Services had a reasonable basis to determine, in this case, that the medical treatment was not medically necessary because there was medical evidence that "indicated that there was no disturbance in thinking, nor suicidal thinking." *Id.* at 282.

In contrast, the Minnesota Supreme Court held in 1977 that it was arbitrary and capricious for a county to implement a total ban on funding sexual conversion surgery. *See Doe v. Minn. Dep't of Pub. Welfare*, 257 N.W.2d 816 (Minn. 1977). Minnesota continues to have state policies banning all transition-related surgical care. *See* Minn. Stat. § 256B.0625, subdiv. 3a (2015). That ban is currently subject to litigation. *See* Complaint, *Outfront v. Piper*, (Minn. 2d Jud. Dist. Dec. 17, 2015); *see also Pinneke v. Preisser*, 623 F.2d 546 (8th Cir. 1980) (overturning Iowa's policy of denying Medicaid benefits to individuals who needed sex reassignment surgery).

The Fifth Circuit considered this issue in 1980 in a case involving Georgia's ban on paying for "transsexual surgery" because the state considered it to be experimental or, alternatively, not warranted for the individual plaintiff. *See Rush v. Parham*, 625 F.2d 1150 (5th Cir. 1980). The court upheld the denial of funding for medical treatment.

The Affordable Care Act can have an impact on those rules. Section. § 1557 of the ACA, 42 U.S.C. 18116 (2006), prohibits discrimination on the basis of race, color, national origin, sex, age, or disability in health care programs that receive funding from Health and Human Services ("HHS"), are administered by HHS or are Health Insurance Marketplaces under the ACA.

On May 13, 2016, HHS issued the final rule implementing § 1557. These rules contained some language specific to transgender individuals. It was illegal to "have or implement a categorical coverage exclusion or limitation for all health services related to gender transition." 81 Fed. Reg. 31,472 (May 18, 2016) (codified at 45 C.F.R. § 92.207(b)(4)), available at https://www.gpo.gov/fdsys/pkg/FR-2016-05-18/pdf/2016-11458.pdf. This language suggested that an exclusion could happen on a case-by-case basis, but a categorical exclusion would be impermissible.

On June 19, 2020, the Trump Administration issued final regulations implementing § 1557 which eliminated the general prohibition on discrimination based on gender identity and sex-stereotyping and specific health insurance protections for transgender individuals. *See* 85 Fed. Reg. 27,160 (June 19, 2020), available at https://www.govinfo.gov/content/pkg/FR-2020-06-19/pdf/2020-11758.pdf. On August 17, 2020, a federal district court judge enjoined the implementation of those rules, finding that HHS was "arbitrary and capricious" in adopting this rule days after the *Bostock* decision was rendered. *See Walker v. Azar,* 480 F. Supp.3d 417 (E.D. N.Y. 2020). *See also Whitman-Walker Clinic, Inc. v. U.S. Department of Health and Human Services,* 485 F. Supp.3d 1 (D. D.C. 2020) (issuing partial preliminary injunction in favor of health care entities on ADA coverage).

On May 10, 2021, the Biden administration announced that health care providers cannot discriminate against transgender individuals. They said that the new policy implemented the *Bostock* decision and would cover all health plans that receive public funding. Thus, it appears that transgender categorical exclusions are, once again, unlawful under public health care such as Medicaid and Medicare. Further, the ACA's nondiscrimination provisions likely require coverage of transgender medical treatment under private health care plans.

Early cases seemed to support the position of the Biden administration. In 2018, before *Bostock* was decided, a Wisconsin district court judge found that a categorical exclusion likely violated the ACA's nondiscrimination requirements. *See Flack v. Wis. Dept. of Health Servs.,* 328 F. Supp.3d 931 (W.D. Wis. 2018) (granting plaintiffs' request for a preliminary injunction).

Similarly, a Florida case supported the position of the Biden administration on this issue. In 2022,

Florida sought to end gender-affirming care under Medicaid for both minors and adults. It first made the change through administrative regulation and then endorsed the change through legislation. On June 21, 2023, a federal district court found that these administrative and statutory changes were unconstitutional and illegal under the Affordable Care Act and the Medicaid Act. Employing either rational basis or intermediate scrutiny, the court found that the denial of Medicaid coverage could not survive scrutiny because those same drugs are available to people who are not transgender. Similarly, the court found that the rules violated the Affordable Care Act's prohibition of discrimination based on sex. With respect to a claim under the Medicaid statute, the court found that these rules were in violation of a rule requiring effective treatment under the appropriate standard of care. Finally, the court found these rules violated Medicaid's comparability requirement because an individual was denied treatment that was less in "amount, duration, or scope" than assistance available to other Medicaid beneficiaries. *See Dekker v. Weida,* 679 F. Supp.3d 1271 (N.D. Fla. 2023). This case is on appeal to the Eleventh Circuit.

In *Skrmetti*, the Court vacated and remanded a consolidated case involving West Virginia's coverage of gender-affirming care. *See Anderson v. Crouch,* 100 F.4th 122 (4th Cir. 2024), *judgment vacated by Folwell v. Kadel*, 2025 WL 1787687 (June 30, 2025).

West Virginia's Medicaid program covered some gender-affirming care but not gender-affirming surgery. The program, however, did cover the same surgical procedures when conducted to treat non-gender dysphoria diagnoses. For example, the program covered mastectomies as a treatment for cancer but not to treat gender dysphoria. *Id.* at 134. Relying on the *Grimm* precedent from the Fourth Circuit, the court considered transgender people to constitute a quasi-suspect class. *Id.* at 143. The Fourth Circuit rejected the state's argument that *Geduldig* required it to conclude that the state's program did not constitute transgender or sex discrimination. *Id.* at 147. The Fourth Circuit held that "gender dysphoria, a diagnosis inextricable from transgender status, is a proxy for transgender identity. And coverage exclusions that bar treatments for gender dysphoria bar treatments on the basis of transgender identity by proxy." *Id.* at 149. Applying intermediate scrutiny, the Fourth Circuit found that West Virginia could not justify its policy.

On remand, the Fourth Circuit will need to follow the holding in *Skrmetti* that the state's ban on gender-affirming health care for minors did not constitute transgender discrimination. One would expect that the Fourth Circuit would have to reconsider the case under rational basis scrutiny rather than heightened scrutiny. West Virginia had argued that the exclusions were justified to save costs and avoid medically ineffective treatments. Because West Virginia said that it "did not know if Medicaid had conducted any research or analysis about the cost of providing access to gender-affirming care," the Fourth Circuit concluded its "proferred rationales were created for the purposes of litigation" and could not justify the policy under a heightened-scrutiny analysis. *Id.* at 157. Under rational basis scrutiny, post-hoc justifications can be permissible. Thus, it is possible that West Virginia will prevail upon remand. *Skrmetti* emphasized the importance of deferring to states in areas in which there is "medical and scientific uncertainty." *Skrmetti,* 145 S. Ct. at 1836. It is too early to predict if the Supreme Court will ultimately conclude that medical treatment for adults is also in an area of "medical uncertainty."

The West Virginia program did not ban all gender-affirming care for transgender individuals; it merely refused to pay for gender-affirming surgery for people on Medicaid. Importantly, the state did not refuse to pay for hormonal and other similar medical treatment. By contrast, *Skrmetti* involved a ban on *all* gender-affirming care for minors, including hormones and puberty blockers. So it is hard to predict how the *Skrmetti* decision impacts the West Virginia case.

In April 2025, the Centers for Medicare and Medicaid Services urged states to not use Medicaid funds for gender-affirming care for minors. At this time (July 2025), the federal government has not banned the use of Medicaid funding for gender-affirming care in adults. The House Budget Bill that passed the House on May 22, 2025, barred Medicaid coverage of all transgender care and prohibited plans offered under the Affordable Care Act's exchanges from covering such care. That language was not adopted by the Senate, and it did not become law.

Eleven states explicitly prohibit Medicaid coverage for gender-affirming care for all ages. Depending on the outcome of the West Virginia Medicaid case, it is possible that more states or the federal government will try to ban such coverage.

B. PRIVATE HEALTH INSURANCE

Enacted in 2010, section 1557 of the Affordable Care Act ("ACA") prohibits health insurance companies from discriminating against individuals on the basis of sex or gender identity. 42 U.S.C. § 18116. HHS was slow to issue regulations implementing Section 1557. In 2016, the Obama administration issued regulations that said that discrimination on the basis of gender identity, as well as discrimination on the basis of termination of pregnancy, was included within the prohibition against sex discrimination. 45 C.F.R. § 92.4.

Religiously-affiliated healthcare providers and states challenged these regulations. In *Franciscan Alliance, Inc. v. Azar,* 414 F. Supp.3d 928 (N.D. Tex. 2019), a judge found that the regulations violated the Administrative Procedures Act and the Religious Freedom Restoration Act. In June 2020, the Trump Administration eliminated the regulatory language that defined sex discrimination as including gender identity and termination of pregnancy discrimination. Then, in January 2021, President Biden sought to reinstate the protections related to gender identity that had existed prior to 2019 by issuing an Executive Order entitled "Preventing and Combating Discrimination on the Basis of Gender

Identity or Sexual Orientation." In May 2024, HHS issued a regulation stating that entities providing broad protection against gender identity discrimination. 45 C.F.R. §§ 92.101(2) & 92.206. But a district court judge quickly issued a preliminary injunction against enforcement of the 2024 regulation. *See Tennessee v. Becerra,* 739 F. Supp.3d 467 (S.D. Miss. 2024). The *Biden* administration relied on *Bostock* to argue that the term "sex discrimination" in the ACA should have the same meaning as Title VII. The court, however, found that "HHS's position is not persuasive [because] . . . *Bostock's* holding hinged on the broad 'but for' causation standard applicable to Title VII." *Id.* at 478.

On January 20, 2025, President Trump rescinded the Biden 2021 Gender Identity and Sexual Orientation Executive Order. At this time, the Trump administration has not issued new regulations interpreting the nondiscrimination provision but has stopped enforcing the Biden era regulations.

Before Trump took office in January 2025, federal courts had been interpreting the ACA's nondiscrimination requirement to preclude the exclusion of gender transition treatment for state employees. *See C.P. v. Blue Cross Blue Shield of Illinois,* 2022 WL 17788148 (W.D. Wash. 2022); *Doe v. Snyder,* 28 F.4th 103 (9th Cir. 2022); *Boyden v. Conlin,* 341 F. Supp.3d 979 (W.D. Wisc. 2018); *Kadel v. Fowell,* 100 F.4th 122 (4th Cir 2024), *vacated and remanded* 2025 WL 1787687 (June 30, 2025); *L.B.*

and M.B. v. Premera Blue Cross, 2025 WL 1149630 (W.D. Wash. 2025); *Doe v. City of Philadelphia*, 2024 WL 3634221 (E.D. Pa. 2024). Further, a federal district court judge has also found that a blanket exclusion of gender transition-related surgical treatment under a state employee's health care plan violated Title VII. *See Fletcher v. Alaska*, 443 F. Supp.3d 1024 (D. Alaska 2020).

Those decisions interpreting the ACA are now in question in light of *Skrmetti*. In fact, the Supreme Court has vacated and remanded *Folwell v. Kadel* "for further consideration in light of [*Skrmetti*]." 2025 WL 1787687 (June 30, 2025). Some courts have upheld exclusions for transgender surgery under private health plans. *See, e.g., Toomey v. Arizona*, 2021 WL 753721 (D. Ariz. Feb. 26, 2021) (denying motion for preliminary injunction for plaintiff who sought hysterectomy as part of gender reassignment surgery). In *Toomey*, a report and recommendation found that a policy exclusion which "discriminates against some natal females but not all . . . is not, on its face, discrimination on the basis of sex." *Toomey*, 2020 WL 8459367 at *4. Possibly, the *Toomey* analysis will become the predominant interpretation of the ACA on remand.

Nonetheless, some states have updated their rules to reflect the ACA nondiscrimination policies regarding sex and gender identity under the Biden administration. Below are examples of some of the more comprehensive state policies. Notice that these policies sometimes refer to which standards should be followed in defining the appropriate standard of care:

- **California:** Plans must provide coverage for medically necessary services for transgender plan participants if those services are covered for other conditions, including services related to gender transition, such as hormone therapy, hysterectomy, mastectomy and vocal training. Plans also must provide coverage for health-care services that are ordinarily provided to plan participants of one gender, regardless of whether plan participants are enrolled in plans as another gender, have undergone gender transition or are in the process of undergoing gender transition.

Cal. Code Regs. tit. 10, §§ 2561.1–.2 (current through July 22, 2016 Reg. 2016, No. 30); Letter from Cal. Health & Human Servs. Agency Dept. of Managed Health Care, No. 12–K (April 9, 2013).

- **Delaware:** Plans cannot deny, exclude, or limit coverage for medically necessary services to treat gender dysphoria and gender identity disorder, including surgeries or other treatments pertaining to gender transition or related services. If a medical provider and a plan participant determine that a procedure is medically necessary, and the procedure would be covered for another plan participant, the insurance company may not deny coverage.

  Plans must provide coverage for conditions related to plan participants' gender identities on the same basis as coverage provided for other health conditions based on medical necessity, without regard to participants' gender identity.

Medical necessity determinations, eligibility, and prior authorization requirements for diagnoses related to plan participants' gender identities must be based on current medical standards, established by nationally recognized transgender health medical experts.

Del. Code Ann. tit. 18, § 304(22) (2015); Del. Dep't. of Ins., Bulletin No. 86 (March 23, 2016).

- **Illinois:** Plans cannot exclude, limit, charge higher rates, or deny claims for surgical treatments for gender dysphoria, if plans provide coverage for the same surgical treatments for non-transgendered plan participants, such as coverage for mastectomy and post-cancer breast reconstruction. Plans also cannot exclude, limit, charge higher rates, or deny claims for emergency room care for complications from surgery for gender dysphoria, if plans provide coverage for emergency room care for complications from surgery for other medical conditions.

  Plans cannot exclude, limit, charge higher rates, or deny claims for hormone therapy for gender transition, if plans provide hormone therapy treatment coverage for other medical conditions, such as endocrine disorders or menopausal symptoms. Plans cannot deny coverage for sex-specific treatments because of plan participants' gender identities, including obstetrics and gynecology care, mammograms and prostate exams. Plans cannot include exclusionary clauses or language that has the effect of targeting transgender plan participants or plan participants with gender dysphoria.

775 Ill. Comp. Stat. 5/1–102(A), 5/1–103; 5/5–101 (2011); Ill. Dep't. of Ins., Co. Bulletin 2014–10 Healthcare for Transgender Individuals (July 28, 2014).

- **Massachusetts:** Plans must provide coverage for plan participants regardless of gender identity or gender dysphoria, including coverage for medically necessary transgender surgery and gender identity or gender dysphoria related health-care services. Gender identity means an individual's gender-related identity, appearance or behavior regardless of whether such identity, appearance or behavior is different from an individual's assigned sex at birth or physiology.

Mass. Gen. Laws ch. 4, § 7 (Supp. 2016); Mass. Div. of Ins., Bulletin 2014–03 (June 20, 2014).

- **Washington D.C.:** Plans must provide coverage for medically necessary treatments for individuals diagnosed with gender dysphoria or gender identity disorder,

> including gender reassignment surgeries. The most recent edition of the World Professional Association must guide medical necessity determinations for Transgender Health Standards of Care and consultations between plan participants and their physicians.

D.C. Code § 31–2231.11(c) (Supp. 2016); D.C. Dept. of Ins., Sec. & Banking, Bulletin 13–IB–01–30/13 (Revised) (Feb. 27, 2014).

§ 3.12 PRISONERS' RIGHTS

In recent years, prisoners who are transgender have sought medical treatment for gender affirmation surgery. When prison officials have denied their requests, they have sued alleging, among other things, that officials violated their Eighth and Fourteenth Amendment rights.

Early litigation involving these theories was unsuccessful. *See, e.g., Meriwether v. Faulkner*, 821 F.2d 408 (7th Cir. 1987); *Maggert v. Hanks*, 131 F.3d 670 (7th Cir. 1997). Relying on case law that said the Eighth Amendment only requires minimum healthcare for prison inmates, these courts found that hormone treatment, which it considered expensive and "esoteric," did not necessarily have to be provided. *Maggert*, 131 F.3d at 671–72.

Nonetheless, one early case, brought under the Eighth Amendment, reached the United States Supreme Court and created some useful precedent. *See Farmer v. Brennan*, 511 U.S. 825 (1994). Plaintiff Dee Farmer was what the Court called a "transsexual." *Id.* at 829. She was the first transgender plaintiff to bring a case before the United States Supreme Court.

Farmer had undergone estrogen therapy and other procedures before being incarcerated in a male prison population. After being beaten and raped by another inmate, she filed an Eighth Amendment complaint, alleging that the defendant prison engaged in a "deliberately indifferent failure to protect petitioner's safety." *Id.* at 831. She had lost in the district court because she had "never expressed any concern" for her safety. *Id.* at 848. The Supreme Court unanimously found that "a prison official may be held liable under the Eighth Amendment for denying humane conditions of confinement only if he knows that inmates face a substantial risk of serious harm and disregards that risk by failing to take reasonable measures to abate it." *Id.* at 847. Further, the Supreme Court found that Farmer's failure to notify prison officials about the risk was not dispositive. "Advance notification" was not found to be a "necessary element of an Eighth Amendment failure-to-protect claim." *Id.* at 849. The Supreme Court remanded for further discovery on the Eighth Amendment claim. *Id.* at 849. The district court granted summary judgment for the defendant prison officials. *See Farmer v. Brennan*, 81 F.3d 1444, 1448 (7th Cir. 1996). The Seventh Circuit reversed the district court's grant of summary judgment, finding that it had not fully considered Farmer's efforts to secure additional discovery. *Id.* at 1452. *Farmer v. Brennan* is important precedent for the cognizability of an Eighth Amendment claim for a transgender prisoner who is subject to the risk of sexual violence.

In recent years, transgender prisoners have often prevailed in cases involving access to health care and access to safe living conditions. For example, in *Fields v. Smith*, 653 F.3d 550 (7th Cir. 2011), the Seventh Circuit found that the factual predicate for the pre-*Farmer* earlier decisions was wrong. Affirming the district court, the Seventh Circuit found that a complete ban of all medical care, irrespective of medical judgment, was facially invalid. *Id.* at 559.

The Ninth Circuit affirmed a district court's grant of a preliminary injunction to a transgender prisoner who sought gender confirmation surgery. The Ninth Circuit affirmed the district court's holding that the treating psychiatrist acted with deliberate indifference to plaintiff's serious medical needs in violation of the Eighth Amendment, when he denied her gender confirmation surgery. *See Edmo v. Corizon,* 935 F.3d 757 (9th Cir. 2019). The Ninth Circuit voted to deny a request for an en banc petition. *See Edmo v. Corizon,* 949 F.3d 489 (9th Cir. 2020).

The Ninth Circuit decision creates a circuit split on the issue of whether a failure to comply with the World Professional Association for Transgender Healthcare (WPATH) guidelines constitutes deliberate indifference under the Eighth Amendment. The Fifth Circuit placed less weight on those guidelines, finding that they "reflect no consensus, but merely one side in a sharply contested medical debate over sex reassignment surgery." *Gibson v. Collier,* 920 F.3d 212, 221 (5th Cir. 2019). *See also Kosilek v. Spencer,* 774 F.3d 63 (1st Cir. 2014) (en banc) (reversing district court grant of injunctive relief to plaintiff who sought gender reassignment treatment).

The Supreme Court denied a petition for certiorari to resolve the circuit split. *See Idaho Department of Correction v. Edmo,* 141 S. Ct. 610 (2020).

Other cases involving the conditions of confinement and have sometimes been successful. Transgender inmate Damien Cole was able to pursue a successful claim against a correctional officer for allegedly allowing her to engage in sexual relations with an HIV positive inmate because the officer was deliberately indifferent to the substantial risk of serious harm. But her other claims about lack of access to hormonal treatment and conditions of confinement were unsuccessful. *See Cole v. Johnson,* No. 14–cv–01059–JPG–PMF, 2015 WL 4037522 (S.D. Ill. June 1, 2015).

Similarly, Tristain Crowder, also known as Candice Crowder, who is a transgender woman, brought a successful action against California prison officials in 2019. She alleged that prison officials failed to intervene when an inmate brutally attacked her in the dining hall and prison officials retaliated against her for filing grievances and a civil suit. The district court judge found that the dining hall incident stated a cognizable Eighth Amendment claim and that some of her equal protection allegations should survive a motion to dismiss as well as some of her retaliation allegations. *See Crowder v. Diaz,* 2019 WL 3892300 (E.D. Calif. August 19, 2019). Similarly, Passion Star brought a successful Section 1983 case against Texas correctional officials for failing to protect her from sexual assault by other inmates. *See Zollicoffer v. Livingston,* 169 F. Supp.3d 687 (S.D. Tex. 2016).

Further, Tay Tay, a transgender woman, brought a successful Section 1983 action against the Illinois Department of Corrections because it insisted on housing her in a men's prison where she was subjected to a substantial risk of serious harm. *See Tay Tay v. Dennison,* 457 F. Supp.3d 657 (S.D. Ill. 2020).

In response to Trump's Executive Order 14168, 90 Fed. Reg. 8615 (Jan. 20, 2025), which required federal prisons to house prisoners based on their sex assigned at birth, three female transgender inmates brought suit challenging that Executive Order. *See Doe v. McHenry, III*, 763 F. Supp.3d 81 (D. D.C. 2025). The district court granted their request for a temporary restraining order, using an Eighth Amendment analysis.

In addition, prisoners have pursued ADA cases against prison officials arguing that delayed medical treatment for gender dysphoria and harassment by deputies and other inmates constituted an ADA violation. *See Williams v. Kincaid,* 45 F.4th 759 (4th Cir. 2022). The Fourth Circuit reversed the district court's dismissal of this case. The Supreme Court denied a petition for certiorari. *Kincaid v. Williams,* 143 S. Ct. 2414 (2023).

Although many of the cases brought by transgender inmates have been successful, there are exceptions to that pattern. *See, e.g., Richardson v. District of Columbia,* 322 F. Supp.3d 175 (D. D.C. 2018) (finding no Eighth Amendment violation in case involving a female transgender prisoner who was housed with male prisoners); *Renee v. Neal*, 483 F. Supp.3d 606 (N.D. Ind. 2020) (largely granting prison's motion for summary judgment on claims related to transgender prisoners on First and Eighth Amendment claims); *Keohane v. Dixon*, No. 4:24–cv–00434–AW–MAF (N.D. Fla. Dec. 27, 2024) (denying request for a preliminary injunction by female transgender prisoner who was concerned that hormone therapy would be discontinued but had not yet experienced that harm).

Another tactic is to sue under the Gender Motivated Violence Act (GMVA). Crystal Schwenk's conditions of confinement case against the Washington state prison system illustrates the use of the Eighth Amendment along with the Gender Motivated Violence Act (GMVA) to seek damages for her alleged attempted rape by prison guard Robert Mitchell. *See Schwenk v. Hartford*, 204 F.3d 1187 (9th Cir. 2000). Despite identifying as a woman, Schwenk was housed in a male housing unit during her incarceration. Schwenk filed a *pro se* complaint in federal court against Mitchell after Mitchell allegedly tried to rape her twice, and Mitchell allegedly placed an illegal item in her cell so that she would lose accumulated good time credit and be sent to segregation for twenty-eight days. She was also moved to a multi-man cell in a maximum security area where she allegedly "live[d] in a constant state of fear and anxiety." *Id.* at 1194. Mitchell defended the case by arguing he was entitled to qualified immunity and that Schwenk did not have a cognizable claim on the merits. The district court ruled in favor of Schwenk and Mitchell appealed to the Ninth Circuit.

Relying on *Farmer v. Brennan*, 511 U.S. 825 (1994), the Ninth Circuit ruled that "a sexual assault on an inmate by a guard" inherently violates the Eighth Amendment. Further, where "guards themselves are responsible for the rape and sexual abuse of inmates, qualified immunity offers *no* shield." *Id.* at 1197 (emphasis in original). The gender of the guard or the prisoner is not a factor in determining whether the Eighth Amendment has been violated. Thus, the Ninth Circuit ruled that the district court acted correctly in denying Mitchell's qualified immunity claim with respect to Schwenk's Eighth Amendment claims.

With respect to the claim under the Gender Motivated Violence Act, the analysis was a bit more complicated. The GMVA provides a cause of action for "crime[s] of violence committed because of gender or on the basis of gender, and due, at least in part, to an animus based on the victim's gender." 42 U.S.C. § 13981(c) (2006). The Ninth Circuit found that Schwenk stated a claim under the GMVA but, because that claim was not clearly established when she brought the claim, the defendant was entitled to qualified immunity. The Ninth Circuit, therefore, reversed the district court's decision on the GMVA claim. *Id.* at 1199.

Under the doctrine of qualified immunity, a public defendant can avoid liability by arguing that the law was not sufficiently clearly established for the defendant to know that he or she was violating the right at issue. In this case, the Ninth Circuit found that "a violation of state laws regarding rape or sexual assault necessarily constitutes a violation of the GMVA regardless of the actor's motivation, state of mind or emotions." *Id.* at 1205. Nonetheless, the court held that the meaning of the phrase "animus based on the victim's gender" within the GMVA was ambiguous so the defendant could successfully argue that he did not know he was violating the GMVA when he targeted Schwenk for a sexual assault because of her transgender status. Prospectively, the Ninth Circuit's opinion, however, would put other guards on notice that an attempted sexual assault of a transgendered inmate would violate the GMVA and not be subject to a qualified immunity defense.

Litigation involved transgender prisoners has continued under the Trump administration. On January 20, 2025, President Trump issued an Executive Order which provides that federal funds "shall not be spent on any medical treatment for the purpose of conforming an inmate's appearance to that of the opposite sex." The Bureau of Prison implemented that order by ending hormone treatment as well as ending "social accommodations" such as clothing and hair removal devices. *See Kingdom v. Trump*, 2025 WL 1568238, *1 (D. D.C.

June 3, 2025). The district court granted plaintiffs' motion to certify a class and their request for a preliminary injunction.

Rather than being decided under the Eighth Amendment, this case was decided under the Administrative Procedures Act. The court said:

> The import of the Opinion is essentially this: Under the APA, the BOP may not arbitrarily deprive inmates of medications or other lifestyle accommodations that its own medical staff have deemed to be medically appropriate without considering the implications of that decision. Even if the BOP *did* support such a decision with the consideration, study, and reasoning that the APA requires of it, its freedom of action may nevertheless be constrained by the Eighth Amendment of the Constitution, but that is a matter better left for another day—whether that be a later stage of litigation, or another case entirely.
>
> *Id.* at *17.

In another words, the district court left the Eighth Amendment argument for another day. One should expect further developments in the prisoners' rights context.

§ 3.13 COMPETITIVE ATHLETICS

Athletic competition has become a new arena for contesting what it means to be "male" or "female."

At the international level, both the International Association of Athletics Federation (I.A.A.F.) and International Olympic Committee (I.O.C.) have sought to develop rules for determining who can compete in the "women's" athletic division. *See generally* Ruth Padawer, *The Humiliating Practice of Sex-Testing Female Athletes*, N.Y. TIMES MAG. (June 29, 2016). In the 1930s, intersex athletes were sometimes accused of being "gender cheats" when they competed as a female in international competition. The I.A.A.F. and I.O.C. began various forms of gender checks in the 1960s, including the "nude parade" where women's genitals were inspected. Then, the I.A.A.F. instituted chromosomal testing with Maria José Martínez Patiño being the first person disqualified under this testing regime. She appealed the ban and won after it was determined that her body was unable to use testosterone even though she had XY chromosomes and internal testes.

The I.A.A.F. then changed its policies to only disqualify an individual from competing as a woman if the person had "hyperandrogenism" (high testosterone) unless, like Patiño, the person was resistant to testosterone's effects. Reportedly, some athletes had their undescended testes surgically removed, or took hormone-suppressing drugs so they could continue to compete as a woman. Although hyperandrogenism could be a ground for a woman being disqualified from competition, there was no analogous rule for men. Men could compete even if they had natural levels of testosterone much higher than is typical for men.

In July 2015, the Court of Arbitration for Sport ruled that the I.A.A.F.'s policy was not justified by current scientific research because the evidence is unclear as to what role testosterone plays in athletic performance compared with other natural or environmental factors, such as nutrition. *See Dutee Chand*, CAS 2014/A/3759 (Ct. of Arbitration for Sport July 25, 2015). The court suspended the existing policy until July 2017 to give the I.A.A.F. time to prove that the degree of competitive advantage for high testosterone in women was such that they should be disqualified. That decision, however, only applied to the I.A.A.F. The I.O.C. has apparently suspended its gender-testing rules for the 2016 Olympics but has encouraged I.A.A.F. to submit evidence to the Court of Arbitration for Sport by 2017 so that the old policy can be re-instated. *See* IOC Consensus Meeting on Sex Reassignment and Hyperandrogenism (Nov. 2015). Thus, this controversy continues.

Meanwhile, a different section of the I.O.C. regulates athletes who are transgendered. Male to female transgendered individuals do not have to have their testicles or external genitalia removed, but they are required to suppress their testosterone levels below the typical male range. That rule is not affected by the Court of Arbitration decision. *Id.*

At the international level, the International Olympic Committee (IOC) has decided to allow each international sports body to set their own rules for transgender athletes' inclusion. This rule change came after transgender athlete Lia Thomas won the

500 year freestyle event in the women's division of the 2022 NCAA championships and announced that she hoped to compete in the Olympics. Swimming's governing body, FINA, decided to ban athletes who have been through any part of male puberty from elite women's competition. This rule seemingly disqualified Thomas from international competition because she reportedly transitioned while in college. But it also put pressure on each sport organization to engage in its own determination of what rules should apply.

In the domestic arena, more than twenty states have considered laws banning transgender women and girls from women's sports teams. *See* David Crary & Lindsay Whitehurst, *Lawmakers can't cite local examples of trans girls in sports,* AP News, March 3, 2021, https://apnews.com/article/lawmakers-unable-to-cite-local-trans-girls-sports-914a982545e943ecc1e265e8c41042e7.

The Biden administration sought to find a middle ground on this issue. On April 6, 2023, the U.S. Department of Education issued a Notice of Proposed Rulemaking. It was open for public comment for 30 days. It applied to all public K–12 schools, as well as colleges, universities or other institutions that receive federal financial assistance. While not permitting categorical bans on transgender students participating on sports teams consistent with their gender identity, the proposed rules seemed to allow some transgender students to be barred from participating on a team consistent with their gender identity. The proposed rule stated:

> If a recipient adopts or applies sex-related criteria that would limit or deny a student's eligibility to participate on a male or female team consistent with their gender identity, such criteria must, for each sport, level of competition, and grade or education level (i) be substantially related to the achievement of an important educational objective, and (ii) minimize harms to students whose opportunity to participate on a male or female team consistent with their gender identity would be limited or denied.

That language was not finalized before Trump became President in January 2025.

One of the organizations that has come out against exclusionary rules at the state level is the National Women's Law Center. They argue that such laws allow state officials to questions whether a student athlete is female, possibly making her undergo invasive testing such as a gynecological exam, blood work or chromosome testing. They referred to a cisgender female athlete with an athletic build who does not typically wear skirts or dresses. They said that her state's statute puts her at risk of invasive testing.

Lindsay Hecox and Jane Doe brought the first case challenging a ban on transgender women athletes from competing on women's teams. Hecox was denied the right to try out for the women's cross country and track teams at Boise State University. Jane Doe was denied the ability to compete as a woman on her high school soccer and track teams. *See Hecox v. Little*, 479

F. Supp.3d 930 (D. Idaho 2020). Because this case was brought while the Trump administration's interpretation of Title IX was still in place, this case was decided on constitutional grounds. The district court judge issued a preliminary injunction under the equal protection clause, finding that the transgender women were likely to succeed on the merits of an equal protection claim. Hecox was allowed to try out for the cross-country team and did not make the team, but she obtained the relief she sought—a fair opportunity to try out for the team. The district court opinion was affirmed by the Ninth Circuit. *See Hecox v. Little,* 104 F.4th 1061 (9th Cir. 2024).

Similarly, a lawsuit was filed on behalf of Becky Pepper-Jackson to challenge West Virginia's anti-trans law regarding K–12 athletics. Becky was a middle school student who had been a cheerleader and wanted to try out for her middle-school cross-country team. West Virginia's law banned her from doing so. The ACLU filed a lawsuit on her behalf, seeking a preliminary injunction. She initially prevailed. *See B.P.J. v. West Virginia State Board of Education,* 550 F. Supp.3d 347 (S.D. W. Va. 2021). After cisgender female college athlete's motion to intervene was granted, the district court dissolved the preliminary injunction. *See B.P.J. v. West Virginia State Board of Education,* 649 F. Supp.3d 220 (S.D. W. Va. 2023) . The Fourth Circuit reversed the district court, finding that state law violated Title IX as applied to a transgender middle school girl who had been taking puberty blocking medication since third grade. *See B.P.J. by Jackson v. West Virginia*

State Board of Education, 98 F.4th 542 (4th Cir. 2024).

The Supreme Court has decided to accept certiorari on both of these state bans on female transgender athletes. *See Little v. Hecox,* 2025 WL 1829165 (U.S. July 3, 2025); *West Virginia v. B.P.J.,* 2025 WL 1829164 (U.S. July 3, 2025). Based on its decision in *Skrmetti,* one might expect the Court to reverse these appellate decisions and permit these state bans. It will be important to see what level of scrutiny attaches to these cases. Will the Court use rational basis scrutiny like it did in *Skrmetti*?

Enforcement actions by the Trump administration may also clarify the rules that are required by Title IX. Lia Thomas (a female transgender athlete) had competed for the University of Pennsylvania. The Trump administration engaged in an investigation of the University of Pennsylvania's athletic department and found that it violated Title IX by allowing Thomas to compete in a female athletic program and occupy female-only intimate facilities. The University of Pennsylvania entered a Resolution Agreement with the Department of Education which eliminated all of Thomas' swimming records. It also agreed to "specify UPenn will adopt biology-based definitions for the word 'male' and 'female' pursuant to Title IX and consistent with President Trump's Executive Orders." *See* https://www.ed.gov/about/news/press-release/us-department-of-education-announces-university-of-pennsylvania-has-entered-resolution-agreement-resolve-its-title-ix-violations.

The Trump administration sued California on July 10, 2025, because it allowed female trans athletes to compete on female teams. (More than 20 states have policies similar to that of California as of July 2025.) In May 2025, California allowed a female trans athlete to compete in the state track and field meet where she placed first in the high jump and triple jump. Meet officials awarded her first place but also awarded medals to the other girls based on where they would have finished had the trans girl not participated. In response to a communication from the Trump administration, the state of California told the Trump administration that it would not change its longstanding policy of allowing female trans athletes to compete as girls. It sought to withdraw $3.8 billion in education funds to California as a result of this lawsuit. *See Justice Department sues California over transgender athlete policies*, https://www.nbcnews.com/nbc-out/out-politics-and-policy/justice-department-sues-california-transgender-athlete-policies-rcna217758.

A different kind of case was brought against participation by transgender athletes on women's sports teams in Connecticut. In *Soule v. Connecticut Association of Schools,* 2021 WL 1617206 (D. Conn. April 25, 2021), two cis-gender plaintiffs brought suit challenging a Connecticut regulation that permits high school students to participate in sex-segregated sports consistent with their gender identity. They argued that the state regulation violated their rights as girls to compete in all-girls' sports. Their case sought to preclude two transgender students, Andraya Yearwood and Terry Miller, from competing as women in high school sports. The case was dismissed on mootness grounds because Yearwood and Miller had graduated. In states, like Connecticut, however, that have not sought to ban participation by transgender athletes on teams that conform to their gender identity, we may see more lawsuits like this one.

With the Supreme Court scheduled to hear a case in the 2025–26 term on the exclusion of female transgender athletes from participation as women, we will likely receive more guidance by July 2026.

§ 3.14 MILITARY

Bans on transgender people in the military are covered in Chapter 6.

CHAPTER 4
REGULATION OF PARENTHOOD

Note: This chapter is written under the assumption that *Obergefell v. Hodges,* 576 U.S. 644 (2015) will remain good law, so that same-sex couples can marry in any jurisdiction in the United States and have that marriage recognized in every state.

§ 4.1 TRADITIONAL SURROGACY

The topic of surrogacy is one that affects many members of our society, some of whom may be in same-sex relationships. It also affects women's own control of their reproductive capacity and sexuality—whether they can engage in an agreement to facilitate the birth of a child who they do not intend to raise. The topic of surrogacy involves two types of arrangements. In "traditional surrogacy," a woman becomes pregnant using the sperm of a male sperm donor and her own egg. She is biologically related to the child she bears. In "gestational surrogacy," a woman becomes pregnant using the sperm of a male sperm donor and the egg of another woman. She is not biologically related to the child she bears. To the extent that individuals who give birth identify as transgender, gender nonbinary or male, the same rules would theoretically apply to them. Because the reported cases involve people who identify as women, that is the noun used in this chapter.

"Traditional surrogacy" came to the public forefront in the 1980s when Mary Beth Whitehead entered into a contract with Richard Stern in 1985 to agree to be artificially inseminated with Richard's semen and then bear a child who she would relinquish to Richard Stern and his wife Elizabeth Stern for $10,000 and the payment of all of her medical expenses. *See In re Baby M.*, 537 A.2d 1227 (N.J. 1988).

After bearing the child, Mary Beth Whitehead changed her mind about relinquishing the child to the Sterns. After the Sterns voluntary gave the baby to Ms. Whitehead for five days, they received an order from the court for Ms. Whitehead to return the baby to Mr. Stern. When the police arrived at the Whitehead residence to enforce this court order, Ms. Whitehead passed the baby out of a window to her husband and soon disappeared for eighty-seven days. *See In re Baby M.*, 525 A.2d 1128, 1145 (N.J. Super. Ct. 1987). Local law enforcement in Florida removed the baby from Ms. Whitehead's Florida residence and transferred the baby to the Sterns. The Sterns brought suit against Mary Beth Whitehead, seeking to enforce the surrogacy agreement and place the child in the father's sole custody. The court held that the surrogate-parenting agreement was valid and enforceable pursuant to the laws of New Jersey. *Id.* at 1166. With respect to the remedy of specific performance, the court further held that such remedy would only be appropriate if it were in the child's best interest. *Id.* at 1166. After considering the best interests of the child, the court gave permanent custody to Mr. Stern and terminated the parental rights of Ms. Whitehead. The court did order Mr.

Stern to pay $10,000 to Ms. Whitehead as provided by the contract. *Id.* at 1175–76.

On appeal, the New Jersey Supreme Court found that the surrogate contract conflicted with laws and public policy prohibiting use of money in connection with parental rights. Nonetheless, the court found that the best interests of the child did justify awarding custody to biological father and his wife, with visitation to biological mother. *In re Baby M.*, 537 A.2d 1227 (N.J. 1988). The court found there was no legal basis in terminating the parental rights of Ms. Whitehead and found that she was entitled "to retain her rights as a mother." *Id.* at 1253. Because the court found that Ms. Whitehead's parental rights should not have been terminated, it did not reach the question of whether Ms. Whitehead had a constitutional right to her parental rights. *Id.* at 1255. The court found that it was in the best interest of the baby for the Sterns to have custody because their home environment appeared to be more secure, and the bulk of the expert testimony concluded it would be in the best interest of the child to be raised by the Sterns. *Id.* at 1260. Although the court said that it was not a significant factor in its decision, it did note that Ms. Whitehead had divorced Mr. Whitehead, had another child, and married another man since the litigation had commenced. *Id.* at 1260 n.18. Finally, the court remanded to the trial court the issue of visitation with instructions that Ms. Whitehead should be awarded *some* visitation. On remand, the court granted unsupervised, uninterrupted, liberal visitation with Ms. Whitehead that included some overnight visitation. *See In re*

Baby M., 542 A.2d 52 (N.J. Super. Ct. 1988). When the child, Melissa, reached the age of maturity, she legally terminated Ms. Whitehead's parental rights.

In a similar case, and in the absence of a statute on the subject, the Tennessee Supreme Court ruled that "compensation is restricted to the reasonable costs of services, expenses, or injuries related to the pregnancy, the birth of the child, or other matters inherent to the surrogacy process." *In re Baby*, 447 S.W.3d 807, 833 (Tenn. 2014) (allowing enforcement of traditional surrogacy contract but not terminating the surrogate's parental rights).

One difficult problem that arises in some surrogacy cases is how a court should deal with the existence of a surrogacy agreement in resolving a voluntary adoption petition. For example, a woman in Oregon gave birth pursuant to a surrogacy agreement in which she had been artificially inseminated with a man's sperm. There was no conflict; the woman and her husband wanted to relinquish the children to be adopted by the sperm donor man and his wife. *See In re the Adoption of Baby A*, 877 P.2d 107 (Or. Ct. App. 1994). Because the birth mother had been paid $14,000, which was more than her pregnancy-related expenses, the trial court refused to grant the petition for adoption. "It concluded that the payment of money to birth mother makes her consent involuntary and invalidates her consent to the adoption." *Id.* at 107–08. Using a best interest of the child test, the court of appeals reversed and permitted the adoption. *Id.* at 108.

At least one case involving a traditional surrogacy agreement also involved a gay male couple in a state that did not recognize paid surrogacy agreements. G. entered an arrangement with C. to bear a child through artificial insemination from G.'s sperm. There was no formal surrogacy agreement, although, there was a fax from C. to G. that suggested the parties' initial intentions. C. initially indicated that she would relinquish custody to G. and his partner E. Following the birth of the baby. She did allow G. and E. to raise the child but then decided to seek custody herself. *See C. ex rel. T. v. G*, 225 N.Y.L.J., No. 9 at 29 (N.Y. Cty. Sup. Ct. Jan. 12, 2001). The court found that a surrogacy agreement would be unenforceable and used a best interest of the child standard to determine the proper outcome. C. raised the argument in the case that the child was suffering from "gender confusion" by being raised by two men. The court heard expert testimony on this issue and accepted the conclusion that such a diagnosis was not even possible for a baby. *Id.* at 30. The court awarded sole custody to G. with liberal visitation rights to C. Other than considering the argument about "gender confusion," the court's analysis did not appear to consider the sexual orientation of G. as a relevant factor.

Following the *Baby M.* decision, as discussed in *Nutshell* § 4.3, many states have enacted statutes regarding surrogacy contracts.

§ 4.2 GESTATIONAL MOTHERHOOD

Cases involving women who are the gestational mother but not the biological mother can raise difficult questions about who is the legally recognized mother. In the absence of a state statute, states have varied responses to this issue.

This issue was first raised in a California case from the early 1990s. *See Johnson v. Calvert*, 851 P.2d 776 (Cal. 1993) (en banc). Mark and Crispina Calvert entered into a surrogacy arrangement with Anna Johnson in which an embryo that had been fertilized from the egg of Crispina and the sperm of Mark would be implanted in Anna. They entered into a surrogacy arrangement under which Anna would be paid $10,000 in a series of installments and agreed to relinquish all parental rights in favor of Mark and Crispina. The California Supreme Court found that the Uniform Parentage Act ("UPA"), Cal. Civ. Code §§ 7000–7021 (West 2012), did not readily determine the outcome in this case because it merely involved "situations in which substantial evidence points to a particular man as the natural father of the child." *Id.* at 781. In this case, however, both women "adduced evidence of a mother and child relationship as contemplated by the Act." *Id.* at 781. Further, the court found no legislative preference "between blood testing evidence and proof of having given birth." *Id.* at 781. The court rejected the suggestion of amicus curiae ACLU that the court should find the child has two mothers and one father. "Even though rising divorce rates have made multiple parent arrangements common in our society, we see no compelling reason to recognize such a situation here." *Id.* at 781 n.8. Because the UPA did not provide an answer to the question of who had a legal claim to being the mother, the court concluded it should examine the "parties' intentions." *Id.* at 782. In other words, an intent test was used as a tiebreaker when the UPA did not resolve the parenting question. While recognizing that Anna changed her mind, the court found "it is safe to say that Anna would not have been given the opportunity to gestate or deliver the child had she, prior to the implantation of the zygote, manifested her own intent to be the child's mother." *Id.* at 782. Thus, the California court did not say that "intent" is always the controlling factor when there is a parenting dispute but did say it resolves the matter when the UPA does not offer a resolution.

The Ohio Supreme Court has permitted the enforcement of a gestational surrogacy contract, finding that it did not violate public policy. *See J.F. v. D.B.*, 879 N.E.2d 740 (Ohio 2007). In that case, eggs from a nonparty donor were artificially inseminated with semen from the male plaintiff. The gestational mother gave birth to triplets. The sperm donor and the gestational mother had a contract that provided compensation to her and required her to agree to the termination of her parental rights. The Ohio Supreme Court found enforcement of the contract did not violate public policy, but the court also suggested the decision might be different if it were a "traditional" surrogacy arrangement where the woman who gave birth was biologically related to the child. *Id.* at 742. An earlier Ohio case also stated:

"The consent to procreation and the surrender of the right to raise a child of one's own genes must be considered the surrender of basic rights." *Belsito v. Clark*, 67 Ohio Misc. 2d 54, 63 (Ohio Ct. C.P. Summit Cty. 1994). Thus, Ohio might not honor the terms of a "traditional" surrogacy contract if the biological mother did not want to relinquish her parental rights but has enforced a gestational surrogacy contract.

In the Ohio and California cases, it was the intent of the parties, as reflected in the contract, that the gestational surrogate would relinquish her parental rights and the courts enforced that intention. A different fact pattern occurred in Tennessee where the female member of an unmarried heterosexual couple gave birth to a child that was biologically related to her male partner but not herself. She was the gestational mother but not the biological mother. Unlike the Ohio case, there was no contract and the parties disagreed about their intentions. *See In re C.K.G.*, 173 S.W.3d 714 (Tenn. 2005).

In the Tennessee case, Charles and Cindy were an unmarried couple who had three children by obtaining eggs donated from an anonymous third-party female, fertilizing the eggs *in vitro* with Charles's sperm, and then implanting the fertilized eggs in Cindy's uterus. Cindy gave birth to three children by caesarian section; the birth certificates identified Charles and Cindy as the children's legal parents. When their relationship deteriorated, Cindy brought a parentage action to receive support from Charles to raise the children. Charles argued that Cindy had no parental rights to the children because she was not biologically related to them. Further, Charles argued that Cindy was merely a gestational surrogate who had given birth to the children for Charles, but that Cindy had no parental rights.

The Tennessee court decided that this case needed to be resolved based on close consideration of the facts. First, it rejected a genetic test, saying that "where a woman has become intimately involved in the procreation process even though she has not contributed genetic material, factors other than genetics take on special significance." *Id.* at 727–28. Second, it found that the intent of the couple was not dispositive but public policy does "favor[ ] taking into account intent in establishing parentage when technological assistance is involved." *Id.* at 728. Third, the court added the factor of gestation as a consideration. *Id.* at 729. Finally, the court noted that this case did not involve a conflict between the gestator and genetic mother. *Id.* at 730. The court did not suggest how this case would have been resolved had that kind of dispute been presented. Applying all these factors, the court found that Charles's genetic paternity "does not give him a parental status superior to that of Cindy." *Id.* at 730. The court then used a best interest of the child standard to allocate the custody and visitation rights of the parents. The dissenting judge would have decided this case on a genetic basis, finding that Cindy had no legal standing to sue for custody or support as a parent. *Id.* at 735–36. The Tennessee case is unusual in that the gestational mother was accorded full parental rights. In the other cases involving a surrogacy contract, where the gestational mother agreed to relinquish her parental rights, she was not accorded any parental rights.

In a case with similar facts to the Tennessee case, a New Jersey Superior Court reached a different decision. *See A.G.R. v. D.R.H.*, No. FD–09–001838–07 (N.J. Super. Ct. CH. Div. Dec. 23, 2009), available at https://graphics8.nytimes.com/packages/pdf/national/20091231_SURROGATE.pdf. D.R.'s sister, A.G.R., agreed to become pregnant by having an egg implanted that had been fertilized with her brother's partner's sperm (S.H.). The parties signed various agreements stating that A.G.R. would relinquish parental rights to D.R. and S.H. Relying heavily on *Baby M.*, the court held that the principles that invalidated the surrogacy agreement in *Baby M.* have equal force in this case, irrespective of the fact that the woman who gave birth to the twins was not biologically related to the children. It found that A.G.R. has parental rights and that the parental agreement that she signed "is void and serves as no basis for termination of parental rights of the plaintiff." *Id.* at 6. The court also found that S.H. was the legal father of the twins. *Id.* at 6. So, in that case, the legal parents were the gestational mother and the male partner of the mother's brother. This case did involve a gay male couple but there is nothing in the court's reasoning that makes that fact relevant.

The New Jersey Supreme Court has not yet addressed a case involving a gestational surrogacy agreement and the lower courts have not been consistent in their treatment of this issue. In *In the Matter of the Parentage of the Child of Kimberly*

Robinson, 383 N.J. Super. 165 (N.J. Super. Ct. 2005), the court found that the mother of a child conceived through alternative insemination and the mother's same-sex partner should be declared the parents pursuant to the state's Artificial Insemination statute. But in *In the Matter of the Parentage of a Child by T.J.S. and A.L.S.*, 419 N.J. Super. 46 (N.J. Super 2011), the court held that the wife could not obtain a pre-birth order directing her name to be listed on birth certificate of husband and anonymous ovum donor carried to term by gestational carrier.

Connecticut courts, like New Jersey courts, were previously split on the issue of whether an intended parent to a gestational surrogacy agreement could be named on the child's birth certificate. In 2011, the Connecticut Supreme Court, in a case involving two gay men, applied an intent test to conclude that the non-biological intended parent should be listed on the birth certificate without requiring an adoption. *See Raftopol v. Ramey,* 299 Conn. 681 (Conn. 2011).

Courts in other states have similarly ruled that the gestational mother's name need not appear on the birth certificate, especially when the individuals involved in giving birth to the child agree to that result. Thus, in Ohio, a lower court allowed the biological mother to be the woman listed on the birth certificate when her sister voluntarily agreed to be a gestational mother. *See Belsito v. Clark,* 67 Ohio Misc.2d 54, 66 (Ohio Ct C.P. Summit Cty. 1994). Similarly, in Maryland, the state court of appeals ruled that the gestational mother's name need not appear on the birth certificate when the biological father and gestational mother agree on that result, even though surrogacy contracts are illegal in Maryland. *See In re Roberto d.B.*, 923 A.2d 115, 130–31 (Md. 2002). The dissenting opinions disagreed with the result in the Maryland case, arguing that there should be more consideration of the child's best interest, including the impact on the child of having no mother. There is no indication of the sexual orientation of the father in the Maryland case and so it is impossible to know if he had a partner who might also share in raising the child. Finally, the Massachusetts Supreme Court permitted the parties to request that the birth certificate include the names of the intended parents at birth where the parties were in agreement and the birth mother was not a biological parent. *See Culliton v. Beth Israel Deaconess Med. Ctr.*, 756 N.E. 2d 1133 (Mass. 2001).

§ 4.3 TRADITIONAL OR GESTATIONAL SURROGACY STATUTES

A. SURROGACY CONTRACTS

Following the *Baby M.* decision, many states enacted statutes to deal with surrogacy contracts. These state laws fall into three categories. First, some states prohibit all surrogacy contracts and even may impose criminal penalties on those who help create such contracts. *See, e.g.*, D.C. Code §§ 16–401–02 (2012) (prohibiting surrogacy contracts); Mich. Comp. Laws Ann. §§ 722.851–.63 (2011) (prohibiting surrogacy contracts and imposing criminal penalties). *See also Doe v. Att'y Gen.*, 487 N.W.2d 484 (Mich. Ct. App. 1992) (finding Michigan surrogacy prohibition to be constitutional). Second, some states prohibit traditional surrogacy contracts but do not prohibit gestational surrogacy arrangements. *See* Ky. Rev. Stat. Ann. § 199.590(4) (2013); N.D. Cent. Code §§ 14–18–05, 08 (West 2009). Third, some states regulate both traditional and gestational surrogacy contracts but do not ban them. *See* N.H. Rev. Stat. Ann. §§ 168–B:1 to B:32 (2014); Va. Code Ann. §§ 20–156 to –165 (2008); Wash. Rev. Code Ann. §§ 26.26.210–.260 (West, 2016). States in the third category typically allow the couple that wishes to raise the child to pay the surrogate for her role in creating a child, but she is not paid to "sell" the child. *See, e.g.*, *Doe v. Att'y Gen.*, 487 N.W.2d 484 (Mich. 1992).

Tennessee is considered to have a unique way of handling surrogacy issues. It does not prohibit the enforcement of surrogacy contracts but will not enforce terms related to the termination of the surrogate's parental rights. In a case involving a gestational carrier, the Tennessee Supreme Court concluded that the gestational carrier was the children's "legal mother" and could seek both custody and child support from the biological father. *See In re C.K.G.*, 173 S.W.3d 714 (Tenn. 2005). Further, in a case in which the mother was a traditional surrogate (i.e., she was biologically related to the child), the Tennessee Supreme court held that there was no legal basis to terminate her parental rights. The case was remanded to the juvenile court to determine visitation and child support. *See In re Baby*, 447 S.W.3d 807 (Tenn. 2014).

By contrast, the Iowa Supreme Court agreed to enforce a surrogacy contract between a gestational surrogate and a married heterosexual couple. The gestational mother had been implanted with an egg from an anonymous donor that was fertilized with the sperm of the husband of the married couple. *See P.M. and C.M. v. T.B. and D.B.*, 907 N.W.2d 522 (Iowa 2018).

Cases involving gestational motherhood can affect both gay men and lesbians. Gay men may hire a gestational surrogate to bear a child with an egg that has been donated from another woman. A lesbian might bear a child that is the result of a donated sperm and her partner (or another woman's) egg. These situations could cause a court to inquire about who are the legally recognized parents. In the cases discussed above, the courts seem to assume that there will be a male and female parent, but one would expect the same principles to apply when the outcome is two male parents or two female parents. There also are no reported cases involving parents who are gender nonbinary. As with cases involving birth certificates and other identity documents, discussed in Chapter 3, one might expect courts to be flexible in applying rules developed under gender binary assumptions to parents who identify as gender nonbinary. The possibility of more than two parents will be discussed in *Nutshell* § 4.11.

B. IN VITRO FERTILIZATION WITHOUT A CONTRACT

Not all individuals who use in vitro fertilization to assist with producing a child have used a contract to specify parental rights. Further, state law may also govern some of these processes. A complicated case from California reflects how state law can help resolve parenting disputes when a lesbian couple uses in vitro fertilization. *See K.M. v. E.G.*, 117 P.3d 673 (Cal. 2005).

K.M. and E.G. were a lesbian couple who had registered as domestic partners and sought to produce a child together. K.M. donated her egg to E.G. who successfully bore twins. When she made the donation, she also signed a written agreement at the clinic where the medical procedure was performed saying she relinquished any claim to offspring born of her donation. *Id.* at 675. Their relationship ended when the twins were about five years old. *Id.* at 683.

Two different statutory provisions had potential relevance to the resolution of this case. Cal. Fam. Code § 7613(b) (2013) provides: "The donor of semen provided to a licensed physician and surgeon for use in artificial insemination of a woman other than the donor's wife is treated in law as if he were not the natural father of a child thereby conceived." E.G. argued that that rule also meant that a woman is not a mother if she provides ova to a woman who is not her wife. Rather, the court found that the Uniform Parentage Act, Cal. Fam. Code § 7600 et seq. (2013) ("UPA") governed the case. The UPA provides that the "parent and child relationship extends equally to every child and to every parent, regardless of the marital status of the parents." Uniform Parentage Act, Cal. Fam. Code § 7602 (2013).

First, the court concluded that § 7613(b) does not apply to exclude K.M. as a parent of the twins, because the California legislature deliberately did not use the word "married" in front of woman in § 7613(b) "so that in California, subdivision (b) applies to all women, married or not." *Id.* at 679. After considering the legislative history of this section (and treating egg donors like sperm donors), the court said: "there is nothing to indicate that California intended to expand the reach of this provision so far that it would apply if a man provided semen to be used to impregnate his unmarried partner in order to produce a child that would be raised in their joint home." *Id.* at 680. In other words, the court interpreted "donor's wife" broadly to include any situation in which a couple lived together and intended to raise a child together even if they were not technically married. It purported to reach that result irrespective of whether a heterosexual or a lesbian couple were unmarried and took advantage of artificial reproduction to produce a child. Colorado reached a similar result in a case involving a man who provided semen to a physician that was used to impregnate an unmarried friend of the man, who had allegedly promised to allow him to be the father of the child. *See In re R.C.*, 775 P.2d 27 (Colo. 1989).

Because § 7613(b) did not preclude K.M. from being a legally recognized parent, the court then applied the UPA. Under the UPA, the court found that both K.M. and E.G. should be recognized as parents. K.M.'s recognition was based on her genetic relationship with the twins; E.G.'s recognition was based on her giving birth to the twins. *K.M.* at 680–81. Although the California Supreme Court had said in *Johnson* that California law recognizes only one natural mother, the *K.M.* court cited with approval a statement from another case that "our decision in *Johnson* does not preclude a child from having two parents both of whom are women." *Id.* at 681 (citing *Elisa B. v. Super. Ct.*, 117 P.3d 660, 666–67 (Cal. 2005)). The court seemed to confine its statement from *Johnson* to a situation where the child would have two mothers *and* a father.

The *K.M.* decision also confined the *Johnson* intent test to a situation where there is a "tie to break." If the case can be decided under the UPA then the California court said there was no need to apply the *Johnson* intent test. *Id.* at 681.

A dissenting opinion agreed that the UPA should resolve this case but accused the majority of rewriting the UPA to achieve the laudable goal of providing the child with two parents:

> The majority amends the sperm-donor statute by inserting a new provision making a sperm donor the legal father of a child born to a woman artificially inseminated with his sperm whenever the sperm donor and the birth mother "*intended that the resulting child would be raised in their joint home*," even though both the donor and birth mother also intended that the donor *not* be the child's father.

Id. at 685 (Kennard, J., dissenting) (emphasis in original). Because many states have versions of the UPA, the reader should watch how other states interpret similar fact patterns under their own UPA. Justice Kennard's dissent appears to be a more straightforward reading of the statutory language. Of course, it may also be possible in the future that the gestational and biological mothers are married, which could also produce a clearer outcome under the UPA. Then, the biological mother would not have been presumed to have waived her parental rights, as Justice Kennard argues in the *K.M.* case.

§ 4.4 UNIFORM PARENTAGE ACT

A. FATHERHOOD

Historically, states adopted statutes to protect married couples, and sperm donors, when the wife became pregnant by using sperm from a third-party donor. The male donor typically did not want to be a legally recognized parent, and the woman's husband did. § 5 of the Uniform Parentage Act (1973) reflected that situation:

> (a) If, under the supervision of a licensed physician and with the consent of her husband, a wife is inseminated artificially with semen donated by a man not her husband, the husband is treated in law as if he were the natural father of a child thereby conceived. The husband's consent must be in writing and signed by him and his wife. The physician shall certify their signatures and the date of the insemination, and

file the husband's consent with the [State Department of Health], where it shall be kept confidential and in a sealed file. However, the physician's failure to do so does not affect the father and child relationship. All papers and records pertaining to the insemination, whether part of the permanent record of a court or of a file held by the supervising physician or elsewhere, are subject to inspection only upon an order of the court for good cause shown.

(b) The donor of semen provided to a licensed physician for use in artificial insemination of a married woman other than the donor's wife is treated in law as if he were not the natural father of a child thereby conceived.

Unif. Parentage Act § 5 (Unif. Law Comm'n 1973). The 2000 and 2017 versions of the Uniform Parentage Act are even simpler. They state: "A donor is not a parent of a child conceived by assisted reproduction." Unif. Parentage Act, § 703. The 2000 version was adopted in 11 states. The 2017 version has been adopted in three states: California, Vermont, and Washington. Thus, it is important to check one's states' laws to see if they still refer to "husband" and "wife" in the rules regarding assisted reproduction.

States that rely on the 1973 version of the Uniform Parentage Act require the use of a licensed physician to facilitate the artificial insemination as well as a written agreement. If the man and woman do not follow these rules, it is possible that the man can seek to be recognized as the legally-recognized parent (or the woman can try to have him established as a legally-recognized parent to sue him for child support). A California court enforced these rules when a woman used artificial insemination to become pregnant with a child who she had intended to raise with another woman. *See Jhordan C. v. Mary K.*, 224 Cal. Rptr. 530 (Cal. Ct. App. 1986). In that case, the parties did not use a physician or enter into a written agreement. Further, their conduct was consistent with Jhordan acting as a member of the family. His name was on the birth certificate and Mary did not object to Jhordan's collection of baby equipment or the creation of a trust fund for the child. *Id.* at 536. The court appeared to place greater emphasis on the lack of physician involvement than on the lack of a written agreement, saying, "We do not purport to hold that an oral or written nonpaternity agreement between the parties would have been legally binding; that difficult question is not before us (and indeed is more appropriately addressed by the Legislature)." *Id.* at 536. It did, however, approve the physician requirement noting that it merely requires that the woman obtain the semen "through a licensed physician" and does not prohibit home-based artificial insemination. *Id.* at 535.

The Uniform Parentage Act can create some dilemmas for gay men who *want* to be the legally recognized father when using artificial insemination. If they use a physician to facilitate the artificial insemination, then they need to be careful to ensure that their state law will not eliminate their parental rights. It would appear that they need to be especially careful not to participate in artificial insemination with a married woman because the use of a physician seems to create a strong presumption that the husband of the married woman is the legally-recognized father rather than the sperm donor.

In interpreting the Uniform Parentage Act, in situations where sperm donors *want* to be the legally recognized father, states have to be mindful of the Supreme Court's decision in *Stanley v. Illinois*, 405 U.S. 645 (1972). In *Stanley*, an unmarried couple had had three children together and lived together intermittently for eighteen years. Upon the mother's death, the children became wards of the state under Illinois law. The father was not given an opportunity to demonstrate he was a fit parent. The statute presumed the father was unfit if the parents were not married. The Supreme Court concluded that the father "was entitled to a hearing on his fitness as a parent before his children were taken from him and that, by denying him a hearing and extending it to all other parents whose custody of their children is challenged, the State denied Stanley the equal protection of the laws." *Id.* at 649. Nonetheless, the Supreme Court also ruled in *Quilloin v. Walcott*, 434 U.S. 246 (1978) that the biological father of an unmarried couple had no constitutional right to challenge an adoption where he had had no role in the child's life for the first eleven years of the child's life and the child's stepfather was seeking to adopt the child. Finally, the Supreme Court also ruled that a California law was constitutional in creating an irrefutable presumption that the husband of a wife who bore a child was the "father" even though blood tests indicated with 98% certainty that another man was the biological father. *Michael H. v. Gerald D.*, 491 U.S. 110 (1989). The Uniform Parentage Act tries to avoid some of these problems by requiring all of the parties to acknowledge their role in the pregnancy and the legally-mandated parental outcomes. When those conditions are not followed, and the sperm donor wishes to be the legally recognized parent, he may face some legal challenges if the woman who gives birth is also married.

A further, and increasingly common, complication is when a gay man uses both an egg donor and a surrogate (who is not the egg donor). In some cases, the surrogate may also be married to a man who does not want to be presumed to have any parental rights. Because of the vast variation from state to state, one would need to explore the legal ramifications of this arrangement on a state-by-state basis. The Legal Professional Group, a professional group of the American Society for Reproductive Medicine, has a very helpful state by state guide. *See Surrogacy Laws by state*, https://connect.asrm.org/lpg/resources/surrogacy-by-state?ssopc=1. They describe California as "a highly surrogacy friendly state" because "pre-birth and post-birth parentage order are permitted and may be obtained regardless of the marital status or sexual orientation of the intended parent/s and regardless of whether they used their own gametes or donated sperm and/or eggs."

B. MOTHERHOOD

The 1973 version of the Uniform Parentage Act can also require some interpretation in other contexts that relate to who might be designated as the "mother." First, the statute referred to the "husband" of the married woman. One would expect that the term "husband" would be construed to include the same-sex "wife" of a woman who uses a third-party donor for artificial insemination. Second, the statute referred only to a donation of "semen." What if a wife receives the third-party donation of a fertilized egg? On equal protection grounds, one would think that such a statute would provide comparable protection to the same-sex married couple—they would not have to worry about a parentage claim by the woman who donated the fertilized egg.

The 2017 version of the UPA avoids these issues by not using terms such as husband and wife. Instead, it refers to individuals who are married to each other. Further, the 2017 version merely refers to a "donor" in assisted reproduction without specifying that the donation must be semen. Presumably, those rules would apply to the donation of a fertilized egg.

The extension of these kinds of artificial insemination statutes beyond their strict language is reflected in a California decision, *In re Marriage of Buzzanca*, 61 Cal. App. 4th 1410 (Cal. Ct. App. 1998). John and Luanne Buzzanca entered into a surrogacy agreement with a woman who agreed to give birth after being implanted with an embryo that was not biologically related to John or Luanne Buzzanca. Before the baby was born, John filed a petition for dissolution of the marriage. Luanne filed a separate petition seeking to establish herself as the child's mother and seeking child support from John. John took the position that neither he nor Luanne were the child's legal parents. While recognizing that the legislature never contemplated this situation when it wrote the artificial insemination statute, the court concluded it should be guided by the same principles:

> If a husband who consents to artificial insemination under Family Code section 7613 is "treated in law" as the father of the child by virtue of his consent, there is no reason the result should be any different in the case of a married couple who consent to in vitro fertilization by unknown donors and subsequent implantation into a woman who is, as a surrogate, willing to carry the embryo to term for them. The statute is, after all, the clearest expression of past legislative intent when the legislature did contemplate a situation where a person who caused a child to come into being had no biological relationship to the child.

Id. at 1418.

Thus, applying the artificial insemination statute (by analogy), the court found that both John and Luanne were the legally recognized parents of the child. The California decision supports the view that courts will try to interpret their statutes on artificial insemination to treat donors similarly, irrespective of whether they donate eggs or sperm. These statutes, however, typically operate in a context in which the donor has expressed an intention in writing *not* to be a legally recognized parent at the time of the donation. Other principles can apply if the donor's intent is less clear.

Section 8 of the 2017 UPA has a provision governing assisted reproductive technology. Its terms fall into the third category of surrogacy statutes, as discussed in *Nutshell* § 4.3, allowing traditional and gestational surrogacy contracts subject to extensive regulation that includes judicial pre-approval, limits on compensation, and provisions concerning the revocation of rights of the parties to the agreement. The 2017 Act also imposes greater restrictions on traditional surrogacy agreements based on the birth mother's status as a genetic parent. The 2002 version of the UPA made no distinction between traditional and gestational surrogacy contracts.

Further, another issue that arises is whether a female, married couple is entitled to have both of their names on the birth certificate. The Seventh Circuit ruled that it would violate the equal protection clause to presume the married man was the father of a child born or conceived in wedlock is the legal parent of the child but to not extend the same presumption to a married woman (whose partner was female). *See Henderson v. Box,* 947 F.3d 482 (7th Cir. 2020). The Supreme Court refused to grant cert. on this issue. *See Box v. Henderson*, 141 S. Ct. 953 (2020).

Finally, an issue that affects many members of the LGBTQ+ community is whether parents can transfer their U.S. citizenship to their children. This is a federal, not state law, issue. Until May 2021, same-sex couples often had difficulty securing U.S. citizenship for their child if the biological parent was not a U.S. citizen or they used a surrogacy agreement to have their child born abroad. For example, Elad Dvash-Banks and his partner, Andrew, had to sue the State Department so that their twin sons, who were born abroad through a surrogacy arrangement, could be considered U.S. citizens. *See E.J. D.-B. v. United States Department of State,* 825 Fed. Appx. 479 (mem) (9th Cir. 2020). Similarly, the oldest son of Allison Blixt and Stefania Zaccari was denied U.S. citizenship at birth because he was conceived and carried to birth by Zaccari, who is Italian. *See, e.g.,* Supplemental Memorandum in Support of Defendants' Motion to Dismiss, *Blixt v. The United States Department of State,* 2019 WL 2152539 (D.D.C. filed March 19, 2019). District courts had ruled in favor of married gay couples in two cases decided in 2020. *See Mize v. Pompeo,* 482 F. Supp.3d 1317 (N.D. Ga. 2020); *Kiviti v. Pompeo,* 467 F. Supp.3d 293 (D. Md. 2020).

The State Department has a website that answers questions about the citizenship status of children born abroad to a surrogate. https://travel.state.gov/content/travel/en/legal/travel-legal-considerations/us-citizenship/Assisted-Reproductive-Technology-ART-Surrogacy-Abroad.html. That website was last updated on October 31, 2024, so it is not known if the Trump administration will follow those guidelines. Further, the birthright citizenship issue is being heard in the courts at this time, with the Trump administration taking the position that children are not automatically U.S. citizens merely because they were born in the United States. It is too early to know if that issue might affect children born in the United

States through surrogacy agreements when the biological parent is not a U.S. citizen.

§ 4.5 CHILD CUSTODY

A. INTRODUCTION

Parents can have a variety of custodial or visitation arrangements. Shared parenting or joint custody is the preferred legal arrangement. In such an arrangement, the parents share major decisions about the child's well-being. Sometimes, the courts vest sole legal custody in one parent, especially if one parent is found to be unfit. Even if the courts vest sole physical custody in one parent, the parents may retain shared legal custody and, therefore, be legally entitled to be involved in major decisions involving the child. When one parent has primary physical custody, there is usually a visitation agreement concerning when the other parent may spend time with the child. If there are concerns about the fitness of the noncustodial parent for visitation, the visitation agreement can sometimes involve supervised visitation. The general standard for custody and visitation is the "best interest of the child" standard. When an arrangement is in place and the other parent wants to modify it, the courts typically require a "changed circumstances" argument to be made. The presumption is that it is best for the child for a custody/visitation schedule to be stable rather than for the parents to be re-opening it frequently.

As will be discussed below, some courts used to conclude that an LGBTQ+ parent was *per se* unfit. Therefore, the LGBTQ+ parent would have all parental rights terminated. Even though the LGBTQ+ parent may not have had legal custody, the courts also had to determine if he or she should have visitation. As will be discussed in *Nutshell* § 4.6, courts used to place visitation restrictions on LGBTQ+ parents to minimize the exposure of the child to an LGBTQ+ "lifestyle." Although the legal principles involving custody and visitation are similar, this *Nutshell* will discuss those legal principles separately in §§ 4.5 and 4.6

B. 1970S AND 1980S

Child custody disputes are supposed to be resolved under a "best interest of the child" standard. Historically, that presumption favored the mother, although, in recent years courts have been more gender-neutral in resolving custody disputes.

In the 1970s and 1980s, it was commonplace for state courts to have a *per se* rule that homosexuality disqualified a parent from custody. *See, e.g., Constant A. v. Paul C. A.*, 496 A.2d 1, 10 (Pa. Super. 1985) ("there are sufficient social, moral and legal distinctions between the traditional heterosexual family relationship and illicit homosexual relationship to raise the presumption of regularity in favor of the licit, when established, shifting to the illicit, the burden of disproving detriment to the children"). *See also Jacobson v. Jacobson*, 314 N.W.2d 78 (N.D. 1981) (affirming consideration of homosexuality as the "overriding factor" in custody determination). Courts began to reject that rule in the 1980s, replacing it with a "nexus test" that required evidence of actual harm to the child to deny custody. *See, e.g.*, *Bezio v. Patenaude*, 410 N.E.2d 1207 (Mass. 1980).

Even as courts relaxed the *per se* rule, they often expressed strong disapproval of children being exposed to a "gay lifestyle." A California court refused to grant custody to a mother because she was openly living with a female companion in the same apartment. *See Chaffin v. Frye*, 119 Cal. Rptr. 22 (Cal. Ct. App. 1975). A Kentucky court reversed a lower court order that had allowed a child to stay with her lesbian mother, because the lower court had failed to consider the "potential for endangering the physical, mental, moral or emotional health of the child." *S. v. S.*, 608 S.W.2d 64, 66 (Ky. Ct. App. 1980). The court concluded: "[T]he failure of the community to accept and support such a condition, forces on the child a need for secrecy and the isolation imposed by such a secret, thus separating the child from his or her peers." *Id.* at 66. *See, e.g.*, *Irish v. Irish*, 300 N.W.2d 739 (Mich. Ct. App. 1981) (providing that no intimate sexual conduct could take place between mother and her lesbian partner in the children's presence and that children could not remain overnight if mother's lover were present overnight).

A Washington court gave custody of their children to two lesbians, after they each separated from their husbands, but required them to live separate and apart and not remove the children from the state. *See*

Schuster v. Schuster, 585 P.2d 130 (Wash. 1978) (en banc). The women rented separate apartments in the same building and raised the children jointly. The fathers argued that the custody decree should be modified to award them custody. The mothers argued that the "changed circumstances" rule should allow them to be able to modify the original agreement and live together openly. The trial court was willing to eliminate the requirement that the mothers live separate and apart, but the Washington Supreme Court reversed that part of the decision. *Id.* at 133.

In a strongly worded dissent, Justice Rosellini argued that the women should not be allowed to maintain custody of the children. He noted that the women have publicized "the homosexual cause in general and their lesbian relationship" and produced a film entitled "Sandy and Madeleine's Family." *Id.* at 135 (Rosellini, J., dissenting). Citing a case which discussed the immorality of a school teacher being openly gay, Justice Rosellini argued: "I am unable to understand how the court can declare that a school teacher who only admitted to his preference as a homosexual and did not engage in any overt act, is guilty of immorality, and yet, in the instant case, can find perfectly moral the conduct of the respondents." *Id.* at 135.

Justice Rosellini then quoted from a 1977 law review article in which the authors emphasized that the "most threatening aspect of homosexuality is its potential to become a viable alternative to heterosexual intimacy." *Id.* at 135 (quoting J. Harvie Wilkinson III & G. Edward White, *Constitutional*

Protection for Personal Lifestyles, 62 CORNELL L. REV. 563, 595 (1977)). Thus, thc willingness of the Supreme Court of Washington to allow the lesbian mothers to maintain custody of their children may have been seen as a positive development despite the significant restrictions made on their lifestyles. Limitations on gay men and lesbians who were awarded full or partial custody was routine after the abandonment of the *per se* rule.

Similarly, a Pennsylvania court concluded that it was appropriate to consider a mother's homosexuality in determining the appropriate custody arrangement. *See Constant A. v. Paul C.A.*, 496 A.2d 1 (Pa. Super. Ct. 1985). The mother had been awarded controlled partial custody and visitation, which the court refused to modify. *Id.* at 10. While rejecting a *per se* rule against custody, the court articulated the following rule in refusing to conclude that changed circumstances justified giving a lesbian mother expanded custody: "[W]here there is a custody dispute between members of a traditional family environment and one of homosexual composition, *the presumption of regularity applies to the traditional relationship* and the burden of proving no adverse effect of the homosexual relationship falls on the person advocating it." *Id.* at 5 (emphasis in original). The court then stated: "Here, the children do not know of the lesbian relationship of their mother, and it is inconceivable that they would go into that environment, be exposed to the relationship, and *not* suffer some emotional disturbance, perhaps severe." *Id.* at 8 (emphasis in original).

A New York court applied the changed circumstances doctrine to remove a child from her mother's custody because of the "existing homosexual relationship being carried on in the home where this ten year old female child resides." *In re Jane B.*, 380 N.Y.S.2d 848, 856 (N.Y. Sup. Ct. 1976). The court transferred custody to the father and imposed restrictions on the mother's visitation rights, such as that she "will not remain overnight . . . . nor is she to be taken there to visit while [the mother's partner] or other homosexuals are present." *Id.* at 860.

In a case involving a parent who transitioned from male to female, the Nevada Supreme Court affirmed a trial judge's order terminating the transitioning parent's parental rights. *See Daly v. Daly*, 715 P.2d 56 (Nev. 1986). At the time of the termination of her parental rights, Suzanne had agreed to have no contact with their daughter, in part because of the daughter's alleged "revulsion" towards Suzanne. *Id.* at 59. Suzanne had, nonetheless, wanted to maintain her legal status as the child's parent to better protect the possibility of re-connection in the future. The court denied that request, finding "given the circumstances concerning [the daughter's] view of Suzanne and the extent of her opposition to further ties with a vestigial parent, it can be said that Suzanne, in a very real sense, has terminated her own parental rights as a father." *Id.* at 59.

The dissent argued that the majority did not follow the governing law for termination of parental rights which required both a finding that the parent's capacity to raise a child was below minimum standards and that the best interests of the child would be served by a termination of parental rights. Both types of grounds must exist to terminate parental rights. *Id.* at 62. The dissent argued that the majority based its conclusion entirely on the likelihood of harm to the daughter if Suzanne were to seek to interact with the daughter, rather than on the basis of actual evidence of poor parenting skills or harm to the child. *Id.* at 63. In 2000, after the Nevada legislature had amended its child custody laws to focus on the best interest of the child, the Nevada Supreme Court overruled the reasoning in *Daly*, saying that the court had placed "too much emphasis on the conduct of the parents instead of on the best interests of the child." *In re Termination of Parental Rights as to N.J.*, 8 P.3d 126, 132 (Nev. 2000). The 2000 case, however, did not involve parents who were members of the LGBTQ+ community so it is hard to say how the court would currently consider a parent's transgender status as part of the "best interests of the child" analysis.

The consideration of the supposed harm to the children stemming from social unacceptance of their parent's same-sex relationship was contrary to how the Supreme Court resolved a similar issue in the race context. In *Palmore v. Sidoti*, 466 U.S. 429 (1984), a unanimous Court found that it was inappropriate for a court to consider the race of the mother's partner in making a custody decision. The Court stated:

> Whatever problems racially mixed households may pose for children in 1984 can no more

> support a denial of constitutional rights than could the stresses that residential integration was thought to entail in 1917. The effects of racial prejudice, however real, cannot justify a racial classification removing an infant child from the custody of its natural mother found to be an appropriate person to have such custody.

Id. at 434. In 1985, the Alaska Supreme Court relied on *Palmore* to overturn the trial court's order and concluded that it was inappropriate to change custody of minor children from the mother (who was a lesbian) to the father under the changed circumstances doctrine. *S.N.E. v. R.L.B.*, 699 P.2d 875, 878–79 (Alaska 1985) ("Simply put, it is impermissible to rely on any real or imagined social stigma attaching to Mother's status as a lesbian.")

Even without citing *Palmore*, other courts in the 1980s did conclude that a parent's homosexuality did not necessarily render them an unfit parent for custody. *See, e.g.*, *Stroman v. Williams*, 353 S.E.2d 704 (S.C. Ct. App. 1987); *Guinan v. Guinan*, 477 N.Y.S.2d 830 (N.Y. App. Div. 1984); *D.H. v. J.H.*, 418 N.E.2d 286 (Ind. Ct. App. 1981).

C. CONTEMPORARY CASE LAW

While some courts began to have a less discriminatory attitude against LGBTQ+ parents, vestiges of overt discrimination remained in the 1990s and the early 2000s. A trial court judge denied custody to An White in a custody dispute with the grandparents of her children and ordered that any visitation be exercised outside the presence of her lesbian partner. *See White v. Thompson*, 569 So.2d 1181 (Miss. 1990). While recognizing the legal presumption in favor of the fitness and suitability of a child's biological parents, the Mississippi Supreme Court affirmed the conclusion that "An White was unfit, morally or otherwise." *Id.* at 1184. Because there was evidence of White's unfitness that was not related to her lesbianism, the court declined to determine if her homosexuality made her "per se" unfit. *Id.* at 1184–85. Further, the court found that the visitation restriction was within "a reasonable exercise of the court's power and discretion." *Id.* at 1185.

One of the most notorious custody cases was from Virginia. *See Bottoms v. Bottoms*, 457 S.E.2d 102 (Va. 1995). In this case, the Virginia Supreme Court affirmed transferring custody from the mother, Sharon Bottoms, to the grandmother, Pamela Kay Bottoms. The grandmother had filed a petition against her daughter, seeking an award of custody of the daughter's two-year-old son, alleging that the child "is currently living in an environment which is harmful to his mental and physical well being [sic]." *Id.* at 104. The trial court "ruled that because Sharon Bottoms lives in a sexually active lesbian relationship and engages in illegal sexual acts, she is an unfit parent as a matter of law." *Bottoms v. Bottoms*, 444 S.E.2d 276, 279 (Va. Ct. App. 1994), *rev'd*, 457 S.E.2d 102 (Va. 1995). The trial court awarded custody to the grandmother and granted visitation rights to the mother. The court of appeals reversed, concluding that the trial court had abused its discretion by transferring custody to a non-parent, because there was insufficient evidence of parental unfitness. *Id.* at 107. The Virginia Supreme Court reversed the Court of Appeals, concluding that "living daily under conditions stemming from active lesbianism practiced in the home may impose a burden upon a child by reason of the 'social condemnation' attached to such an arrangement, which will inevitably afflict the child's relationships with its 'peers and with the community at large.' " *Bottoms v. Bottoms*, 457 S.E.2d at 108, (citing *Roe v. Roe*, 324 S.E.2d 691, 694 (Va. 1985)).

Similarly, the Supreme Court of Alabama found that a court of appeals had been incorrect in reversing a trial court decision in a case involving a divorced couple where the mother was living in an open lesbian relationship with another woman. *See Ex Parte J.M.F.*, 730 So. 2d 1190 (Ala. 1998). The court of appeals had based its decision on the legal rule that a transfer of custody should only occur with evidence that the mother's alleged misconduct had a detrimental effect upon the child. *Id.* at 1194. The Alabama Supreme Court used a different legal rule. It said that the evidence of detrimental effect upon the child is only necessary when the noncustodial parent argues that the other parent had engaged in sexual misconduct. In this case, the father argued that he had known of his former wife's lesbian relationship at the time of the divorce and never argued that her sexual orientation made her *per se* unqualified to be the custodial parent. Instead, he argued "changed circumstances" to suggest that his recent re-marriage and the mother's "openly homosexual home environment" constituted evidence that a change in custody "would materially promote the child's best interests." *Id.* at 1194.

In 2004, an Alabama Court of Appeals also affirmed the transfer of custody to the father in a similar case in which the biological mother lived with her lesbian partner and the father had remarried. *See L.A.M. v. B.M.*, 906 So. 2d 942 (Ala. Ct. App. 2005). The openness of the homosexual parent's lifestyle was also a factor in a mother successfully persuading the North Carolina courts to change the custody agreement from joint legal custody to sole legal custody. *See Pulliam v. Smith*, 501 S.E.2d 898 (N.C. 1998). While claiming not to invoke a *per se* rule against a father who lived in an open relationship with his male partner, the Idaho Supreme Court affirmed a magistrate's decision to transfer custody to the mother and restrict visitation when the father's male partner was present. *See McGriff v. McGriff*, 99 P.3d 111 (Idaho 2004).

On similar facts, a Florida Court of Appeals refused to change a custody arrangement from a mother to a father merely because of community's bias against the mother's lifestyle and the father's forthcoming re-marriage. *See Jacoby v. Jacoby*, 763 So. 2d 410 (Fla. Dist. Ct. App. 2000) (requiring direct evidence of negative impact on children to change the child custody arrangement). Similarly, in 2003, the North Dakota Supreme Court overruled *Jacobson v. Jacobson*, 314 N.W.2d 78 (N.D. 1981) in which it had previously allowed homosexuality to be an "overriding factor" in a custody determination. *See*

Damron v. Damron, 670 N.W.2d 871, 875 (N.D. 2003).

Other courts have refused to modify a child custody arrangement due to a parent's openly gay lifestyle. For example, in *In re the Marriage of: R.S.*, 677 N.E.2d 1297 (Ill. App. Ct. 1996), the court of appeals reversed a modification of a child custody arrangement by the trial court that had been based on the mother's relationship with a live-in lesbian partner. The court of appeals found there was no evidence of harm and that the theoretical potential of "social condemnation as a result of the mother's relationship" with her partner "was not a sufficient basis for modifying custody." *Id.* at 1301–02. The court also noted that "the risk of such condemnation would not be eliminated by awarding custody of the children to their father." *Id.* at 1302. Similarly, in *Teegarden v. Teegarden*, 642 N.E.2d 1007 (Ind. Ct. App. 1994), the court of appeals ruled that the trial court judge did not have authority to restrict mother's "homosexual activity" as a condition of custody in a custody dispute between the biological mother and the stepmother following the death of the children's biological father. Further, the Indiana Court of Appeals ruled that was no rational basis for an order prohibiting a mother from cohabiting with her same-sex partner while living with her children. *See Downey v. Muffley*, 767 N.E.2d 1014 (Ind. Ct. App. 2002). And, in Alabama, a court refused to modify a custody agreement based on an allegation that the mother allowed the child to visit her aunt and the aunt's alleged lesbian partner. *See Davis v. Blackstock,* 160 So.3d 310 (Ala. Civil App. 2014). But the court was also careful to distinguish the case from *Ex parte J.M.F.*, by mentioning that "the facts do not involve a parent who is engaging in homosexual activity; the father has not alleged that the mother is homosexual or that the child is living in a home with [a lesbian couple]." *Id.* at 320. Thus, as recently as 2014, an Alabama court was open to considering a "homosexual lifestyle" as being a negative factor in a custody case.

In both *White* and *Bottoms*, the party seeking custody was not the biological parent, yet the court awarded custody to this third party over the lesbian mother. These kinds of decisions require evidence that the mother is *unfit* which, in theory, is a high legal standard. The Mississippi and Virginia courts broadly construed the definition of "unfitness" to take custody away from the lesbian mother. Today, such decisions in favor of non-biological parents would be less likely in light of the Supreme Court decision in *Troxel v. Granville*, 530 U.S. 57 (2000). In that decision, the United States Supreme Court ruled that a Washington state statute was unconstitutional, in permitting the child's paternal grandparents to seek visitation rights, because the statute violated the substantive due process rights of the biological mother to control the care, custody and control of her children. Although *Troxel* involved visitation, its conclusion that the mother had a fundamental due process interest in the care, custody and control of her children would be equally applicable in a custody dispute between a mother and grandparents, as occurred in *White* and *Bottoms*. *See, e.g.*, *In re Strome*,

120 P.3d 499 (Or. Ct. App. 2005) (rejecting custody petition by mother of a gay father).

§ 4.6 VISITATION

When one parent has legal custody of the child, the other parent will typically have visitation rights to spend time with the child. Absent a finding of unfitness, so that no visitation is appropriate, the legal standard is a best interest of the child standard. As we will see below, courts have the discretion to impose restrictions on visitation privileges, such as limiting whether overnight visitors are present or whether the parent attends certain kinds of activities with the child.

A. 1970s AND 1980s

Some courts, in the 1980s, began to apply the *Palmore* rule to cases involving gay men and lesbians, and refused to affirm a visitation decision based on social stigma. *See, e.g., Conkel v. Conkel*, 509 N.E.2d 983 (Ohio Ct. App. 1987). Nonetheless, while citing *Palmore*, the Ohio court left in place a restriction that Conkel could not have the children overnight if his male partner were present. *Id.* at 984. *But see Inscoe v. Inscoe*, 700 N.E.2d 70 (Ohio Ct. App. 1997) (refusing to modify child custody agreement based merely on evidence that father was living in an openly homosexual relationship).

A California court refused to restrict a father's visitation rights "without a link to detriment to the child." *See In re Marriage of Birdsall*, 243 Cal. Rptr. 287, 291 (Cal. Ct. App. 1988). Because of the lack of evidence of harm from the father having a male, overnight visitor, the court vacated that part of the lower court's judgment which had forbidden Birdsall from having overnight visitation from his child "in the presence of any friend, acquaintance or associate who is known to be homosexual." *Id.* at 291. The court was unwilling to presume detriment merely because Birdsall was a gay man. Other courts followed that rule in the 1980s. *See In re Marriage of Cabalquinto*, 718 P.2d 7 (Wash. Ct. App. 1986) (holding that limitation of father's visitation decree to prevent his association with homosexual companion during minor son's visit was improper). *See also In re Marriage of Cabalquinto*, 669 P.2d 886 (Wash. 1983) (remanding trial court judge's denial of father's visitation request because the trial judge's reasoning was unclear and could have been based on father's homosexual lifestyle).

Not all courts followed the *Birdsall* approach to visitation in the 1980s. For example, a Missouri trial court had modified an earlier visitation order so that the father could continue to have the child for ten days every other month, but could not have his lover, or any other male with whom the father resided, in the child's presence or in the father's home during the child's visits. *See J.P. v. P.W.*, 772 S.W.2d 786 (Mo. Ct. App. 1989). Rather than require proof of a detriment, the court of appeals found "it is established that expert testimony is not a necessary basis for a determination that exposure to a homosexual influence will adversely affect a child." *Id.* at 793. Further, the court modified the visitation rules established by the trial court because it would be impractical to have supervised visitation in Austin, Texas for ten days. On remand, the "trial court may determine that, in view of the age of the child, it would be impractical to provide for such supervised visitation in Austin." *Id.* at 794. Thus, the father's cross-appeal of the supervised restriction resulted in even *more* restrictions being put in place.

Other courts also imposed restrictions on an LGBTQ+ parent's visitation rights in the 1970s and 1980s. A New Jersey court restricted a father's visitation to daytime hours only due to his deep involvement in the gay rights movement. *See In re J. S. & C.*, 324 A.2d 90 (N.J. Super. Ct. Ch. Div. 1974). A Missouri court restricted a gay father's visitation rights by denying him the right to have the child overnight. *See J.L.P.(H.) v. D.J.P.*, 643 S.W.2d 865 (Mo. Ct. App. 1982). These restrictions were affirmed on appeal with the court of appeals concluding: "There is substantial evidence . . . . to find that the potential for physical and emotional harm exists if the restrictions on visitation are not imposed." *Id.* at 869. An Ohio Court of Appeals overruled a trial court judge's visitation order because it did not sufficiently limit the homosexual father's visitation rights. *See Roberts v. Roberts*, 489 N.E.2d 1067 (Ohio Ct. App. 1985) (while not requiring trial court judge to terminate visitation with the father, requiring father not to reveal his "homosexual lifestyle" to his children).

B. CONTEMPORARY CASE LAW

Beginning in the 1990s, appellate courts typically reversed lower court orders that sought to eliminate or significantly curtail a parent's visitation rights due to a parent's homosexual lifestyle. *See, e.g., North v. North*, 648 A.2d 1025 (Md. Ct. Spec. App. 1994) (finding that circuit court abused its discretion by denying father overnight visitation based on fear that he would display or discuss his homosexual lifestyle with the children); *Pleasant v. Pleasant*, 628 N.E.2d 633 (Ill. App. Ct. 1993) (reversing trial court decision that had limited mother's visitation because she was openly involved in a lesbian relationship); *In re Marriage of Black,* 392 P.3d 1041 (Wash. 2017) (finding that trial court abused its discretion in considering wife's sexual orientation as a factor when determining the parenting plan).

Nonetheless, some appellate courts did continue to affirm restrictions placed on parents related to their homosexuality. In *Marlow v. Marlow*, 702 N.E.2d 733 (Ind. Ct. App. 1998), the trial court judge awarded sole custody to the mother and imposed two restrictions on the father's visitation rights: (1) he could not have a non-blood related person in the house overnight when the children were present and (2) he could not include the children in any activities that promoted a "homosexual lifestyle." *Id.* at 735. The court of appeals affirmed that order concluding that it was based on the best interest of the children rather than private bias against the father's homosexuality. Similarly, in *A.O.V. v. J.R.V.*, Nos. 0219–06–4, 0220–06–4, 2007 WL 581871 (Va. Ct.

App. Feb. 27, 2007), the trial court judge had awarded joint custody to the parents but primary physical custody to the mother. The father was granted visitation for one weekend a month, some holidays, and four weeks in the summer. *Id.* at *2. The mother appealed the custody determination arguing that she should have been granted sole custody and the father should have been prohibited from exposing the children to his homosexual lifestyle. The court of appeals affirmed those aspects of the trial court order, finding the trial court judge did not abuse his discretion. *Id.* at *11. It is likely that *Obergefell* renders those determinations as inappropriate, but it would also be hard to use the federal courts to contest such determinations. For further discussion of *Obergefell, see Nutshell* § 5.6.

In a more recent case involving a visitation conflict, the Arizona Court of Appeals concluded that the lower court had erred in granting a visitation plan that divided the child's time equally between two women who had jointly raised the child for seven years before ending their 17-year sexual relationship. *See Egan v. The Honorable Elaine Fridlund-Horne*, 221 Ariz. 229 (Ariz. Ct. App. 2009). While recognizing that the nonbiological parent was not entitled to equal visitation rights, the court remanded for what it considered to be a reasonable order under state law. The Arizona court rejected the approach taken in Washington under *In re Parentage of L.B.*, discussed at *Nutshell* § 4.8, because "we sharply disagree with the bold pronouncement . . . . that, if a person can establish standing as a de facto parent, then that person has a fundamental liberty interest in the care, custody, and control of the child, to the same extent as the legal parent." *Id.* at 237. Thus, sharp disagreements continue to exist from state to state in how to treat children raised in a nontraditional family environment.

§ 4.7 ADOPTION

A. OVERVIEW

Cases involving the LGBTQ+ community and adoption have occurred in two different kinds of situations. First, gay men and lesbians have sought to adopt children as "single adults" (in the days before they were permitted to legally marry). Although all states currently allow such individuals to adopt, this issue, like the custody and visitation issue, has evolved over the years. Second, gay men and lesbians have sought to become the second parent to a child where their partner is already a legally-recognized parent. Various barriers, including the historical bar to same-sex marriages, have sometimes made this difficult.

B. ADOPTIONS AS SINGLE PARENTS

The LGBTQ+ community has faced statutory and common law bars to adoption although most of those restrictions have now been eliminated.

1. Florida Statute

Florida enacted a law in 1977 that provided: "No person eligible to adopt under this statute may adopt if that person is a homosexual." Fla. Stat. § 63.042(3) (found unconstitutional 2010). Foster parents and guardians who wished to adopt the children in their care but were precluded from doing so because they were gay men or lesbians, challenged this statute. The district court ruled for the state finding that the foster parents had no liberty interest in adopting children and that the law was constitutional under rational basis review under the Equal Protection Clause. The Eleventh Circuit affirmed. *See Lofton v. Sec'y of the Dep't of Children and Soc. Serv.*, 358 F.3d 804 (11th Cir. 2004). Despite the ruling of the Eleventh Circuit, a state court judge ruled in 2008 that the ban violated the state's equal protection clause. *See In re Adoption of Doe*, No. [Redacted] 2008 WL 5070056 (Fla. Cir. Ct. Aug. 29, 2008). Similarly, the Florida District Court of Appeal found the statute banning adoptions by homosexuals to be unconstitutional under the Florida Constitution. *See Florida Dep't of Children and Families v. In re Adoption of X.X.G. and N.R.G.*, 45 So. 3d 79 (Fla. Dist. Ct. App. 2010). The state did not appeal this ruling and the Florida Department of Children and Families no longer inquires about prospective parents' sexual orientation in determining their fitness to be parents. In 2017, Florida agreed to settle a federal lawsuit over birth certificates issued to children born into same-sex marriages. *See* Dara Kam, *Florida settles birth certificate suit, agrees to recognize same-sex married parents,* MIAMI HERALD, Jan. 11, 2017, available at https://www.miamiherald.com/news/local/community/gay-south-florida/article 125929324.html. Presumably, this decision would also give more latitude to same-sex couples to jointly adopt children and have both names listed on the birth certificate.

Other states have passed, and then repealed, such bans on adoptions by gay men and lesbians. *See, e.g.*, 1987 N.H. Laws ch. 343, codified at N.H. Rev. Stat. Ann. § 170–B:4 (repealed in 1999) (legislature "finds that, as a matter of public policy, the provision of a healthy environment and a role model for our children should exclude homosexuals, as defined by this act, from participating in governmentally sanctioned programs of adoption [and foster care]").

2. Mississippi Statute

Mississippi Code § 93–17–3(5) states: "Adoption by couples of the same gender is prohibited." This language was added to the legislative code in 2000. *See* S. 3074, 2000 Reg. Sess. (Miss. 2000). Two lesbian couples seeking a private adoption involving the biological child of one of the partners and two other lesbian couples desiring adoption through Mississippi's foster-care system challenged the law as unconstitutional. *See Campaign for Southern Equality v. Mississippi Department of Human Services,* 175 F. Supp.3d 691 (S.D. Miss. 2016). The district court concluded that the unconstitutionality of the state ban flowed directly from *Obergefell*. "It also seems highly unlikely that the same court that held a state cannot ban gay marriage because it would deny benefits—expressly including the right to adopt—would then conclude that married gay couples can be denied that very same benefit." *Id.* at

710. The case doesn't resolve whether such rules could be applied exclusively to *unmarried* couples.

3. Utah Statute

In 2000, the same year that Mississippi enacted its ban on adoption by same-sex couples, Utah enacted a statute that prohibited adoption to any person who is "cohabiting in a relationship that is not a legally valid and binding marriage." Utah Code Ann. § 78–30–9 (repealed 2008). At the time Utah passed this measure, it was not possible for same-sex couples to have their marriages recognized in Utah. Utah repealed this provision in 2008. The statutory justification for this rule was that such adoptions were not in a "child's best interest."

Now that same-sex couples, like heterosexual couples, have the option of getting married, it is hard to know if the Utah statute could withstand constitutional challenge. (Before same-sex couples could marry, one could argue that the statute was invalid under *Romer v. Evans,* 517 U.S. 620 (1996) as being based on an invidious anti-gay purpose.) In both *United States v. Windsor*, 570 U.S. 744 (2013) and *Obergefell v. Hodges*, 576 U.S. 644 (2015), the Supreme Court emphasized that gay men and lesbians could be excellent parents and it was inappropriate of society to deny children the opportunity to live with married parents, who could both be legally recognized parents. For example, the *Obergefell* Court said:

> A third basis for protecting the right to marry is that it safeguards children and families and

> thus draws meaning from related rights of childrearing, procreation, and education. *See, e.g., Pierce v. Society of Sisters*, 268 U.S. 510, 45 S. Ct. 571, 69 L. Ed. 1070. Without the recognition, stability, and predictability marriage offers, children suffer the stigma of knowing their families are somehow lesser. They also suffer the significant material costs of being raised by unmarried parents, relegated to a more difficult and uncertain family life. The marriage laws at issue thus harm and humiliate the children of same-sex couples. *See Windsor, supra,* at ___, 133 S. Ct., at 2694–2695.

Obergefell, 576 U.S. at 667–68.

That language has two different, plausible readings in connection with the Utah statute. On the one hand, that language suggests that it is impermissible to have a presumption that it is not in a child's best interest to live with a same-sex couple irrespective of whether they are married. On the other hand, the language suggests that children raised in a nonmarital family unit are "relegated to a more difficult and uncertain family life." *Id*. at 2590. The Utah legislature could defend such legislation by saying they are trying to avoid having the child raised in such a difficult situation. Nonetheless, there is some case law protecting the rights of nonmarital couples and, possibly, that case law could be used to say it is inappropriate to discriminate against nonmarital couples. *See, e.g., Eisenstadt v. Baird*, 405 U.S. 438 (1972) (overturning law that limited contraceptives to persons in marital relationships).

4. Common Law Barriers

Rather than have a statutory ban against LGBTQ+ people adopting children, most states have a "best interest of the child" standard for determining if potential adoptive parents are qualified to adopt. That subjective determination can sometimes be used to consider a prospective parent's sexual orientation. *See, e.g., In re Appeal in Pima Cty. Juvenile Action B-10489*, 727 P.2d 830 (Ariz. Ct. App. 1986) (considering fact that adoption applicant was bisexual was one of several factors used to conclude that he was not an acceptable person to adopt children).

In re Adoption of Charles B., 552 N.E.2d 884 (Ohio 1990) reflects how these rules can sometimes be used to consider the sexual orientation of a prospective parent. Charles B. was one of three children who became eligible for adoption in 1985 after his biological parents signed a voluntary permanent surrender of each of them. *Id.* at 886. Charles B. had significant disabilities as well as leukemia. In early 1987, Mr. B. indicated a general interest in adopting a child and, specifically, in adopting Charles. A year later, Mr. B. filed a petition for the adoption of Charles in probate court. The guardian recommended that the court approve the adoption. The state opposed the adoption, simply testifying that Mr. B. did not meet their "characteristic profile of preferred adoptive placement." *Id.* at 888. Hearing the testimony, the trial court granted the petition for adoption. *Id.* at 889. The state appealed and the court of appeals reversed the judgment of the trial court, "finding that, as a matter of law, homosexuals are not eligible to adopt." *Id.* at 885. The Ohio Supreme Court reversed, finding that the trial court had not abused its discretion in granting the petition for adoption.

Justice Alice Robie Resnick dissented, arguing that Mr. B., as a gay man, is at risk of becoming HIV-positive. She said:

> Mr. B was aware of this problem and was tested, proving to be HIV negative. However, we must remember that adoption is not just for today but forever. Mr. B falls within a high-risk population for AIDS. Why place a child whose immune system has already been altered in such an environment? It was best stated by Kathleen Handley, Administrator of Social Services for the Licking County Department of Human Services, at the hearing that "[o]ur feeling is that professionally it would be an adoption risk * * * to place a child in a setting where there is no practiced precedent to give us support. We do not view this as a child that needs experimentation. He has too many other issues that he has to conquer in his life."

Id. at 891.

Even though no other individual had come forward who was willing to adopt Charles, Justice Resnick thought it was better for him to stay in the care of the state rather than be adopted by Mr. B. Her views, as well as those of the state agency, reflect how individuals can use such pretexts to bar the LGBTQ+ community from adopting children, even if there is no statutory bar to such adoptions.

C. SECOND-PARENT ADOPTIONS

Most jurisdictions provide that someone cannot adopt a child unless the biological parents relinquish their parental rights. The exception is stepparents where the parent who wishes to adopt is married to the person who is the only legally recognized parent. In that case, the stepparent is allowed to adopt the child so that the child has two parents.

This rule has often made it difficult for the LGBTQ+ community to co-parent a child when only one of them is the biological parent of the child. For example, if Ruth becomes pregnant through artificial insemination and raises a child with her partner, Cara, they cannot both be legally recognized parents unless Ruth and Cara are married. In the post-*Obergefell* world, Ruth and Cara might marry to solve this problem. But many cases occurred before *Obergefell* was decided where lesbian couples argued that they both should be the legally recognized parents without the biological parent relinquishing her parental rights.

One of those cases was part of the consolidated *Obergefell* case. April DeBoer and Jayne Rowse were a lesbian couple who had each adopted various children over the years. *See DeBoer v. Snyder*, 973 F. Supp. 2d 757, 760 (E.D. Mich.), *rev'd*, 772 F.3d 388

(6th Cir. 2014), *rev'd sub nom.*, *Obergefell v. Hodges*, 576 U.S. 644 (2015). When they sought to jointly adopt each other's children, they were barred by Mich. Comp. Laws § 710.24 (2012), which restricts adoptions to either single persons or married couples. They claimed that the adoption law violated the Equal Protection Clause "because it impermissibly discriminates against unmarried couples." *Id.* at 760. The district court judge invited the plaintiffs to amend their complaint to challenge the state ban on same-sex marriage rather than to challenge the ban on single persons jointly adopting children. *Id.* at 760. They eventually succeeded in their challenge to the marriage ban. Michigan law continues to restrict joint adoptions to married couples. April Deboer and Jayne Rowse were married in August 2015 and reportedly said, "This is the first step in the final step we're looking to achieve, which is to complete the second-parent adoption." *See* Katrease Stafford, *From Supreme Court to Southfield: Deboer and Rowse Marry*, DETROIT FREE PRESS, Aug. 22, 2015, available at https://www.freep.com/story/news/local/michigan/oakland/2015/08/22/april-deboer-wedding-gay-marriage/32193359/.

Other plaintiffs have succeeded in persuading judges to allow unmarried couples to jointly adopt (before same-sex marriage became possible). *See, e.g.*, *In re M.M.D.*, 662 A.2d 837 (D.C. Ct. App. 1995). The trial court judge had interpreted the D.C. statute to preclude the unmarried couple from jointly adopting the child. The court of appeals interpreted the phrase "any person" to include the term "any persons" so that D.C. law could be used to permit *two* people to jointly adopt a child without being married to each other. After an exhaustive recitation of principles of statutory interpretation, the court of appeals concluded they could adopt and take advantage of the stepparent rule so long as they were an unmarried couple "living together in a committed personal relationship, whether of the same sex or of opposite sexes." *Id.* at 862. A similar result has been reached in other courts through principles of liberally construing state statutes to facilitate adoptions. *See In re Petition of K.M.*, 653 N.E.2d 888 (Ill. App. Ct. 1995); *In re Adoption of Tammy*, 619 N.E.2d 315 (Mass. 1993); *In re Adoption of Child by J.M.G.*, 632 A.2d 550 (N.J. 1993); *In re Adoption of Evan*, 583 N.Y.S.2d 997 (Surr. Ct. N.Y. Co. 1992); *In re Jacob*, 660 N.E.2d 397 (N.Y. Ct. App. 1995); *In re Adoption of B.L.V.B.*, 628 A.2d 1271 (Vt. 1993); *In re Adoption of L.O.F.*, S. Ct. Civ. No. 2013–0087, 2015 WL 2406304 (V.I. May 20, 2015).

Some judges who approved second-parent adoptions by unmarried same-sex partners have found that the underlying statute should be construed liberally to avoid constitutional problems. For example, the New York Court of Appeals stated:

> Given that section 117 is open to two differing interpretations as to whether it automatically terminates parental rights in all cases, a construction of the section that would deny children like Jacob and Dana the opportunity of having their two *de facto* parents become their legal parents, based solely on their biological mother's sexual orientation or marital status,

> would not only be unjust under the circumstances, but also might raise constitutional concerns in light of the adoption statute's historically consistent purpose-the best interests of the child. (*See, e.g., Gomez v. Perez,* 409 U.S. 535, 538, 93 S. Ct. 872, 875, 35 L.Ed.2d 56 [Equal Protection Clause prevents unequal treatment of children whose parents are unmarried]; *Plyler v. Doe,* 457 U.S. 202, 220, 120 S.Ct 2382, 2396, 72 L.Ed.2d 786 [State may not direct the onus of parent's perceived "misconduct against his (or her) children"]; *Matter of Burns,* 55 N.Y.2d 501, 507–510, 450 N.Y.S.2d 173, 435 N.E.2d 390 [New York statute requiring child born out of wedlock to prove "acknowledgment" by deceased parent did not further legitimate State interest]; *see also, Matter of Best,* 66 N.Y.2d 151, 160, n. 4, 495 N.Y.S.2d 345, 485 N.E.2d 1010, *supra).*

In re Jacob, 660 N.E.2d 397, 405 (N.Y. Ct. App. 1995).

The New York court suggested that a narrow reading of the adoption statute would constitute discrimination on the basis of sexual orientation or marital status. At the time that decision was written, same-sex couples could not marry in New York. Even though same-sex couples can now marry, one could arguably still claim, as the court stated above, that the parent's "misconduct" (in deciding not to marry) should not be used to harm the child who would benefit from having two legally-recognized parents.

Nonetheless, some judges continue not to interpret state law to facilitate joint adoptions by unmarried couples. For example, the Nebraska Supreme Court ruled that their adoption statute requires a biological parent to relinquish his or her parental rights for a child to be eligible for adoption by a party other than the biological parent's spouse. *See In re Adoption of Luke*, 640 N.W.2d 374 (Neb. 2002). *See also In re Adoption of Baby Z.*, 724 A.2d 1035 (Conn. 1999) (biological mother and same-sex cohabitant not permitted to be named as parents under Connecticut law). The Connecticut decision was reversed on October 1, 2000 by the state legislature. *See* H.R. 5830, Public Act 00–228, amending Conn. Gen. Stat. § 45a–724 (Conn. 2000). At this time, nearly all states permit second-parent adoption, although, as will be discussed below, it is sometimes necessary to make arguments about "parenthood by estoppel" or "de facto parenting" for the second parent's rights to be recognized when a second-parent adoption is not permitted under state law.

Some states have sought to preclude second-parent adoptions by gay men and lesbians. For example, Oklahoma law prohibits state agencies and courts from "recogniz[ing] an adoption by more than one individual of the same sex from any other state or foreign jurisdiction." Okla. Stat. tit. 10, § 7502–1.4(A) (2009). The Tenth Circuit found that this rule violated the Full Faith and Credit Clause. *See Finstuen v. Crutcher*, 496 F.3d 1139, 1156 (10th Cir. 2007). That decision is consistent with a subsequent Full Faith and Credit decision by the United States Supreme Court. *See V.L. v. E.L.*, 577 U.S. 404 (2016). But the Tenth Circuit issue does not resolve the question of whether it is constitutional for states to prohibit second-parent adoptions for unmarried couples.

§ 4.8 DE FACTO PARENT

The concept of "de facto" parenting has sometimes been used to allow a former partner to seek visitation or custody rights after the dissolution of a relationship where a second-parent adoption has not taken place.

One of the earliest examples of this legal theory occurred in Wisconsin. *See In re Custody of H.S.H.-K*, 533 N.W.2d 419 (Wis. 1995). After co-parenting a child for five years, a lesbian couple separated. The biological mother terminated her former partner's relationship with the child and filed a restraining order seeking to prohibit all contact. As a nonparent, the former partner had no standing to seek custody or visitation. Further, she could not seek custody rights as a product of dissolution of a marriage because the couple had never been married (a legal impossibility at the time). Nonetheless, the Wisconsin Supreme Court granted visitation under its equitable authority finding that the nonparent had a "parent-like relationship with the child" and that "a significant triggering event justifies state intervention." *Id.* at 421. Similarly, the Massachusetts Supreme Court embraced a *de facto* parent theory in granting visitation rights to a former lesbian partner who had helped raise the child for three years. *See E.N.O. v. L.M.M.*, 711 N.E.2d 886 (Mass. 1999).

In embracing the *de facto* parent rule, the Washington Supreme Court adopted the following four criteria:

> (1) the natural or legal parent consented to and fostered the parent-like relationship, (2) the petitioner and the child lived together in the same household, (3) the petitioner assumed obligations of parenthood without expectation of financial compensation, and (4) the petitioner has been in a parental role for a length of time sufficient to have established with the child a bonded, dependent relationship, parental in nature.

In re Parentage of L.B., 122 P.3d 161, 176 (Wash. 2005).

The counterargument for recognition of parental rights in the de *facto* parenting situation is the constitutional rights of the biological parent as recognized in *Troxel v. Granville*, 530 U.S. 57 (2000). The Washington Supreme Court responded to the *Troxel* argument by finding:

> The State is not interfering on behalf of a third party in an insular family unit but is enforcing the rights and obligations of parenthood that attach to *de facto* parents; a status that can be achieved only through the active encouragement of the biological or adoptive parent by affirmatively establishing a family unit with the *de facto* parent and child or children that accompany the family.

In re Parentage of L.B., 122 P.3d at 179.

The Washington state case shows how difficult arguments about *de facto* parenting can be. As noted by the dissent, the biological mother and the sperm donor married after this litigation began and the sperm donor signed a paternity affidavit, requesting the birth certificate be amended. *Id.* at 164 n.3. The sperm donor, however, was not a party to the dispute and the court did not adjudicate his rights.

Not all courts accept the *de facto* parenting argument. As discussed in *Nutshell* § 4.7, Arizona rejects that concept. Similarly, the Vermont Supreme Court rejected *de facto* parenting in *Titchenal v. Dexter*, 693 A.2d 682 (Vt. 1997). Diane Dexter had adopted a child during her relationship with Chris Titchenal. Chris did not seek to adopt the child because she thought such an adoption was not permissible under the state's adoption statute. When Diane stopped allowing Chris to visit the child after the dissolution of their relationship, Chris brought an action requesting the superior court to exercise its equitable jurisdiction to establish visitation rights between Chris and the child. One factor in the court denying Chris the opportunity to obtain an equitable visitation order was that the court concluded she could have sought a second-parent adoption. Because a statutory option had existed, which Chris had not exercised, the court declined to exercise its equitable jurisdiction. It is too early to know if the availability of marriage and second-parent adoptions to same-sex couples will cause courts to be less willing in the future to recognize *de facto* parenting.

New York had rejected *de facto* parenting arguments in *Matter of Alison D. v. Virginia M.*, 77 N.Y.2d 651 (1991). It reversed that decision in *In the Matter of Brooke S.B. v. Elizabeth A.*, 28 N.Y.3d 1 (N.Y. Ct. Appeals 2016). The New York Court of Appeals held that the non-biological, non-adoptive partner has standing to seek visitation and custody under state domestic relations law where the partner shows by clear and convincing evidence that the parties agreed to conceive a child and to raise the child together. In this case, the non-biological partner alleged that the parties had entered into a pre-conception agreement to conceive and raise a child as co-parents. While declining to determine what other kinds of allegations could meet this test, the court held that those allegations, if proven by clear and convincing evidence, would be sufficient to seek standing to attain visitation and custody rights. The court declined to issue a broad "functional" test and preferred to limit the decision to the facts before it.

§ 4.9 CHILD SUPPORT

In many of the preceding cases, a same-sex couple has sought to be recognized by the courts as the parents of a child. Sometimes, however, one member of a same-sex couple will seek to avoid having legal responsibility for a child who was conceived or born during their relationship. The biological parent may bring suit for child support or, if the biological parent has sought public assistance, the state may sue the former partner for child support.

The key phrase in the Uniform Parentage Act that these courts often consider is the rule that an unmarried man can be declared a child's father if he "receives the child into his home and openly holds the child out as his own." When a biological mother is in an unmarried relationship with another woman, she has sometimes argued that the other woman should be considered a parent for the purpose of child support if they jointly welcomed her biological child into their home and held the child out as their child. The courts often examine the facts carefully to determine if that factor has been met.

The Washington state courts have reached a different result in two different cases involving a lesbian couple with the timing of their separation being a crucial fact. In *State ex rel. D.R.M.*, 34 P.3d 887 (Wash. Ct. App. 2001), the couple (Kelly McDonald and Tracy Wood) separated about a month after McDonald was inseminated. Although Wood initially made payments to McDonald, she stopped making the payments ten months after the birth and McDonald went on public assistance. The State filed a petition to establish parentage and a child support obligation on Wood. McDonald also filed an action seeing an equitable distribution of property and enforcement of the parties' written agreement for financial support for two and one-half years. The court ruled in favor of Wood, concluding that "McDonald is not being treated differently [under the UPA] than an unmarried woman who has a male partner under otherwise similar facts." *Id.* at 893.

By contrast, in *In re Parentage of L.B.*, 122 P.3d 161 (Wash. 2005), the lesbian couple lived together for the first six years of their child's life. Distinguishing *D.R.M.*, and applying the principles of *de facto* parent, the court found that both women were legally recognized parents. *Id.* at 169 n.9. Despite the language in *D.R.M.* about application of the Uniform Parentage Act, the court relied on the common law *de facto* parent principle. The dissent in *L.B.* argued that it is up to the legislature to create such parental recognition, not the courts. *See Id.* at 182 (Johnson, J., dissenting).

The California Supreme Court directly applied the Uniform Parentage Act to find a support obligation where the lesbian couple had lived together when the children (twins) were born. *See Elisa B. v. Super. Ct.*, 117 P.3d 660 (Cal. 2005). Like *D.R.M.*, the county filed a support action against the former lesbian partner (Elisa) after the biological mother (Emily) sought public assistance to raise the children. Emily gave birth to twins in March 1998 and the couple separated in November 1999. Applying the provision of the UPA that refers to a parent receiving "the child into his home and openly hold[ing] out the child as his natural child," the court asked if Elisa's relationship with the twins met that test. *Id.* at 667. The court found those factors applied noting that Elisa "actively assisted Emily in becoming pregnant with the expressed intention of enjoying the rights and accepting the responsibilities of parenting the resulting children. She accepted those obligations and enjoyed those rights for years." *Id.* At 669. The court also noted that Elisa and Emily were "in a committed relationship . . . . when they decided to have children together." *Id.* at 670. The court also emphasized, drawing on previous decisions, that "a natural parent within the meaning of the UPA could be a person with no biological connection to the child." *Id.* at 671.

Thus, it appears that children born to a lesbian couple, who hold the children out as their mutual children, may be jointly responsible for child support under the UPA, even if the couple never marries and both parents' names are never entered on the birth certificate. Currently, there have been no analogous cases involving men.

§ 4.10 FULL FAITH AND CREDIT: ADOPTIONS AND CUSTODY ACROSS STATE BORDERS

Custody, visitation and adoption disputes in the LGBTQ+ community can become especially complicated when interstate issues arise. One such example occurred in the *de facto* parenting context; another occurred in the adoption context. In both cases, the courts ultimately employed traditional principles of Full Faith and Credit to enforce the family law decision of the state in which the child resided.

The case that involved *de facto* parenting issues (and received international attention) was *Miller-Jenkins v. Miller-Jenkins*, 912 A.2d 951 (Vt. 2006). Lisa Miller-Jenkins and Janet Miller-Jenkins had entered a civil union in Vermont in 2000. Lisa and

Janet were living in Virginia when Lisa gave birth to IMJ in April 2002; they subsequently moved to Vermont until they separated in the fall of 2003. Lisa filed a petition to dissolve the civil union in November 2003, and the family law court awarded custodial rights to Lisa and parent-child contact to Janet. *Id.* at 956. Rather than comply with the court order, Lisa moved to Virginia and requested a Virginia court to establish IMJ's parentage. The Virginia court determined that the Virginia civil union was null and void under Virginia law and found that Lisa was the sole biological and natural parent of IMJ. *Id.* at 957.

The Parental Kidnapping Prevention Act ("PKPA") determines when one state must give Full Faith and Credit to a child custody determination of another state. Finding the original determination by the Vermont court to be a valid use of the *de facto* parent test in the context of a second-parent custody determination, the Vermont Supreme Court concluded that the visitation order was valid, and that Lisa should be held in contempt for willfully violating the visitation order. *Id.* at 974. After Lisa continued to fight Janet seeing their daughter for three years, the Vermont Supreme Court ruled that Janet should be given sole custody over their daughter with the caveat that the court should reevaluate Janet's relationship with IMJ before transitioning custody because of the long period of time in which Janet had no contact with IMJ. *Miller-Jenkins v. Miller-Jenkins*, 12 A.3d 768, 780 (Vt. 2010). Nonetheless, the Vermont Supreme Court also indicated that Lisa had once again disappeared with

IMJ and that her attorneys were unable to reach her. *Id.* at 773 n.2. Lisa allegedly fled to Nicaragua with the help of a Mennonite pastor. *See Mennonite Pastor Convicted of Helping Mom Lisa Miller Flee to Nicaragua with Daughter*, NBC NEWS, Aug. 14, 2012.

In a *per curiam* opinion, the United States Supreme Court insisted that an Alabama state court must give Full Faith and Credit to a Georgia court's adoption order in a dispute between a same-sex couple. *See V.L. v. E.L.*, 577 U.S. 404 (2016). A Georgia court had approved the second-parent adoption of three children that V.L. and E.L. had raised together in Georgia before moving to Alabama. E.L. had given birth to twins in 2002 and another child in 2004. E.L. had consented to V.L.'s adoption of the children as a second parent. After the two women separated in 2011, while living in Alabama, V.L. asked an Alabama court to recognize the Georgia adoption order and award her custody or visitation rights. *Id.* at 1019. The Alabama Supreme Court refused to extend Full Faith and Credit to the Georgia ruling, concluding that the Georgia court had not had proper jurisdiction over the parties to render the judgment. While acknowledging that the Georgia court's jurisdiction was ambiguous, the Supreme Court cited the "time-honored" rule that "where the Full Faith and Credit Clause is concerned, a court must be 'slow to read ambiguous words, as meaning to leave the judgment open to dispute, or as intended to do more than fix the rule by which the court should decide.'" *Id.* at 410 (quoting *Fauntleroy v. Lum*, 210 U.S. 230, 234–35 (1908)).

The *V.L. v. E.L.* decision is important because Full Faith and Credit was applied even though the underlying Georgia statute did not seem to permit a second-parent adoption. Georgia law states that "a child who has any living parent or guardian may be adopted by a third party . . . . only if each such living parent and each such guardian has voluntarily and in writing surrendered all of his or her rights to such child." Ga. Code Ann. § 19–8–5(a) (2015). Despite that language, a Georgia family law judge had permitted the second-parent adoption. And that order, by virtue of the Supreme Court's interpretation of the Full Faith & Credit Clause, was followed in Alabama.

§ 4.11 POLYPARENTING

To some extent, the concept of polyparenting already exists under the law. When parents are divorced, they often enter new relationships in which they jointly raise a child. In the surrogacy context, many kinds of voluntary relationships are often followed, which may result in more than two people helping to raise a child. Grandparents, aunts, or uncles raise many children, with their biological parents playing a continuing role in their lives. Three or four *de facto* parents are not unusual in a child's life, although, it is rare for a state to allow more than two people to have their names on a birth certificate as the legally-recognized parents.

The concept of polyparenting challenges the heterosexual duality that forms the basis of much of family law. Sometimes, individuals want legal recognition of more than two parents. Other times, individuals want to restrict custody or visitation by a third of fourth person who claims parental rights. Litigation tends to occur when there is a dispute; thus, it is hard to document successful, voluntary polyparenting arrangements. Two examples can reflect the kinds of issues that may arise in polyparenting situations. *See In re Thomas S. v. Robin Y.*, 209 A.D.2d. 298 (N.Y. App. Div. 1994); *LaChapelle v. Mitten*, 607 N.W.2d 151 (Minn. Ct. App. 2000).

In re Thomas S. v. Robin Y. reflects the kinds of legal problems that can occur when a lesbian couple uses a known sperm donor and consents to the sperm donor having an involvement in the child's life (but don't want him to be a legally recognized parent). The lesbian couple used a known sperm donor who lived in California. Pursuant to an agreement they had with the sperm donor, they introduced their daughter to their sperm donor when the daughter was around three years old. The daughter saw the sperm donor between sixty and one hundred and forty-eight days over the next six years. When the daughter was around ten years old, the sperm donor indicated that he wanted to develop a paternal relationship with her. Applying the principle of equitable estoppel, the trial court refused to enter an order of filiation and dismissed the proceedings. The trial judge was also influenced by a psychiatrist's report and a law guardian's conclusion that it was in the daughter's best interest not to have the sperm donor recognized as her father. Because the second female parent had not adopted the daughter, and there was no doubt that the sperm donor was the biological father, the court of appeals reversed the trial court. "Having initiated and encouraged, over a substantial period of time, the relationship between petitioner and his daughter, respondent is estopped to deny his right to legal recognition of that relationship." *Id.* at 306–07. In a strongly worded dissent, Justice Ellerin argued that the trial court was correct, and that the doctrine of equitable estoppel must be applied to preclude the issuance of a filiation order due to the sperm donor's ten years of failure to "assume the responsibilities of parenthood." *Id.* at 316.

In the *Thomas S.* case, the court did not literally award "polyparenting" rights, but Robin's partner was an important parent in the child's life. In one of the few decisions of its kind, a Minnesota court of appeals did recognize the parental rights of two mothers and a sperm donor in a case in which the lesbian couple separated after having a second-parent adoption. *See LaChapelle v. Mitten*, 607 N.W.2d 151 (Minn. Ct. App. 2000). Like the *Thomas S.* case, this decision reflects the uncertainty that can exist when lesbian couples do not take advantage of a state's sperm donor statute when bearing a child through artificial insemination. It is possible that the sperm donor will be able to assert parental rights. In this case, the sperm donor sought parental rights after the couple separated and the biological mother moved to a different state. In a highly unusual decision, the court of appeals affirmed a trial court judgment that: (1) the biological mother has sole physical custody but only on the condition that she move back to Minnesota from Michigan, (2) that both the former lesbian partner and the sperm donor should have joint legal custody with respect to the right to make important decisions regarding the child, and (3) that the biological mother *not* be allowed to change the child's surname to match hers. The court ruled that it does not violate a custodial parent's constitutional right to travel or right to privacy to have a custody decision require her to change her state of residency. Also, one highly unusual aspect of this case is that the lesbian couple had petitioned for adoption and that petition had been granted. *Id.* at 157. The court vacated that adoption, finding that it was fraudulent because the parties failed to inform the court of the father's identity or that they had agreed that the sperm donor would have a "significant relationship" with the child. *Id.* at 157. The non-biological mother's legal rights were, therefore, implicitly predicated on a *de facto* parent theory rather than a second-parent adoption theory.

LaChapelle v. Mitten is an unusual case in which a court recognized the legal rights of the biological mother, former lesbian partner and sperm donor. The overall framework was a "best interest of the child" framework that raises the larger issue of what kind of parenting arrangement is in a child's best interest. Some might argue that it is difficult for more than two adults to work together to serve a child's best interests. Others might argue that the presumption that two parents is the ideal arrangement is based on heteronormative assumptions and not empirical data. In theory, the resolution in individual cases is based on an assessment of what is best for that individual child but, in some of the cases discussed above, the court overrode a report by the guardian ad litem or psychiatrist who examined the child.

In a more recent case involving a biological mother, a biological father and the father's husband, a New York court found that the father's husband had standing to seek custody and visitation, along with the biological parents. *See In the Matter of David S. v. Samantha G.*, 59 Misc.3d 960 (N.Y. Family Ct. 2018). In this case, the parties had informally agreed to a tri-parenting agreement before the child was born. Although they had engaged an attorney to draft an agreement, no agreement was ever signed. When a conflict arose about custody and visitation, the parties took their case to family court. Everyone agreed that the father's husband should have some custody and visitation rights, but the biological mother disputed his claim to be a "third legal parent." Following the precedent of *Brooke S.B.*, discussed in *Nutshell* § 4.8, the court found "where the three parties entered and followed through with a preconception plan to raise a child together in a tri-parent arrangement, the biological father's spouse had standing to seek custody and visitation as a parent pursuant to *Brooke S.B.*" *Id.* at 965.

In ruling in favor of the husband of the father, the New York court recognized the implication of its decision to other same-sex couples:

> It is worth noting that the situation before the court—where three parties are involved in raising a child—is likely to recur. Realistically, where same-sex couples seek to conceive and rear a child who is the biological child of one member of the couple, there is always a third party who provides either the egg or the sperm. While in many cases, an anonymous donor is used or all persons involved agree that the donor will not be a parent, this is *not* the situation in the instant case and in many other cases where the parties agree that the provider of the egg or sperm *will* be a parent.

Id. at 966.

Thus, the possibility of more than two individuals being recognized as the parents of a child in New York is explicitly accepted. Other states may follow that lead.

§ 4.12 REGULATION OF PARENTS OF TRANSGENDER CHILDREN

A recent development is attempts by states to regulate parental decisions of the parents of transgender children.

The most well-publicized example is Texas. On February 18, 2022, the Texas Attorney General issued an opinion that concluded that certain " 'sex change' procedures and treatments .... when performed on children, can legally constitute child abuse." Relying on this opinion, Governor Abbott sent a letter to the Commissioner of the Texas

Department of Family and Protective Services (DFPS) expressing his view that "sex change" procedures can constitute child abuse and that DFPS should follow this directive. A married couple and a doctor filed suit challenging this action as a violation of Texas law with regard to notice and comment before the implementation of a new rule. The state trial court issued a temporary injunction restraining enforcement of the rule as against the plaintiffs. The state appealed and the appellate court issued a temporary injunction against any enforcement of the rule. *See Abbott v. Doe,* 2022 WL 837956 (Ct. App. March 21, 2022).

Texas petitioned for a writ of mandamus, directing the appellate court to vacate its order. The Texas Supreme Court conditionally granted the petition as to the portions of the order that purported to have statewide application, because the appellate court lacked authority to grant such a broad remedy. The Court maintained the injunction applicable to the individual plaintiffs. It also found that the Governor has no authority to take enforcement actions. The statements by the Governor and Attorney General should therefore be considered nonbinding under Texas law. *See In Re Abbott,* 645 S.W.3d 276 (Tex. 2022).

The Texas Supreme Court gave little attention to the constitutional rights of parents if DFPS would seek to take steps to intervene in their lives. It did acknowledge that parental decisions "enjoy some measure of constitutional protection whether the government agrees with them or not." *Id.* at 282. The

Court also made passing reference to the power of the legislature to constrain DFPS's discretion while noting those constraints are "subject to constitutional limitations." *Id.* at 281. Justice Lerhmann's concurrence also notes that the plaintiffs asserted various constitutional violations in support of its position but emphasized that no member of the Court has reached those issues. *Id.* at 285. Thus, although the Texas controversy has received considerable publicity, the decision of the Texas Supreme Court has little applicability in other jurisdictions.

Further, the narrow Texas Supreme Court decision does not appear to have stopped DFPS from investigating families whose children have received gender-affirming care. Reporters have documented ongoing investigations of parental action. *See* Jo Yurcaba, *Texas resumes some investigations into parents of transgender youth,* NBCNEWS.COM, May 24, 2022, https://www.nbcnews.com/nbc-out/out-politics-and-policy/texas-resumes-investigations-parents-transgender-youths-rcna30382.

This issue is likely to continue in Texas or other states and the reader should seek more current information on the application of constitutional law to the rights of these parents.

As discussed in Chapter Three, many states have sought to ban gender-affirming care for minors and the Supreme Court has upheld such bans. *See United States v. Skrmetti,* 145 S. Ct. 1816 (2025). In upholding the ban under rational basis review, the Court emphasized that a state legislature is allowed to give weight to the risks, including the minor becoming "irreversible sterile, having increased risk of disease and illness, or suffering from adverse and sometimes fatal psychological consequences" in banning gender-affirming care for minors. *Id.* at 1826. It is unknown at this time if a state could cite those concerns at this time to remove a minor from a child if the parents supported gender-affirming care.

CHAPTER 5
REGULATION OF MARRIAGE

§ 5.1 THE CONSTITUTIONAL, HISTORICAL STATUS OF MARRIAGE

The marriage equality issue relies on two sets of rights that will be discussed in this chapter—the right to marry and the freedom to choose your marital partner on a nondiscriminatory basis. When states failed to recognize same-sex marriage, they were violating both rights. Technically, members of the lesbian and gay community could *marry* because they could marry someone of the "opposite sex" but, realistically, they could not choose to marry the person they loved. As we will see in *Nutshell* §§ 5.5 and 5.6, when the Supreme Court finally concluded that states and the federal government could not refuse to recognize same-sex marriages, it relied on both of those constitutional principles.

In a case involving the right of a parent to choose to send their child to a school where the child would be taught a foreign language, the Supreme Court found that the liberty interest protected by the Fourteenth Amendment included:

> [N]ot merely freedom from bodily restraint but also the right of the individual to contract, to engage in any of the common occupations of life, to acquire useful knowledge, *to marry*, establish a home and bring up children, to worship God according to the dictates of his own conscience, and generally to enjoy those privileges long

> recognized at common law as essential to the orderly pursuit of happiness by free men.

Meyer v. Nebraska, 262 U.S. 390, 399 (1923) (emphasis added).

More than forty years later, the Supreme Court again mentioned the right to marry in a decision that found a state could not constitutionally bar access to contraceptives for married women. *See Griswold v. Connecticut*, 381 U.S. 479, 495 (1965) ("The entire fabric of the Constitution and the purposes that clearly underlie its specific guarantees demonstrate that the rights to marital privacy and to marry and raise a family are of similar order and magnitude as the fundamental rights specifically protected.").

Then, in 1967, the Supreme Court decided the landmark case, *Loving v. Virginia*, 388 U.S. 1 (1967), in which it concluded that a state's anti-miscegenation statute violated both the Equal Protection and Due Process clauses of the Fourteenth Amendment. With respect to the right to marry, the Court stated that "marriage is one of the 'basic civil rights of man,' fundamental to our very existence and survival." *Id.* at 12 (quoting *Skinner v. Oklahoma*, 316 U.S. 535, 541 (1942)). Further, the Court recognized that "restricting the freedom to marry solely because of racial classifications violates the central meaning of the Equal Protection Clause." *Id.* at 12. *Loving*, therefore, made it clear that the freedom to marry is violated not merely when one is precluded from marrying altogether but also when one is precluded from marrying the partner of one's choice (on the basis of race).

Following *Loving*, the Supreme Court applied the right to marry in a case involving a Wisconsin statute that unconstitutionally precluded someone from marrying who had prior child-support obligations, *Zablocki v. Redhail*, 434 U.S. 374 (1978), and in a case involving a Missouri prison regulation that precluded prisoners from marrying other inmates or civilians, *Turner v. Safley*, 482 U.S. 78 (1987). While the level of scrutiny was arguably lower in *Turner* because the plaintiffs were incarcerated, the *Zablocki* case articulated the heightened scrutiny standard that one would expect to apply in a case involving a fundamental liberty interest. "When a statutory classification significantly interferes with the exercise of a fundamental right, it cannot be upheld unless it is supported by sufficiently important state interests and is closely tailored to effectuate only those interests." *Zablocki*, 434 U.S. at 388. The Wisconsin statute failed this test with the Court finding that it was "grossly underinclusive" and "substantially overinclusive as well." *Id.* at 390. "Since the support obligation is the same whether the child is born in or out of wedlock, the net result of preventing the marriage is simply more illegitimate children." *Id.* at 390.

While that line of cases could have been interpreted to extend the right to marry to same-sex couples, not all courts were willing to render that interpretation until the Supreme Court decided that issue. As the Sixth Circuit said (in a case that was eventually reversed by the Supreme Court):

> A similar problem confronts the claimants' reliance on other decisions treating marriage as a fundamental right, whether in the context of a statute denying marriage licenses to fathers who could not pay child support, *Zablocki v. Redhail*, 434 U.S. 374, 383 (1978), or a regulation restricting prisoners' ability to obtain marriage licenses, *Turner v. Safley*, 482 U.S. 78, 94–95 (1987). It strains credulity to believe that a year after each decision a gay indigent father could have required the State to grant him a marriage license for his partnership or that a gay prisoner could have required the State to permit him to marry a gay partner. When *Loving* and its progeny used the word marriage, they did not redefine the term but accepted its traditional meaning.

DeBoer v. Snyder, 772 F.3d 388, 411–12 (6th Cir. 2014), *rev'd sub nom. Obergefell v. Hodges*, 576 U.S. 644 (2015).

§ 5.2 UNSUCCESSFUL SAME-SEX MARRIAGE CASES

In the 1970s, plaintiffs lost cases where they sought to marry someone of the same sex, with the courts typically invoking dictionary definitions or everyday meanings to determine that "marriage has always been considered as the union of a man and a woman." *See Jones v. Hallahan*, 501 S.W.2d 588, 589 (Ky. Ct. App. 1973); *Baker v. Nelson*, 191 N.W.2d 185, 186 (Minn. 1971), *appeal dismissed*, 409 U.S. 810 (1972) ("The institution of marriage as a union of man and woman, uniquely involving the procreation and rearing of children within a family, is as old as the book of Genesis."). Baker appealed his case to the United States Supreme Court, which issued a one-line order stating that the appeal did not raise "a substantial federal question." *Baker v. Nelson*, 409 U.S. 810 (1972). That one-line decision was arguably precedent that must be followed by the lower courts in the absence of contravening case law by the Supreme Court.

In *Singer v. Hara*, the Washington Court of Appeals also rejected an equality argument under its state's constitution. It also relied on the definitional argument to reject that legal theory:

> Given the definition of marriage which we have enunciated, the distinction between the case presented by appellants and those presented in Loving and Perez is apparent. In Loving and Perez, the parties were barred from entering into the marriage relationship because of an impermissible racial classification. There is no analogous sexual classification involved in the instant case because appellants are not being denied entry into the marriage relationship because of their sex; rather, they are being denied entry into the marriage relationship because of the recognized definition of that relationship as one which may be entered into only by two persons who are members of the opposite sex. As the court observed in Jones v. Hallahan, *supra*, 501 S.W.2d at 590: 'In substance, the relationship proposed by the

> appellants does not authorize the issuance of a marriage license because what they propose is not a marriage.' Loving and Perez are inapposite.

Singer v. Hara, 522 P.2d 1187, 1192 (Wash. Ct. App. 1974) (footnote omitted).

Although the reasoning in these cases was cursory, the *Baker v. Nelson* opinion was often cited to preclude a lower federal court from recognizing same-sex marriage until the Supreme Court overturned *Baker*. For example, in *DeBoer v. Snyder*, the Sixth Circuit said that

> *Baker v. Nelson*:
>
> "[D]oes confine lower federal courts in later cases. It matters not whether we think the decision was right in its time, remains right today, or will be followed by the Court in the future. Only the Supreme Court may overrule its own precedents, and we remain bound even by its summary decisions 'until such time as the Court informs [us] that [we] are not.") (quoting *Hicks v. Miranda*, 422 U.S. 332, 345 (1975).

DeBoer v. Snyder, 772 F.3d 388, 400 (6th Cir. 2014), *rev'd sub nom. Obergefell v. Hodges*, 576 U.S. 644 (2015). As we will see below, not all lower courts agreed with that assessment of the binding nature of *Baker v. Nelson*.

Some southern state courts, as recently as 2015, refused to recognize same-sex marriage before *Obergefell v. Hodges*, 576 U.S. 644 (2015) created nationwide marriage equality. *See Ex parte State of Alabama*, 200 So.3d 495 (Ala. 2016) (emergency writ of mandamus to prohibit all probate judges in state from issuing marriage licenses to same-sex couples). That decision was abrogated by *Obergefell*.

§ 5.3 SUCCESSFUL SAME-SEX MARRIAGE CASES UNDER STATE CONSTITUTIONS

Because of the arguable binding nature of *Baker v. Nelson*, the early successful challenges to state bans on same-sex marriage came in state courts, relying on state constitutional law arguments.

The first successful same-sex marriage case, which was brought under a state constitution, was *Baehr v. Lewin*, 852 P.2d 44 (Haw. 1993). Six individuals had filed a complaint for injunctive and declaratory relief in Hawaii state court, declaring that the refusal to grant marriage licenses to people of the same sex violated the right to privacy and the right to Equal Protection. The lower court granted a judgment on the pleadings to the state; the plaintiffs appealed that ruling to the Hawaii Supreme Court. The Hawaii Supreme Court ruled that the right to same-sex marriage is not "so rooted in the traditions and collective conscience of our people that failure to recognize it would violate the fundamental principles of liberty and justice that lie at the base of all our civil and political institutions." *Id.* at 57. Nonetheless, the Court also ruled that "the applicant couples are free to press their equal protection claim. If they are successful, the State of Hawaii will no longer be permitted to refuse marriage licenses to couples merely on the basis that they are of the same sex." *Id.* at 57. Finding that this claim should be decided under the strict scrutiny standard under the state's constitution, the Hawaii Supreme Court said:

> Accordingly, we hold that sex is a "suspect category" for purposes of equal protection analysis under article I, section 5 of the Hawaii Constitution and that HRS § 572–1 is subject to the "strict scrutiny" test. It therefore follows, and we so hold, that (1) HRS § 572–1 is presumed to be unconstitutional (2) unless Lewin, as an agent of the State of Hawaii, can show that (a) the statute's sex-based classification is justified by compelling state interests and (b) the statute is narrowly drawn to avoid unnecessary abridgements of the applicant couples' constitutional rights.

Id. at 67.

Because of the Hawaii Supreme court decision, the trial court conducted a full trial with testimony from expert witnesses. In 1996, the trial court ruled that the state had demonstrated no reason to deny same-sex marriage, so that same-sex couples should be allowed to marry. *See Baehr v. Miike*, Civ. No. 91–1394, 1996 WL 694235 (Cir. Ct. Haw. Dec. 3, 1996). On April 29, 1997, both houses of the Hawaii legislature passed House Bill No. 117 proposing an amendment to the Hawaii Constitution stating: "The legislature shall have the power to reserve marriage to opposite-sex couples." The state electorate ratified the amendment in November 1998. *See generally*

Baehr v. Miike, No. 20371, 1999 WL 35643448 at *1 (Haw. Dec. 9, 1999). In light of that amendment, the Hawaii Supreme Court ruled that the marriage amendment rendered the plaintiffs' complaint moot. *Id.* at *1. As will be discussed in Part D, below, the Hawaii decision generated an enormous national backlash against the Hawaii trial court decision (before the state marriage amendment was adopted).

The next positive development at the state level was in Vermont. The Vermont Supreme Court in *Baker v. Vermont*, 744 A.2d 864 (Vt. 1999), ruled that exclusion of same-sex couples from benefits and protections incident to marriage under state law violated the common benefits clause of the state Constitution. The Court did not go so far as to say the state had to extend *marriage* to same-sex couples. Instead, it said:

> [T]he State is constitutionally required to extend to same-sex couples the common benefits and protections that flow from marriage under Vermont Law. Whether this ultimately takes the form of inclusion with the marriage laws themselves or a parallel 'domestic partnership' system or some equivalent statutory alternative, rests with the Legislature.

Id. at 867. The Vermont legislature responded by enacting a civil union statute in April 2000, Vt. Stat. Ann. tit. 15, §§ 1201–1207 (2010 & Supp. 2014), which Lambda Legal described at the time as "groundbreaking." *See* Lambda Legal, *Baker v. Vermont*, available at https://www.lambdalegal.org/news/ny_20000630_vt-civil-unions-law-to-take-effect. While not providing same-sex couples with the opportunity to have their relationship recognized by other states or the federal government, this development did allow same-sex couples to begin to benefit from some of the benefits of marriage. In 2009, Vermont recognized same-sex marriage through legislative action. *See* Vermont S. 115, available at https://static.votesmart.org/static/bill text/24500.pdf.

New Jersey proceeded on a parallel path to Vermont. In 2006, the New Jersey Supreme Court concluded that same-sex couples should be afforded the same rights and benefits enjoyed by opposite-sex couples, and ordered the state legislature to amend the marriage statutes or enact a statutory structure affording same-sex couples the same rights and benefits enjoyed by married opposite-sex couples. *Lewis v. Harris*, 908 A.2d 196 (N.J. 2006). Like Vermont, New Jersey enacted the Civil Union Act on December 21, 2006. Legislative attempts to replace that statute with full marriage equality for same-sex couples were unsuccessful but a legal challenge in *Garden State Equality v. Dow*, 82 A.3d 336 (N.J. Super. Ct. Law Div. 2013) was finally successful. After unsuccessful attempts to stay the enforcement of that ruling, same-sex marriages became possible in New Jersey on October 21, 2013. *See Garden State Equality v. Dow*, 433 N.J. Super. 347 (N.J. Super. Ct. Law Div. 2013) (denying stay); *Garden State Equality v. Dow*, 216 N.J. 314 (N.J. 2013) (denying stay).

With the historic decision in *Goodridge v. Department of Public Health*, 798 N.E.2d 941 (Mass.

2003), Massachusetts became the first state to permit same-sex couples to fully enter the institution of marriage (rather than merely enter civil unions). The plurality opinion of the Massachusetts Supreme Court found that "[l]imiting the protections, benefits, and obligations of civil marriage to opposite-sex couples violates the basic premises of individual liberty and equality under law protected by the Massachusetts Constitution." *Id.* at 968. The Court then turned to the issue of relief and determined that it made sense to extend marriage to same-sex couples rather than invalidate the ability of any couple to marry. Nonetheless, it stayed entry of its judgment for 180 days to give the legislature 180 days "to take such action as it may deem appropriate in light of this opinion." *Id.* at 969–70. The decision was rendered on November 18, 2003.

When the Massachusetts Supreme Court decided *Goodridge*, it wasn't clear if Massachusetts, like Vermont, would move towards civil unions rather than marriages. In response to the *Goodridge* decision, the Massachusetts Senate on December 11, 2003, requested an advisory opinion from the Massachusetts Supreme Court on the constitutionality of a bill that prohibited same-sex couples from entering marriage but allowed them to form civil unions with all the benefits, protections, rights, and responsibilities of marriage. The Massachusetts Supreme Court concluded on February 3, 2004, that the bill violated the equal protection and due process requirements of the Massachusetts Constitution. It "maintains an unconstitutional, inferior, and discriminatory status for same-sex couples. . . ." *In re Opinions of the Justices to the Senate*, 802 N.E.2d 565, 572 (Mass. 2004). With no legislation passing the Massachusetts legislature that implemented the previous Massachusetts Supreme Court decision, the lower court entered judgment for the plaintiffs on May 17, 2004, 180 days after the original *Goodridge* opinion. *Goodridge v. Dep't of Pub. Health*, No. 01–1647–A, 2004 WL 5064000 (Mass. Super. Ct. May 17, 2004). The lower court refused to delay implementation while some voters sought to amend the Massachusetts State Constitution to preclude same-sex marriage. Same-sex marriages began to occur on May 17, 2004, despite some continued debate about whether Massachusetts law allowed out-of-state couples to marry in Massachusetts when such marriages were prohibited in their home state. *See Cote-Whitacre v. Dep't of Pub. Health*, 844 N.E.2d 623 (Mass. 2006) (permitting local clerks to issue marriage licenses to out-of-state couples unless there is a determination that same-sex marriage is prohibited in those states).

Alaska state courts were also a hospitable forum for same-sex marriage claims. In 1998, an Alaska Superior Court ruled that the recognition of one's choice of a life partner is a fundamental right, so the state must demonstrate a compelling interest to preclude same-sex couples from marrying. *See Brause v. Bureau of Vital Statistics*, No. 3AN–95–6562 CI, 1998 WL 88743 (Alaska Super. Ct. Feb. 27, 1998). That victory, however, was short-lived as the Alaska Constitution was amended on November 3, 1998, to state that a "marriage may exist only between one man and one woman." Alaska Const. art. 1, § 25 (effective January 3, 1999). Following the *Windsor* decision, this provision was found to be unconstitutional by a federal district court in 2014. *See Hamby v. Parnell*, 56 F. Supp.3d 1056 (D. Alaska 2014).

The New York Court of Appeals held that the New York Constitution does not compel recognition of marriages between members of the same sex, and said that any changes should be made by the legislature. *Hernandez v. Robles*, 821 N.Y.S.2d 770 (N.Y. 2006). Nonetheless, the state of New York began recognizing marriages consummated in *other* states, as well as Canada, as early as 2004. *See Godfrey v. Spano*, 920 N.E.2d 328 (N.Y. 2009) (describing 2004 informal opinion letters of the Attorney General and State Comptroller of New York which concluded that "New York law presumptively requires that parties to such [same-sex] unions must be treated as spouses for purposes of New York law" and "[t]he Retirement System will recognize a same-sex Canadian marriage in the same manner as an opposite-sex New York Marriage, under principle of comity"). This recognition of Canadian marriages, even though New York itself was not marrying same-sex couples, was an important aspect of Edie Windsor's landmark same-sex marriage case against the federal government. *See Windsor v. United States*, 833 F. Supp. 2d 394, 398 (S.D.N.Y. 2012), *aff'd*, 699 F.3d 169 (2d Cir. 2012), *aff'd*, 570 U.S. 744 (2013) (recognizing validity of Windsor's same-sex marriage in Canada under the laws of New York).

§ 5.4 DEFENSE OF MARRIAGE ACT

In response to the decision of the Hawaii Supreme Court, discussed in Part C, above, the United States Congress enacted the Defense of Marriage Act ("DOMA").

Section 2(a) of DOMA, provided that, "No state . . . . shall be required to give effect to any public act, record, or judicial proceeding of any other State . . . . respecting a relationship between persons of the same sex that is treated as a marriage under the laws of such other State. . . ." Defense of Marriage Act, Pub. L. No. 104–199, 110 Stat. 2419 (1996) (codified at 28 U.S.C. § 1738C (1996)).

In response to the Hawaii marriage equality decision and the enactment of DOMA, § 2, thirty-one states banned same-sex marriage and twenty-eight of those states did so by constitutional amendment. These provisions allowed these states to take advantage of DOMA, § 2, and not recognize marriages consummated in other states (or foreign countries). *See* Steve Sanders, *Mini-DOMAs as Political Process Failures: The Case for Heightened Scrutiny of State ANTI-Gay Marriage Amendments,* 109 NORTHWESTERN L. REV. 12 (2014). The constitutionality of these state statutes and constitutional amendments was successfully challenged in *Obergefell*, as discussed in *Nutshell* § 5.6, and thereby also invalidated § 2 of DOMA.

Section 3(a) of DOMA, provided that:

> In determining the meaning of any Act of Congress, or any ruling, regulation, or

> interpretation of the various administrative bureaus and agencies of the United States, the word 'marriage' means only a legal union between one man and one woman as husband and wife, and the word 'spouse' refers only to a person of the opposite sex who is a husband or a wife

Defense of Marriage Act, Pub. L. 104–199, 110 Stat. 2419 (1996) (codified at 1 U.S.C. § 7 (1996)). The effect of this provision was that same-sex couples, who had gotten married in their state, could not take advantage of the myriad of federal benefits available to same-sex partners. The constitutionality of this provision was successfully challenged in *United States v. Windsor*, 570 U.S. 744 (2013), discussed in *Nutshell* § 5.5, below.

§ 5.5 UNITED STATES V. WINDSOR

In a 5–4 opinion, authored by Justice Kennedy, the Supreme Court invalidated § 3 of DOMA in *United States v. Windsor,* 570 U.S. 744 (2013). Under § 3 of DOMA, the federal government did not recognize Edith Windsor's marriage to Thea Spyer, so that Windsor was ineligible to take advantage of the unlimited, spousal federal estate tax exemption.

The procedural history of this case was a bit complicated. Windsor and Spyer traveled to Canada in 2007 to get married. At that time, the state of New York did not permit same-sex couples to marry. When Spyer died in 2009, the federal government refused to recognize the legitimacy of their marriage and required Windsor to pay $363,053 in estate taxes.

On November 9, 2010, Windsor filed suited against the federal government, seeking a refund of the estate tax and a declaration that § 3 of DOMA was unconstitutional. In February 2011, Attorney General Holder announced that the Department of Justice would no longer defend DOMA's constitutionality. *Windsor v. United States*, 833 F. Supp. 2d 394, 397 (S.D.N.Y. 2012). Further, the Attorney General took the position that this issue should be resolved under a heightened review of scrutiny. The House of Representatives then formed the Bipartisan Legal Advisory Group ("BLAG") to intervene to defend the constitutionality of DOMA. Their motion to intervene was granted. *Id.* at 397.

To have standing to sue, Windsor had to demonstrate that her marriage was recognized under New York law in 2009, the relevant tax year, because the law of the state of domicile ordinarily determines whether two persons are married at the time of death. This argument was made somewhat difficult by the fact that a 2006 state court decision had concluded that the "New York Constitution does not compel recognition of marriages between members of the same sex." *See Hernandez v. Robles*, 821 N.Y.S.2d 770, 774 (N.Y. 2006). Nonetheless, the *Windsor* district court found that New York would recognize their marriage based on the unanimous views of the state courts and governmental officials that New York would recognize a marriage consummated in another jurisdiction. *Windsor*, 833 F. Supp. 2d at 399.

In other words, New York did not grant marriages to same-sex partners, but it recognized the validity of same-sex marriages that were consummated in other jurisdictions. Concluding that Windsor did have standing to pursue her claim, the federal district court granted her motion for summary judgment, concluding that § 3 of DOMA could not even meet the lenient rational basis test for Equal Protection review, as recognized by the Fifth Amendment's Due Process Clause. *Id.* at 402.

Following the district court's opinion, the United States, in its role as a nominal defendant, and BLAG filed a notice of appeal. The Second Circuit denied a motion filed by BLAG to strike the United States' notice of appeal, because the United States continued to enforce DOMA (and not give Windsor her refund). *Windsor v. United States*, 699 F.3d 169, 176 (2d Cir. 2012). On appeal, BLAG continued to press the argument that Windsor did not have standing to challenge DOMA because New York did not recognize her marriage at the time of Spyer's death. The Second Circuit had the option of certifying this question to the New York Court of Appeals, but it declined to do so. *Id.* at 177.

Unlike the district court, the Second Circuit, in an opinion authored by Chief Judge Dennis Jacobs and which was joined by Judge Christopher Droney, reviewed DOMA under heightened scrutiny. They concluded that gay men and lesbians have been historically subjected to discrimination, have a defining characteristic that frequently bears on their ability to perform or contribute to society, exhibit the characteristics of a discrete and immutable group, and lack political power. *Id.* at 181. Applying an intermediate level of scrutiny, the Second Circuit concluded that § 3 of DOMA violates Equal Protection and is, therefore, unconstitutional. *Id.* at 188.

Judge Chester John Straub dissented from the Second Circuit's decision. He concluded that the majority's decision was foreclosed by the Supreme Court's summary dismissal in *Baker v. Nelson*, 409 U.S. 810 (1972). Because *Baker* was a decision on the merits, not a mere denial of certiorari, he concluded that it was binding until the Supreme Court informed lower courts that it was not binding. *Id.* at 193. The majority had concluded that *Baker* had "no bearing on this case" because, when *Baker* was decided, the Supreme Court had not yet developed intermediate scrutiny nor found that a state classification that discriminated against gay men and lesbians could not survive rational basis scrutiny. *Id.* at 179. Finally, Judge Straub's dissent concluded that § 3 of DOMA could satisfy rational basis review because it advances the governmental interest in:

> (1) maintaining a uniform federal definition of marriage, (2) preserving the public fisc and respecting prior legislative judgments, (3) exercising caution, (4) recognizing opposite-sex couples' unique ability to procreate, (5) incentivizing the raising of children by their biological parents, and (6) encouraging

> childrearing in a setting with both a mother and a father.

Id. at 197–98.

Judge Straub concluded his dissent by emphasizing the importance of the legislature, rather than the courts, deciding the marriage equality issue:

> Whether connections between marriage, procreation, and biological offspring recognized by DOMA and the uniformity it imposes are to continue is not for the courts to decide, but rather an issue for the American people and their elected representatives to settle through the democratic process. Courts should not intervene where there is a robust political debate because doing so poisons the political well, imposing a destructive anti-majoritarian constitutional ruling on a vigorous debate. Courts should not entertain claims like those advanced here, as we can intervene in this robust debate only to cut it short.

Id. at 211.

The Supreme Court accepted certiorari to consider the constitutionality of § 3 of DOMA. A threshold issue that had to be resolved by the Court was whether the federal government or BLAG were entitled to appeal the Second Circuit decision. Although the Department of Justice argued that § 3 of DOMA was unconstitutional, the Supreme Court ruled that it retained a sufficient stake in the controversy to be a party to the litigation because it had refused to pay Windsor the refund she sought. *United States v. Windsor,* 570 U.S. 744, 757 (2013).

While the Court agreed to hear the case on the merits, it recognized that the Attorney General's position created some unusual problems. The Court could have chosen not to hear the case on prudential grounds even though the plaintiff had suffered a real injury.

> Still, there is no suggestion here that it is appropriate for the Executive as a matter of course to challenge statutes in the judicial forum rather than making the case to Congress for their amendment or repeal. The integrity of the political process would be at risk if difficult constitutional issues were simply referred to the Court as a routine exercise.

Id. at 762–63. Justice Scalia's dissent (which was joined by Justices Roberts and Thomas) strongly disagreed with the determination that the Court should hear the case at all. He described the determination that the Court should hear the case as "jaw-dropping" because it "is an assertion of judicial supremacy over the people's Representatives in Congress and the Executive. It envisions a Supreme Court standing (or rather enthroned) at the apex of government, empowered to decide all constitutional questions always and everywhere 'primary' in its role." *Id.* at 779.

Proceeding to the merits, the Supreme Court held that § 3 of DOMA was unconstitutional, relying both on principles of federalism and equality. It found that

§ 3 of DOMA "rejects the long-established precept that the incidents, benefits, and obligations of marriage are uniform for all married couples within each State. . . ." *Id.* at 768. Although the majority could have struck down § 3 of DOMA as violating basic federalism principles, it found that that determination was "unnecessary" because the provision violated basic equality principles.

Relying on its animus-based equal-protection reasoning from *Romer v. Evans,* 517 U.S. 620 (1996), the Court held that the "avowed purpose and practical effect of the law here in question are to impose a disadvantage, a separate status, and so a stigma upon all who enter into same-sex marriages made lawful by the unquestioned authority of the States." *Id.* at 2693. It described the interference with the "dignity" of same-sex marriages as the "essence" of the statute. *Id.* at 770. It found that the "federal statute is invalid, for no legitimate purpose overcomes the purpose and effect to disparage and to injure those whom the State, by its marriage laws, sought to protect in personhood and dignity." *Id.* at 2696.

While the majority opinion in *Windsor* certainly had language suggesting that states, themselves, violated the Equal Protection Clause by not recognizing same-sex marriages, the Court declined to go that far in its holding. Instead, it ended the opinion by noting: "By seeking to displace this protection and treating those persons as living in marriages less respected than others, the federal statute is in violation of the Fifth Amendment. This opinion and its holding are confined to those lawful marriages." *Id.* at 775. Chief Justice Roberts, in his dissent, emphasized this disclaimer as reflecting that the Court had not yet determined the constitutionality of states' refusal to recognize same-sex marriages, but Justice Scalia described that sentence as a "bald, unreasoned disclaime[r]." *Id.* at 798.

While Scalia was correct to predict the Supreme Court ultimately applying the *Windsor* decision to state bans on same-sex marriage, the opinion may be more limited than was apparent at the time. In his concurrence in *Skrmetti*, Justice Thomas emphasizes that *Windsor* (along with other similar precedents) was not premised on the Court's conclusion that " 'sexual orientation discrimination is just a form of sex discrimination' warranting heightened constitutional scrutiny." *Skrmetti*, 145 S. Ct. at 1838 (quoting Justice Kavanaugh's dissent in *Bostock*). *Skrmetti*, of course, dealt with transgender discrimination, not sexual orientation discrimination, but Justice Thomas made his claim as a signal to future litigation in the sexual orientation arena. For further discussion of *Skrmetti*, see *Nutshell* § 3.6.

On the same day as the Court announced the decision in *Windsor*, it also held that procedural obstacles precluded it from hearing *Hollingsworth v. Perry*, 570 U.S. 693 (2013), which involved the constitutionality of a state ban on same-sex marriage.

Following *Windsor*, four courts of appeals found that states could not constitutionally ban same-sex marriage. *See Bostic v. Schaefer*, 760 F.3d 352 (4th Cir. 2014) (violates fundamental right to marry); *Baskin v. Bogan*, 766 F.3d 648 (7th Cir. 2014) (violates rational basis review under Equal Protection Clause); *Latta v. Otter*, 771 F.3d 456 (9th Cir. 2014) (violates heightened scrutiny under Equal Protection Clause and fundamental right to marry); *Bishop v. Smith*, 760 F.3d 1070 (10th Cir. 2014) (violates fundamental right to marry).

By contrast, reversing four district court decisions, the Sixth Circuit consolidated each of those cases and concluded that it was inappropriate for a court of appeals to invalidate state bans on same-sex marriage given the unwillingness of the Supreme Court to explicitly overrule *Baker v. Nelson*. *DeBoer v. Snyder*, 772 F.3d 388 (6th Cir. 2015). Judge Jeffrey Suttons' majority opinion for the Sixth Circuit (joined by Judge Deborah Cook), which reversed the lower courts and upheld the state bans on same-sex marriage, ended with this plea for judicial caution:

> In just eleven years, nineteen States and a conspicuous District, accounting for nearly forty-five percent of the population, have exercised their sovereign powers to expand a definition of marriage that until recently was universally followed going back to the earliest days of human history. That is a difficult timeline to criticize as unworthy of further debate and voting. When the courts do not let the people resolve new social issues like this one,

> they perpetuate the idea that the heroes in these change events are judges and lawyers. Better in this instance, we think, to allow change through the customary political processes, in which the people, gay and straight alike, become the heroes of their own stories by meeting each other not as adversaries in a court system but as fellow citizens seeking to resolve a new social issue in a fair-minded way.

Id. at 421.

Judge Martha Craig Daughtrey dissented. She began her dissent by stating:

> The author of the majority opinion has drafted what would make an engrossing TED Talk or, possibly, an introductory lecture in Political Philosophy. But as an appellate court decision, it wholly fails to grapple with the relevant constitutional question in this appeal: whether a state's constitutional prohibition of same-sex marriage violates equal protection under the Fourteenth Amendment.

Id. at 421.

Judge Daughtrey devoted much of her opinion to discussing the harm to children from being denied the opportunity to live in a household with married parents, merely because their parents are a same-sex couple. She noted that the proponents of the bans on same-sex marriage spent almost their entire oral arguments on the "irresponsible procreation" theory—that limiting marriage to opposite-sex couples "is rational, even necessary, to provide for 'unintended offspring' by channeling their biological procreators into the bonds of matrimony." *Id.* at 422.

Nonetheless, she claimed that a reader of the majority opinion would ask: "But what about the children?" and be concerned that they had ignored "the destabilizing effect of its absence in the homes of tens of thousands of same-sex parents throughout the four states of the Sixth Circuit." *Id.* at 422. Citing Judge Richard Posner's Seventh Circuit opinion in *Baskin*, she observed:

> How ironic that irresponsible, unmarried, opposite-sex couples in the Sixth Circuit who produce unwanted offspring must be "channeled" into marriage and thus rewarded with its many psychological and financial benefits, while same-sex couples who become model parents are punished for their responsible behavior by being denied the right to marry. As an obviously exasperated Judge Posner responded after puzzling over this same paradox in *Baskin*, "Go figure."

Id. at 422.

She closed her opinion with this observation:

> More than 20 years ago, when I took my oath of office to serve as a judge on the United States Court of Appeals for the Sixth Circuit, I solemnly swore to "administer justice without respect to persons," to "do equal right to the poor and to the rich," and to "faithfully and impartially discharge and perform all the duties incumbent upon me . . . . under the Constitution

> and laws of the United States." *See* 28 U.S.C. § 453. If we in the judiciary do not have the authority, and indeed the responsibility, to right fundamental wrongs left excused by a majority of the electorate, our whole intricate, constitutional system of checks and balances, as well as the oaths to which we swore, prove to be nothing but shams.

Id. at 436–37.

The Sixth Circuit opinion in *DeBoer v. Snyder* virtually guaranteed that the Supreme Court would grant certiorari on the issue of whether states could deprive same-sex couples of the right to marry. And, it did so, in *Obergefell v. Hodges,* 576 U.S. 644 (2015), discussed next.

§ 5.6 OBERGEFELL V. HODGES

The *Obergefell* case was the consolidated appeal of various cases from the Sixth Circuit: *Obergefell v. Hodges* (Ohio), *Tanco v. Haslam* (Tennessee), *DeBoer v. Snyder* (Michigan), and *Bourke v. Beshear* (Kentucky). *See Obergefell v. Hodges,* 576 U.S. 644 (2015).

After John Arthur's diagnosis with ALS, he and James Obergefell travelled to Baltimore, Maryland, to be married inside a medical transport plane. Nonetheless, Ohio refused to allow Obergefell to be listed as the surviving spouse on Arthur's death certificate. *Id.* at 658.

The Tennessee case involved Army Reserve Sergeant First Class Ijpe DeKoe and his partner

Thomas Kostura. They married in New York before DeKoe was deployed to Afghanistan. They moved to Tennessee, where DeKoe worked full time for the Army Reserve. Tennessee refused to recognize their marriage. *Id.* at 659.

April DeBoer and Jayne Rowse were foster and adoptive parents who wanted to marry so that they could jointly adopt the children they were raising together. Michigan law precluded their marriage and joint adoption. *Id.* at 658–59.

The Kentucky case involved four same-sex couples who were validly married outside Kentucky but could not get Kentucky to recognize their marriages. *See Bourke v. Beshear*, 996 F. Supp. 2d 542 (W.D. Ky. 2014), *rev'd*, *DeBoer v. Snyder*, 772 F.3d 388 (6th Cir. 2014), *rev'd*, *Obergefell v. Hodges*, 576 U.S. 644 (2015).

The Supreme Court granted cert. on two questions: (1) "whether the Fourteenth Amendment requires a State to license a marriage between two people of the same sex" and (2) "whether the Fourteenth Amendment requires a State to recognize a same-sex marriage licensed and performed in a State which does grant that right." *Id.* at 656.

Justice Kennedy delivered the opinion of the Court, which was joined by Justices Ginsburg, Breyer, Sotomayor, and Kagan. Chief Justice Roberts filed a dissenting opinion, which was joined by Justices Scalia and Thomas. Justice Scalia filed a dissenting opinion, which was joined by Justice Thomas. Justice Thomas filed a dissenting opinion, which was joined by Justices Scalia and Alito. Justice Alito filed a dissenting opinion, which was joined by Justices Scalia and Thomas.

After describing the procedural posture of the case in Part I, Justice Kennedy began his opinion in Part II A by describing the facts of some of the cases, which he argued illustrated the "urgency of the petitioners' cause." *Id.* at 648. Obergefell's case reflected that a state-imposed separation caused them to "remain strangers even in death." DeBoer's case reflected that the court had to be concerned about how "tragedy" might befall them and provide them with considerable "uncertainty" in their lives. DeKoe "must endure a substantial burden" after serving "this Nation to preserve the freedom the Constitution protects." *Id.* at 659. In sum, their "stories reveal that they seek not to denigrate marriage but rather to live their lives, or honor their spouses' memory, joined by its bond." *Id.* at 659.

In Part II B of his opinion, Justice Kennedy discussed how the "ancient origins of marriage" have "evolved over time." *Id.* at 659. At the end of this discussion, he mentioned that many lower courts have considered the issue of same-sex marriage in recent years and have based "their decisions on principled reasons and neutral discussions, without scornful or disparaging commentary." *Id.* at 663–64. He also observed that most of the lower courts (and some state courts) have concluded that "same-sex couples must be allowed to marry." *Id.* at 663.

Part III of the opinion grounded the right to same-sex marriage in both the Due Process Clause and the

Equal Protection Clause of the Fourteenth Amendment. This part of the opinion was grounded in a non-originalist conception of judicial interpretation. In discussing the scope of the right to marry as protected by the right to "liberty," he noted that "rights come not from ancient sources alone. They rise, too, from a better informed understanding of how constitutional imperatives define a liberty that remains urgent in our own era." *Id.* at 671–72.

Most of Part III was devoted to defending the right to marry as a liberty interest protected by the Fourteenth Amendment's Due Process Clause, drawing on Justice Harlan's dissent in *Poe v. Ullman*, 367 U.S. 497 (1961) (Harlan, J., dissenting). He articulated "four principles and traditions" that "demonstrate that the reasons marriage is fundamental under the Constitution apply with equal force to same-sex couples." 576 U.S. at 646.

These four premises were: (1) "the right to personal choice regarding marriage is inherent in the concept of individual autonomy," *Id.* at 646; (2) "the right to marry is fundamental because it supports a two-person union unlike any other in its importance to the committed individuals," *Id.* at 646; (3) "it safeguards children and families and thus draws meaning from related rights of childbearing, procreation, and education," *Id.* at 646; and (4) "marriage is a keystone of our social order." *Id.* at 646. While recognizing that people might have "decent and honorable religious or philosophical premises" to oppose same-sex marriage, he concludes that the state's imprimatur behind the exclusion of same-sex marriage "demeans or stigmatizes those whose own liberty is then denied." *Id.* at 672.

Justice Kennedy then noted the interrelation that can exist between liberty and equality rights, concluding that the right to marry is a right that "reflect[s] this dynamic." *Id.* at 672. Drawing on the Court's precedent from both the race and gender areas, he reflected "that new insights and societal understandings can reveal unjustified inequality within our most fundamental institutions that once passed unnoticed and unchallenged." *Id.* at 673. (Again, Justice Kennedy embraced a non-originalist perspective in understanding what kind of conduct violates the Constitution.) Applying this perspective to same-sex marriage, he observed that bans on marriage by same-sex couples both burden liberty and "abridge central precepts of equality." *Id.* at 675. "The imposition of this disability on gays and lesbians serves to disrespect and subordinate them." *Id.* at 675.

In Part IV, Justice Kennedy responded to the argument that the Court should be cautious and let the legislative branch resolve this issue. In concluding that caution was inappropriate, he returned to his conclusion in *Lawrence v. Texas* that *Bowers v. Hardwick* was wrong when it was initially decided. That error in *Bowers*, he argued, caused gay men and lesbians to face "pain and humiliation." *Id.* at 678. "Dignitary wounds cannot always be healed with the stroke of a pen." *Id.* at 2606. Further, he rejected the argument that "allowing same-sex couples to wed will harm marriage as an institution by leading to fewer opposite-sex marriages." *Id.* at 2606. He called that argument "counterintuitive" and "unrealistic." *Id.* at 678.

Finally, Justice Kennedy responded to the argument that the existence of same-sex marriage would impinge on some people's religious freedom or rights of free speech. He noted that the First Amendment would still protect those who choose to teach religious principles and discuss their views "in an open and searching debate." *Id.* at 680. Nonetheless, the Constitution "does not permit the State to bar same-sex couples from marriage on the same terms as accorded to couples of the opposite sex." *Id.* at 680.

Having determined that states, themselves, could not bar same-sex couples from getting married, it only took Justice Kennedy a few paragraphs to likewise conclude that states must recognize same-sex marriages validly performed out of state. *Id.* at 681. The states' lawyers had conceded that fact at oral argument. *Id.* at 681.

As mentioned above, *Nutshell,* § 5.5, with respect to Kennedy's opinion in *Windsor,* the Court never holds that sexual orientation discrimination deserves heightened scrutiny, or can be considered a type of sex discrimination that thereby receives heightened scrutiny.

The first dissenting opinion was authored by Chief Justice Roberts and joined by Justices Scalia and Thomas. The Roberts dissent focused on the question of *who* should decide whether same-sex couples could marry—the courts or the legislature. Repeatedly citing *Lochner v. New York*, 198 U.S. 45 (1905), the Roberts' opinion accused the majority of using an "aggressive application of substantive due process [that] breaks sharply with decades of precedent and returns the Court to the unprincipled approach of *Lochner*." 576 U.S. at 697. The Roberts opinion also questioned whether the majority opinion could be used to challenge the decision by states to limit marriage to the union of two people. He characterized the move from two-person unions to plural unions as a "shorter" leap than the move from opposite-sex unions to same-sex unions. "If the majority is willing to take the big leap, it is hard to see how it can say no to the shorter one." *Id*. at 704. The Roberts opinion also discussed the religious liberty issues that he considered raised by the majority opinion. He characterized the majority opinion's use of terms like "disparage" and "disrespect" as "apparent assaults on the character of fairminded people." *Id*. at 712.

Justice Scalia wrote a separate dissent that was joined by Justice Thomas. He used much stronger language than the Chief Justice to argue that the majority opinion was an inappropriate example of judicial activism. He said that the majority's opinion robs the people of "the freedom to govern themselves." *Id*. at 714. He also criticized the language of the majority opinion as reflecting "showy profundities [that] are often profoundly incoherent." *Id*. at 719. For example, he argued that "[f]reedom of [i]ntimacy" is "abridged rather than expanded by marriage. . . . [A]nyone in a long-lasting marriage will attest that that happy state constricts, rather than expands, what one can prudently say." *Id.* at 719.

Justice Alito did not join either of those two dissents but wrote his own dissent that was joined by Justices Scalia and Thomas. He argued that the Constitution leaves the question of same-sex marriage to the people of each state. He was concerned about what he called the usurpation of the right of the people to decide these issues, but his language was milder than that of Justice Scalia. He also did not engage in the lengthy historical discussion found in Justice Scalia's opinion. He argued that "[e]ven enthusiastic supporters of same-sex marriage should worry about the scope of the power that today's majority claims." *Id.* at 742.

Following the *Obergefell* decision, most states began to offer same-sex couples the opportunity to get married. Puerto Rico sought to resist adhering to the Court's decision. In *Conde-Vidal v. Garcia-Padilla*, 54 F. Supp.3d 157 (D.P.R. 2014), the district court judge held that Puerto Rico, through its legislature, was free to shape its own marriage policy. When the First Circuit vacated and remanded that decision, the district court judge again refused to enter judgment in favor of the plaintiffs. *See Conde Vidal v. Garcia-Padilla,* 167 F. Supp.3d 279 (D. P.R. 2016). The First Circuit issued a writ of mandamus to require Puerto Rico to recognize same-sex marriages. *See In re Conde Vidal*, 818 F.3d 765 (1st Cir. 2016).

Alabama also resisted. On January 23, 2015, a federal district court judge ruled that Alabama's prohibition against same-sex marriage violated same-sex couples' rights under the Fourteenth Amendment's Due Process and Equal Protection clauses. *Searcy v. Strange*, 81 F. Supp.3d 1285 (S.D. Ala. 2015). *Searcy* involved plaintiffs who had married in other states and wanted the state of Alabama to recognize their marriages.

In response to the *Searcy* decision, public interest groups filed an emergency petition for writ of mandamus to prohibit all probate judges from issuing marriage licenses to same-sex couples. On March 3, 2015, the Alabama Supreme Court granted that writ of mandamus. *See Ex parte State of Alabama,* 200 So.3d 495 (Ala. 2016). The Alabama Supreme Court concluded that "[n]othing in the United States Constitution alters or overrides" the duty of Alabama probate judges to engage in their "ministerial duty not to issue any marriage license contrary to [Alabama] law." *Id.* at 552.

Following the Alabama Supreme Court decision, which tried to confine the decision in *Searcy* to the discrete plaintiffs before the district court, a different set of plaintiffs filed a class-action lawsuit to obtain a preliminary injunction to prevent the state from refusing to recognize same-sex marriages. *See Strawser v. Strange,* 105 F. Supp.3d 1323 (S.D. Ala. 2015), *appeal dismissed as moot*, No. 15–12508–CC (11th Cir. October 20, 2015). The district court granted the preliminary injunction on May 21, 2015, but stayed its implementation until the Supreme Court decided *Obergefell.*

After *Obergefell* was decided, Alabama Chief Justice Roy S. Moore tried to resist implementation of the *Obergefell* decision. He issued an administrative order on January 6, 2016, stating that "Alabama probate judges have a ministerial duty not to issue any marriage license contrary to [the Sanctity of Marriage Amendment or the Alabama Marriage Protection Act]." *See Administrative Order of the Chief Justice of the Alabama Supreme Court* (Jan. 6, 2016), available at https://www.splcenter.org/wp-content/uploads/files/roymoore-adminorder_jan6-2016.pdf. In response to this and other actions by Justice Moore, the Judicial Inquiry Commission of the State of Alabama filed a complaint on May 6, 2016, against Justice Moore and suspended him from serving as a Justice of the Alabama Supreme Court. This was the second time in his career that he was removed from office. He was re-elected to the position in 2012 after having been removed from the position in 2003. *See* Niraj Chokshi, *Alabama's Top Judge is Suspended, and May Lose Job, After Blocking Gay Marriage*, WASH. POST, May 7, 2016, available at https://www.washingtonpost.com/news/post-nation/wp/2016/05/07/alabamas-top-judge-is-suspended-and-may-lose-job-after-blocking-gay-marriage/.

The final legal action in the Alabama matter was a case filed by Alabama resident Austin Burdick against the members of the Supreme Court majority in *Obergefell*. *See Complaint, Burdick v. Kennedy*, No. 2:16–cv–00313–TMP, 2016 WL 734630 (N.D. Ala. Feb. 24, 2016). This complaint argued that the *Obergefell* majority violated their constitutional oath by rendering the Constitution a "nullity." *Id.* The Justices filed a motion to dismiss. *See* Defendants'

Motion to Dismiss, *Burdick v. Kennedy*, No. 2:16–cv–00313–MHH (N.D. Ala. May 5, 2016).

The other major piece of resistance to *Obergefell* was in Kentucky, where clerk Kim Davis refused to issue marriage licenses. That resistance will be discussed in *Nutshell* § 9.6.

The *Obergefell* decision creates some thorny issues to be considered in divorce cases if the parties choose to terminate their marriage. For example, Mary Elizabeth LaFrance and Gail Cline were Nevada residents who desired to be married before same-sex marriage became available in Nevada. In 2000, they traveled to Vermont to have their relationship legally recognized as a civil union. In 2003, they traveled to Canada to marry. In 2014, they decided to dissolve their marriage. Nevada is a community property state. The legal question was—when did their marital "community" begin? The Nevada Supreme Court ruled that it began on the date they were married in Canada, not the date they attained a civil union in Nevada, because they never registered their Vermont civil union with the state of Nevada. Thus, the state applied *Obergefell* retroactively for a marriage consummated out of state. *See LaFrance v. Cline,* 477 P.3d 369 (Table), 2020 WL 7663476 (Nevada 2020).

While the current Supreme Court has not explicitly said that it plans to overrule *Obergefell*, that possibility is supported by the views of some members of the Court. In *Skrmetti*, Justice Thomas' concurrence quoted Justice Kavanaugh's dissent in *Bostock* in which Kavanaugh said: "in those cases,

[*Obergefell* and *Windsor*] the Court never suggested that sexual orientation discrimination is just a form of sex discrimination." *Skrmetti,* 145 S. Ct. at 1838 (Thomas, J., concurring). On the other hand, Justice Barrett's concurrence (with Justice Thomas) makes it clear that *Skrmetti* is not resolving the issue whether being transgender constitutes a suspect class. Similarly, there continues to be no constitutional precedent as to whether being gay, lesbian or bisexual constitutes a suspect or quasi-suspect class. But it is also the case that Justice Barrett's concurrence lays out the factors that need to be met in order for suspect class treatment to occur. She says that the historical existence of private discrimination is not enough. "For purposes of the Fourteenth Amendment, the relevant question is whether the group has been subject to a longstanding pattern of discrimination *in the law*. In other words, we ask whether the group has suffered a history of *de jure* discrimination." *Id.* at 1853. To the extent that arguments are made in the future about the constitutionality of state bans on same-sex marriage, we can expect the Barrett opinion in *Skrmetti* to be a source that plaintiffs use in fashioning their arguments.

§ 5.7 NON-MARITAL FORMS OF RECOGNITION

A. ORAL CONTRACT

Until recently, same-sex partners did not have the option of entering a legally-recognized marriage and, sometimes, tried to take advantage of other legal arrangements to obtain some of the protections that might be available to married couples. These efforts obtained mixed results.

The leading case that spurred many of these legal developments was a case involving a heterosexual couple, *Marvin v. Marvin*, 557 P.2d 106 (Cal. 1976) (en banc). In the *Marvin* case, Michelle and Lee Marvin had lived together for six years, holding themselves out to the public as husband and wife. Michelle Marvin claimed they had an oral agreement that she was entitled to half the property that had been acquired during their relationship, as well as support payments in the event of the dissolution of the relationship. The California Supreme Court held that the court should enforce the contract so long as it was not explicitly based on an "unlawful meretricious consideration." *Id.* at 122.

That legal theory was not immediately available to same-sex couples in California. James Daly and Randal Jones entered a relationship in March 1976. Jones moved into Daly's condominium, and with facts like that of Michelle Marvin, quit his job and served as a companion to Daly. They, too, had an alleged oral contract. When James Daly died in July 1978, Randal Jones sued for half of the cohabitors' equitable property. Because the cohabitors' agreement supposedly included a term that indicated that Jones would be Daly's "lover," the court found that it was an unenforceable agreement involving unlawful meretricious consideration. *Jones v. Daly*, 122 Cal. App. 3d 500, 508. (Cal. Ct. App. 1981).

Seven years later, the California Court of Appeals reached a different result in a case involving two men. *See Whorton v. Dillingham*, 248 Cal. Rptr. 405 (Cal. Ct. App. 1988). Donnis Whorton alleged that he entered an oral contract with Benjamin Dillingham, during the seven years in which they cohabited. Although the two cases seem quite similar, the court of appeals distinguished them by saying that Jones' contract was limited to "lover, companion, homemaker, traveling companion, housekeeper and cook" while Whorton's contract included the additional items of "chauffeur, bodyguard, secretary, and business partner." *Id.* at 410. A more recent California case simply says that "*Jones* was wrongly decided because *Marvin* states homemaking services are lawful consideration for an agreement relating to earnings, property or expenses." *Bergen v. Wood*, 14 Cal. App. 4th 854, 859 (Cal. Ct. App. 1993). The *Bergen* decision also describes *Whorton* as "better reasoned" than *Jones*. *Id.* at 859.

The New York courts have refused to follow the *Marvin v. Marvin* legal theory when there is no legally enforceable contract. But a New York state court has enforced a written contract between a lesbian couple which was ratified by continued performance for three years after the court concluded that there was no duress or lack of consideration. *See Silver v. Starrett,* 176 Misc.2d 511 (N.Y. Sup. Ct. 1998).

B. STATUTORY INTERPRETATION

Miguel Braschi and Leslie Blanchard were living together in a rent-controlled apartment in New York City from 1975 until Blanchard's death in 1986. Their landlord sent Braschi an eviction notice following Blanchard's death. New York City law provided eviction protection to "family members within traditional, legally recognized familial relationships." *See Braschi v. Stahl Assocs. Co.*, 74 N.Y.2d 201, 207 (N.Y. 1989). Rather than conclude that the residents of an apartment must be married to benefit from the eviction protection, the New York Court of Appeals concluded that a court should examine the following factors: "[T]he exclusivity and longevity of the relationship, the level of emotional and financial commitment, the manner in which the parties have conducted their everyday lives and held themselves out to society and the reliance placed upon one another for daily family services." *Id.* at 212–13. Ruling on a preliminary injunction motion, the court easily concluded that Braschi met those factors because the two men had lived together for more than ten years, held themselves out to their families as life partners and shared all their financial obligations. Braschi was also the primary beneficiary of Blanchard's will and life insurance policy.

This case involved a question of statutory interpretation. What did the local ordinance mean when it used the term "family member?" Did it intend to include a same-sex couple who had made a long-term commitment to each other? Following the decision in *Braschi*, the Division of Housing and

Community Renewal ("DHCR") amended its regulations so that the rent stabilization rules included a gay life-partner within the definition of family. *See Silberman v. Biderman*, 735 F. Supp. 1138, 1150 n.26 (E.D.N.Y. 1990). The *Braschi* decision was based on statutory principles, not constitutional law principles.

Another case, which engendered considerable publicity, was also based on principles of statutory interpretation. Sharon Kowalski and Karen Thompson were lesbian partners at the time of Kowalski's automobile accident, which left her severely disabled. *See In re Guardianship of Kowalski*, 478 N.W.2d 790 (Minn. Ct. App. 1992). Following the accident, both Thompson and Kowalski's father, Donald Kowalski, petitioned for guardianship. Thompson agreed to the appointment of Mr. Kowalski as the guardian, expecting to have certain visitation rights and input into major medical decisions. However, Mr. Kowalski immediately asserted complete control of his daughter and terminated all of Thompson's visitation rights. After Mr. Kowalski requested to be removed as guardian, due to his own medical problems, a guardianship hearing was held. Rather than appoint Thompson as guardian, the trial court appointed Karen Tomberlin—a friend of the Kowalski family—as the guardian. *Id.* at 792.

State law governs guardianship proceedings. In this case, state law required an appointment that would be in the "best interests of the ward." *Id.* at 792. The trial court appointed Tomberlin, in part, because it was concerned that Thompson had breached Kowalski's privacy by publicly revealing the nature of their relationship and had taken her to public events, which were described as "exploit[ative]." *Id.* at 796. The court of appeals, however, concluded that the record revealed that Thompson's actions were consistent with Kowalski's best interests. *Id.* at 796. It, therefore, concluded that the trial court had abused its discretion in granting guardianship to Tomberlin. "Abuse of discretion" is a high legal standard and reflects what might be considered the bias of the trial court in evaluating the nature of the couple's commitment to each other. The court of appeals had to determine that the trial court's findings were clearly erroneous to find that an abuse of discretion had occurred. Such a conclusion is highly unusual. *See, e.g.*, *In re Guardianship of Wells*, 733 N.W.2d 506 (Minn. Ct. App. 2007) (refusing to reverse trial court's guardianship decision).

§ 5.8 MARRIAGE CONVERSION STATUTES

Before states began to make same-sex marriage available, they created civil unions and domestic partnerships. These other mechanisms provided registered same-sex partners with some of the state-level benefits available to married partners such as health insurance benefits.

When same-sex marriage became available, state legislatures had to contend with what to do with these other legal arrangements. Four states have passed legislation requiring same-sex couples to become legally married to retain any state-sanctioned benefits as couples. Some of these statutes have even gone further and converted the registered domestic partnership to a marriage unless the parties take steps to dissolve the relationship. *See generally* Kaiponanea T. Matsumura, *A Right Not to Marry*, 84 FORDHAM L. REV. 1509 (2016). In other words, state-registered domestic partnerships have been often eliminated as same-sex marriage has become permissible. The elimination of state-registered domestic partnerships affects both same-sex and opposite-sex partners who might want to receive some state benefits or protections without entering the legal category of marriage.

Connecticut law provides that parties who have previously registered for a civil union will be considered married unless they dissolve or annul their civil union by October 1, 2010. *See* Conn. Gen. Stat. Ann. § 46b–38rr (West Supp. 2016). Similarly, Delaware law provides that individuals who are in a civil union after July 1, 2013, shall be considered married unless they have begun to undertake the dissolution of their civil union. *See* Del. Code Ann. tit. 13 § 218 (Supp. 2014). Further, New Hampshire law has similar rules, effective January 1, 2011. *See* N.H. Rev. Stat. Ann. § 457:46 (Supp. 2015). The state of Washington has a similar law, with the effective marriage conversion occurring on June 30, 2014, but it has an exception for people who are sixty-two years of age or older. (Their domestic partnerships appear to be dissolved but they are not automatically deemed married.) *See* Wash. Rev. Code Ann. § 26.60.100 (West 2016). The category of "civil union" no longer exists under Connecticut, Delaware, New Hampshire, or Washington law.

The legal issue raised by these statutes is whether people have the right to choose *not* to get married. It is unusual for someone's legal status to convert to the status of marriage without that person taking any pro-active steps. There have been no legal challenges to these state statutes.

CHAPTER 6
UNITED STATES MILITARY

§ 6.1 RACIAL AND GENDER SEGREGATION OF ARMED FORCES

The ability to serve in the military has always been considered an important aspect of United States citizenship. Thus, women and African-American people have sought the right to participate in the armed forces on the same basis as white men in order to demonstrate their full participation in American life.

The exclusion of women and those of African descent from the military was embedded in our earliest laws. The militia law of 1792 stated that every "free able-bodied white male citizen" shall be enrolled in the militia. *See Dred Scott v. Sandford*, 60 U.S. 393, 420 (1856). Professor Kenneth Karst has argued that the African-American men who volunteered to serve in the Union army during the Civil War perceived that service as crucial to their request for full citizenship. *See* Kenneth L. Karst, *The Pursuit of Manhood and the Desegregation of the Armed Forces*, 38 UCLA L. REV. 499 (1991) (*Dred Scott* was not overturned until the Fourteenth Amendment was ratified in 1868 to give full citizenship to African-Americans.) Nonetheless, the United States military was not desegregated until President Harry Truman issued Executive Order 9981 on July 26, 1948. Even after the Executive Order was issued, many troops remained segregated until October 30, 1954, when the Secretary of

Defense announced that the last racially segregated unit had been abolished. *See* Exec. Order No. 9981 (1948), available at https://www.trumanlibrary.gov/library/executive-orders/9981/executive-order-9981.

Despite the official exclusion of women from the military, women have managed to serve in the military, including combat roles, since the Revolutionary War. *See* Lucinda J. Peach, *Women at War: The Ethics of Women in Combat*, 15 HAMLINE J. PUB. L. & POL'Y 199, 201 (1994). The first major step in using women in the military was passage of Pub. L. No. 77–554 and Pub. L. No. 77–689, which created women's auxiliary forces in 1942. Women officially became eligible to enlist in the Regular Armed Forces as a result of the passage of the Women's Armed Services Integration Act of 1948, Pub. L. No. 80–625. This statute, however, limited women's participation to two percent of the armed forces and imbedded other conditions of inequality in women's participation in the military, including significant restrictions on their ability to be promoted. In 1967, during the Vietnam Conflict, Pub. L. No. 90–130, available at http://uscode.house.gov/statutes/pl/90/130.pdf, removed many of the promotion restrictions as well as the two percent cap on women's participation.

The first legal challenge to women's unequal participation in the military occurred in 1971 when First Lieutenant Sharron A. Frontiero, a physical therapist assigned to Maxwell Air Force Base Hospital in Alabama, challenged her level of veterans' benefits under federal law. *See Frontiero v.*

Laird, 341 F. Supp. 201 (M.D. Ala. 1972), *rev'd*, 411 U.S. 677 (1973). Under existing law, a married man automatically received certain benefits, but a married woman had to establish that her husband received at least one-half of his support from her for the female service member to receive the extra benefits. Distinguishing *Reed v. Reed*, 404 U.S. 71 (1971), which had struck down a state probate statute that used gender as a tie-breaker for reasons of administrative convenience, the three-judge district court concluded (with one dissent) that the military's rule could be upheld because it provided a vehicle through which female service members could seek the extra benefits. In an 8–1 decision, with the plurality opinion authored by Justice Brennan, the Supreme Court reversed the district court. *Frontiero v. Richardson*, 411 U.S. 677 (1973). Justice Brennan was willing to invoke strict scrutiny, but the various concurrences were not willing to take that step. Nonetheless, the case marked an important step towards equality in the military by overturning the "differential treatment to male and female members of the uniformed services for the sole purpose of achieving administrative convenience." *Id.* at 690–91. A few years later, the Court clarified that sex-based discrimination is subject to "intermediate level scrutiny," not embracing the approach suggested by Justice Brennan in *Frontiero*. *See Craig v. Boren*, 429 U.S. 190, 218 (1976) (requiring gender-based discrimination to be justified by being "substantially related to achievement of the statutory objective").

Despite the Court's decisions in *Frontiero* and *Craig*, the Supreme Court upheld gender-based rules in the military when they arguably benefitted female service members. In *Schlesinger v. Ballard*, 419 U.S. 498 (1975), Justice Stewart authored a 5–4 decision upholding a statutory scheme whereby women receive a mandatory thirteen-year tenure of commissioned service before mandatory discharge for lack of promotion, whereas men might be discharged before reaching that thirteen-year mark for lack of promotion. Overturning a three-judge district court, the Supreme Court justified that distinction by noting that male and female officers are not similarly situated with respect to opportunities for advancement; therefore, it was reasonable to give women more years to secure a promotion before discharging them for failing to do so.

Similarly, the Supreme Court upheld the exclusion of women from the draft-registration requirement. *See Rostker v. Goldberg*, 453 U.S. 57 (1981). Although the three-judge district court had ruled that the Military Selective Service Act violated the Due Process Clause of the Fifth Amendment (which applies equal protection principles to the federal government), the Supreme Court reversed in a 6–3 opinion authored by Justice Rehnquist. (Justice Rehnquist had been the lone dissenter in *Frontiero*.) Applying traditional principles of military deference, the Court found that it was appropriate for Congress to exclude women from mandatory registration since they were also not eligible for combat. The decision to exempt women from registration was not the "accidental by-product of a traditional way of thinking about females." *Id.* at 74.

On January 23, 2013, Secretary of Defense Leon Panetta rescinded the ban on women serving in ground combat units and set forth a plan to implement this policy change, although, the military branches were given three years to implement these changes. *See* Elisabeth Bumiller & Thom Shanker, *Pentagon Is Set to Lift Combat Ban for Women*, N.Y. TIMES, Jan. 23, 2013.

The elimination of the combat restrictions draws into question the constitutionality of the draft-registration restriction. In 2016, Congress created the National Commission on Military, National, and Public Service [NCMNPS] to study whether Selective Service registration should be conducted "regardless of sex." National Defense Authorization Act for Fiscal Year 2017, §§ 551(a), 555(c)(2)(A), 130 Stat. 2130, 2135. On March 25, 2020, the Commission released its final report which recommended the elimination of male-only registration. *See Inspired to Serve*, available at https://digital.library.unt.edu/ark:/67531/metadc1724232/m2/1/high_res_d/Executive_Summary.pdf. On June 7, 2021, the Supreme Court voted not to grant cert. on a case involving the constitutionality of the male-only registration system. Justices Sotomayor, Breyer and Kavanaugh explained their decision to vote against a grant of cert. as predicated on deference to Congress on matters of national defense and military affairs "while Congress actively weighs the issue." *National Coalition for Men v. Selective Service System*, 141 S. Ct. 1815, 1816 (2021) (Sotomayor, J., joining with Breyer and Kavanaugh).

§ 6.2 MILITARY'S HISTORICAL EXCLUSION OF LGBTQ+ COMMUNITY

The military has a long record of seeking to exclude homosexuals from military service. The first recorded court martial for engaging in sodomy was 1778, when Private Lieutenant General Frederick Enslin was found guilty of the charge "attempting to commit sodomy." *See* Maureen Renee Zieber, *Frederick Gotthold Enslin: An Obscure Military Life.*

Until 1920, when the Articles of War, 41. Stat. 787, listed sodomy as an offense, homosexual soldiers were pushed out of the military on charges of conduct unbecoming an officer. One of the most infamous examples of an anti-gay witch-hunt was the Newport sex scandal. After Chief Machinist's Mate Ervin Arnold spent some time being treated for severe rheumatism at the naval training station's hospital in February 1919, he initiated a wide-scale investigation of the apparent immoral conditions in Newport. His witch-hunt involved the use of young men who acted like "streetwalkers" and other young men who "allowed their bodies to be used 'in unspeakable ways.'" Not satisfied with gathering court-martial evidence against fifteen sailors, they went after those who lived within a ten-mile zone of any military installation including the well-respected Reverend Samuel Neal Kent. According to John Loughery, the defense attorney "humiliated Arnold's operatives, hammering away at their inexact memories and dwelling on the extent to which they had solicited and enjoyed the attentions of the many men they reported on." John Loughery, *The Other*

Side of Silence: Men's Lives and Gay Identities: A Twentieth-Century History, (Chapter 1) (1999). Reverend Kent was found not guilty at two separate trials. By the early 1920s, it appears that the men who were imprisoned were released and were allowed to resume their civilian lives. Loughery considers the Newport episode to reflect that "the old social order with its strict gender roles was being questioned long before Stonewall and the counterculture of the 1960s appeared." *Id.*

Following the Newport scandal, Congress amended the Articles of War in 1920 to specifically make consensual sodomy subject to court martial. Article 93:

> Any person subject to military law who commits manslaughter, mayhem, arson, burglary, housebreaking, robbery, larceny, embezzlement, perjury, forgery, sodomy, assault with intent to commit any felony, assault with intent to do bodily harm with a dangerous weapon, instrument, or other thing, or assault with intent to do bodily harm, shall be punished as a court-martial may direct.

The Articles of War, ch. 2, art. 93 (1920).

Following World War I, the military favored a medical model for screening homosexuals out of the military. For example, Army standards listed " 'sexual perversion," which included oral and anal sex among men, as one sign of 'functional' degeneracy." *See* RHONDA EVANS, U.S. MILITARY POLICIES CONCERNING HOMOSEXUALS:

DEVELOPMENT, IMPLEMENTATION AND OUTCOMES: REPORT PREPARED FOR THE CENTER FOR THE STUDY OF SEXUAL MINORITIES IN THE MILITARY, 8. The military's screening standards were not consistently implemented but it did continue to administratively discharge and court martial soldiers for committing sodomy. The rate of discharge grew in the 1950s due to a general crackdown on homosexuals throughout the federal government. "In 1953, President Eisenhower signed Executive Order 10450, which made 'sexual perversion' grounds for dismissal from federal employment." *Id.* at 12.

Challenges to these rules, before the 1980s, focused on whether the rules comported with due process requirements, not whether they were substantively constitutional. For example, Leonard Matlovich successfully challenged whether the Air Force had provided him with sufficient opportunity to demonstrate that an "unusual circumstances" exception should apply that would allow him to stay in the military despite his acknowledged homosexuality. *See Matlovich v. Sec'y of the Air Force*, 591 F.2d 852 (D.C. Cir. 1978). Following the *Matlovich* decision, however, the military tightened the exclusionary rule so that the military would not be required to consider exceptions in individual cases.

§ 6.3 MILITARY'S DEFINITIONAL CHALLENGES

The military's historical attempt to exclude the LGBTQ+ community from serving in the military has been plagued with definitional challenges. A close examination of this exclusion both documents the historical exclusion as well as the definitional problems that institutions face when they try to exclude a category of people.

President Harry Truman signed the Uniform Code of Military Justice in 1950, which set up discharge rules for homosexual service members until the passage of "Don't Ask, Don't Tell" in 1993. *See A history of 'don't ask, don't tell,'* WASH. POST, Nov. 30, 2010. Pursuant to such rules, the Navy, for example, in 1972, had a policy of separating members of the service who were "involved in homosexuality." "Homosexuality" was defined as including the "expressed desire, tendency, or proclivity toward [homosexual] acts whether or not such acts are committed." *See Woodward v. United States*, 871 F.2d 1068, 1069 n.1 (Fed. Cir. 1989).

This definition led to significant enforcement questions. Does it cover a person who admits to being a homosexual but has not been found to engage in any homosexual conduct, a bisexual person, and an avowed heterosexual who has some same-sex sexual experiences?

A. HOMOSEXUAL STATUS

Cases involving individuals who acknowledge being a homosexual but who have not been found to engage in any sexual conduct have been difficult for the courts. Often, the courts found it appropriate to nonetheless allow them to be covered by the "conduct" military regulation. *See, e.g., Woodward v.*

United States, 871 F.2d 1068, 1074 n.6 (Fed. Cir. 1989). The military branches amended their disqualification rules to make it clear that no evidence of a homosexual act needs to be present to discharge someone for homosexuality. The new Army regulation, for example, specifically included "an individual who is an admitted homosexual but as to whom there is no evidence that they have engaged in homosexual acts either before or during military service, or has committed homosexual acts. *See BenShalom v. Marsh*, 703 F. Supp. 1372, 1374 (E.D. Wis. 1989), *rev'd*, 881 F.2d 454 (7th Cir. 1989) (sustaining rule as constitutional).

Midshipman Joseph Steffan unsuccessfully challenged the Department of Defense's regulation that caused his discharge from the Naval Academy merely because he admitted that he was a homosexual. *See Steffan v. Perry*, 41 F.3d 677 (D.C. Cir. 1994) (en banc). An en banc panel of the D.C. Circuit upheld the regulation against constitutional challenge under the rational basis test that: "Particularly in light of this [military] deference, we think the class of self-described homosexuals is sufficiently close to the class of those who engage or intend to engage in homosexual conduct for the military's policy to survive rational basis review." *Id.* at 686–87. The D.C. Circuit similarly stated: "It is sufficient to recognize that the government's presumption, as embodied in the Academy regulations, is certainly rational given that the human sexual drive is enormously powerful, and that an open declaration that one is a homosexual is a rather reliable indication as to the direction of one's drive." *Id.* at 690. Although the government had already revised its regulations to "Don't Ask, Don't Tell," under which a person's homosexual status might no longer be grounds for discharge, the D.C. Circuit concluded that those new regulations did not "conced[e] that the Academy regulations (and former DOD Directives) were irrational." *Id.* at 690. In a sharply worded dissent, Judge Wald (who was also joined by Judge Edwards and Judge Rogers) said: "The government's contention in this case smacks of precisely the sort of stereotypical assessment forbidden by *Stanton* and *Reed* . . . . at bottom, the government and the majority seem to be saying that gay servicemembers—unlike heterosexuals—must be presumed incapable of controlling their sexual 'desires' in conformity with the law." *Id.* at 712.

B. BISEXUALS

In an opinion authored by then-Circuit Judge Anthony Kennedy, the Ninth Circuit affirmed the constitutionality of the Navy's ban as applied to bisexuals. *See Beller v. Middendorf*, 632 F.2d 788 (9th Cir. 1980). Plaintiff Dennis Beller described himself as a bisexual and admitted having sexual activities with males after his enlistment in the Navy. *Id.* at 794. The Ninth Circuit concluded he was properly discharged under the existing military regulations.

C. PURPORTED HETEROSEXUALS

The issue of whether these regulations covered individuals who claimed to be heterosexuals, yet engaged in homosexual conduct, was also raised in the *Beller* case. Plaintiff James Miller admitted to engaging in homosexual activity while serving in the military, yet a medical officer concluded that "he did not appear to be 'a homosexual,' and that [there was] no evidence of psychosis or neurosis." *Id.* at 794. Although both Beller and Miller were discharged under the applicable rules, the Navy subsequently modified its rules to provide:

> A member who has solicited, attempted, or engaged in a homosexual act on a single occasion and who does not profess or demonstrate proclivity to repeat such an act may be considered for retention in light of all relevant circumstances.

See id. at 801 n.9 (quoting SECNAV Instruction 1900.9C).

§ 6.4 CHALLENGES TO MILITARY RULES

The most successful challenge to the military's automatic discharge of homosexuals was short-lived but reflected in Judge Norris's opinion in *Watkins v. U.S. Army*, 847 F.2d 1329 (9th Cir. 1988), which was withdrawn in a hearing en banc in *Watkins v. U.S. Army*, 875 F.2d 699 (9th Cir. 1989) (holding that Army was estopped from barring soldier's reenlistment solely because of his acknowledged homosexuality).

The Watkins case was an excellent fact pattern upon which to overturn the military regulations because Sergeant Perry Watkins had served in the military for many decades as an open homosexual with no apparent detriment to unit cohesion. When Perry Watkins enlisted in the Army in 1967 at age nineteen, he candidly marked "yes" in response to a question whether he had homosexual tendencies. *Id.* at 1330. After fourteen years of exemplary performance, the Army felt compelled to discharge him in 1981 pursuant to new regulations that mandated the disqualification of all homosexuals irrespective of the length or quality of their service. The only evidence of Watkins' homosexual conduct was his statement in 1968. The case, therefore, raised the direct question whether the military could treat someone disfavorably merely because of the person's status as a homosexual, without any evidence that the person had violated the military's code of conduct.

In overturning the Army regulation, the Ninth Circuit panel concluded that homosexuals constitute a suspect class under equal protection jurisprudence, applying the factors the Court has traditionally used to make that determination. First, the Ninth Circuit concluded that homosexuals have "suffered a history of purposeful discrimination," *Id.* at 1345, as reflected in their history of experiencing violence as well as being excluded from "jobs, schools, housing, churches, and even families." *Id.* at 1345. Second, this discrimination can be characterized as "invidious," because the trait has no relevance "to the quality of a person's contribution to society." *Id.* at 1346. Third, "sexual orientation is immutable for the purposes of equal protection doctrine." *Id.* at 1347. Fourth, the group "lacks the political power necessary to obtain redress from the political branches of government." *Id.* at 1348.

The Ninth Circuit especially wrestled with the immutability factor because it concluded that "the causes of homosexuality are not fully understood." *Id.* at 1347. The Ninth Circuit panel then engaged in the following thought experiment:

> Scientific proof aside, it seems appropriate to ask whether heterosexuals feel capable of changing *their* sexual orientation. Would heterosexuals living in a city that passed an ordinance banning those who engaged in or desired to engage in sex with persons of the *opposite* sex find it easy not only to abstain from heterosexual activity but also to shift the object of their sexual desires to persons of the same sex? It may be that some heterosexuals and homosexuals can change their sexual orientation through extensive therapy, neurosurgery or shock treatment. . . . But the possibility of such a difficult and traumatic change does not make sexual orientation "mutable" for equal protection purposes. To express the same idea under the alternative formulation, we conclude that allowing the government to penalize the failure to change such a central aspect of individual and group identity would be abhorrent to the values animating the constitutional ideal of equal protection of the laws.

Id. at 1347–48.

This decision of the Ninth Circuit, however, was withdrawn and Perry Watkins was allowed to stay in the military through an estoppel analysis. *See Watkins v. U.S. Army*, 875 F.2d 699 (9th Cir. 1989). But the withdrawn opinion was an important example of a court trying to elevate sexual orientation discrimination to strict scrutiny status, such as used in the race discrimination area.

§ 6.5 ENACTMENT OF "DON'T ASK, DON'T TELL"

In 1992, while running for President, candidate Bill Clinton promised to lift the ban on homosexuals serving openly in the military. After running into opposition from Congress, President Clinton agreed to sign into law what was called "Don't Ask, Don't Tell," because it was consistent with President Clinton's directive that military applicants should no longer be asked about their sexual orientation when enlisting in the military. The new policy, however, continued to provide broad grounds for discharge if a service member sought to be open about his or her homosexuality. Below is an excerpt of that policy:

10 U.S.C.A. § 654

§ 654. Policy concerning homosexuality in the armed forces

(a) Findings.—Congress makes the following findings:

. . . .

(2) There is no constitutional right to serve in the armed forces.

. . . .

(13) The prohibition against homosexual conduct is a longstanding element of military law that continues to be necessary in the unique circumstances of military service.

. . . .

(15) The presence in the armed forces of persons who demonstrate a propensity or intent to engage in homosexual acts would create an unacceptable risk to the high standards of morale, good order and discipline, and unit cohesion that are the essence of military capability.

(b) Policy.—A member of the armed forces shall be separated from the armed forces under regulations prescribed by the Secretary of Defense if one or more of the following findings is made and approved in accordance with procedures set forth in such regulations:

(1) That the member has engaged in, attempted to engage in, or solicited another to engage in a homosexual act or acts unless there are further findings, made and approved in accordance with procedures set forth in such regulations, that the member has demonstrated that—

(A) such conduct is a departure from the member's usual and customary behavior;

(B) such conduct, under all the circumstances, is unlikely to recur;

(C) such conduct was not accomplished by use of force, coercion, or intimidation;

(D) under the particular circumstances of the case, the member's continued presence in the armed forces is consistent with the interests of the armed forces in proper discipline, good order, and morale; and

(E) the member does not have a propensity or intent to engage in homosexual acts.

(2) That the member has stated that he or she is a homosexual or bisexual, or words to that effect, unless there is a further finding, made and approved in accordance with procedures set forth in the regulations, that the member has demonstrated that he or she is not a person who engages in, attempts to engage in, has a propensity to engage in, or intends to engage in homosexual acts.

(3) That the member has married or attempted to marry a person known to be of the same biological sex.

. . . .

(e) Rule of construction.—Nothing in subsection (b) shall be construed to require that a member of the armed forces be processed for separation from the armed forces when a determination is made in accordance with regulations prescribed by the Secretary of Defense that—

(1) the member engaged in conduct or made statements for the 'purpose of avoiding or terminating military service; and

(2) separation of the member would not be in the best interest of the armed forces.

(f) Definitions.—In this section:

(1) The term "homosexual" means a person, regardless of sex, who engages in, attempts to engage in, has a propensity to engage in, or intends to engage in homosexual acts, and includes the terms "gay" and "lesbian".

(2) The term "bisexual" means a person who engages in, attempts to engage in, has a propensity to engage in, or intends to engage in homosexual and heterosexual acts.

(3) The term "homosexual act" means—

(A) any bodily contact, actively undertaken or passively permitted, between members of the same sex for the purpose of satisfying sexual desires; and

(B) any bodily contact which a reasonable person would understand to demonstrate a propensity or intent to engage in an act described in subparagraph (A).

* * *

10 U.S.C.A. § 654 (repealed 2010).

That policy was upheld under a First Amendment challenge, when an Air Force Captain was discharged because he admitted his homosexuality to his commanding officer. *See Richenberg v. Perry*, 73 F.3d 172 (8th Cir. 1995). The lower courts repeatedly ruled that "Don't Ask, Don't Tell" did not violate substantive due process, the Equal Protection Clause, procedural due process, or the First Amendment. *See, e.g., Holmes v. California Army National Guard*, 124 F.3d 1126, 1136 (9th Cir. 1997); *Philips v. Perry*, 106 F.3d 1420, 1425–26 (9th Cir. 1997); *Thomasson v. Perry*, 80 F.3d 915 (4th Cir. 1996) (en banc). Applying rational basis scrutiny and military deference, the courts readily determined that these rules rationally related to legitimate legislative ends.

A dissenting opinion in the *Thomasson* case, however, argued that these policies could be found to be unconstitutional because they were clearly based on "prejudice against homosexuals." *Id.* at 951. (Hall, J., dissenting, joined by Ervin, Michael & Motz, JJ.) The dissent ended with this observation:

> Lt. Paul Thomasson's career is over because it is presumed that he will misbehave in a manner that is assumed to incite the prejudices of his colleagues, whom it is speculated will abandon their duties to defend the United States rather than tolerate him in their midst. There is no proof of any of these hypotheses in the record, and there is abundant disproof.

Id. at 954.

These challenges were further pursued after the Supreme Court decided in *Lawrence v. Texas*, 539

U.S. 558 (2003) that the state of Texas could not criminalize consensual sodomy. In *United States v. Marcum*, 60 M.J. 198 (C.A.A.F. 2004), the United States Court of Appeals for the Armed Forces considered the implications of the *Lawrence* decision on Technical Sergeant Eric Marcum's conviction for committing consensual sodomy. Rather than consider a facial challenge to the military regulation, the court considered an "as applied" challenge. Because Marcum acknowledged having a sexual relationship with someone he supervised, the court found that his conduct was not protected by *Lawrence*. His sexual partner was "a person 'who might be coerced' or who was 'situated in [a] relationship[ ] where consent might not easily be refused.' *Lawrence*, 539 U.S. at 578. Thus, based on this factor, Appellant's conduct fell outside the liberty interest identified by the Supreme Court." *Id.* at 208.

In 2008, the Ninth Circuit revisited its decisions upholding "Don't Ask, Don't Tell" in light of the Supreme Court's decision in *Lawrence v. Texas*, 539 U.S. 558 (2003). *See Witt v. Dep't of Air Force*, 527 F.3d 806 (9th Cir. 2008). The Ninth Circuit construed the *Lawrence* decision as creating an intermediate level of scrutiny under substantive due process. It, therefore, vacated and remanded the district court's decision on that legal theory because it had been inappropriately deferential to the government in assessing the validity of the "Don't Ask, Don't Tell" rule. While conceding that the government articulated an important governmental interest, it concluded that the government offered insufficient evidence that application of the rule to Major Witt significantly furthered that government interest and whether less intrusive means could have substantially achieved the government's interest. *Id.* at 821. On remand, the district court concluded that application of "Don't Ask, Don't Tell" to plaintiff violated her substantive due process rights. *See Witt v. U.S. Dep't of Air Force*, 739 F. Supp. 2d 1308 (W.D. Wash. 2010).

By contrast, the First Circuit concluded that "Don't Ask, Don't Tell" survived a constitutional challenge in a case brought by twelve former members of the United States military who were separated from service under the act. *See Cook v. Gates*, 528 F.3d 42 (1st Cir. 2008). The First Circuit emphasized the deference that is accorded Congress in matters relating to the military and, relying heavily on the Court's analysis in *Rostker v. Goldberg*, 453 U.S. 57 (1981), concluded that the statute survived constitutional challenge because of Congress' "detailed legislative record":

> This record makes plain that Congress concluded, after considered deliberation, that the Act was necessary to preserve the military's effectiveness as a fighting force, 10 U.S.C. § 654(a)(15), and thus, to ensure national security. This is an exceedingly weighty interest and one that unquestionably surpasses the government interest that was at stake in *Lawrence*.

Id. at 60.

In dissent, Judge Saris argued that the statute could not survive a First Amendment challenge. He took issue with the Department of Defense directive that provided: "A statement by a Service member that he or she is a homosexual or bisexual, or words to that effect, creates a *rebuttable presumption* that the Service member engages in, attempts to engage in, has a propensity to engage in, or intends to engage in homosexual acts." *Id.* at 66. Reluctantly conceding that the directive could be content-neutral, he nonetheless concluded that plaintiffs were entitled to seek to demonstrate on remand that the directive was overly restrictive of the plaintiffs' speech to serve the government's alleged substantial interest in preventing the occurrence of homosexual acts in the military. Plaintiffs argued that the directive was a dead letter in practice (rather than an actual rebuttable presumption) because it is "functionally impossible" to rebut the presumption short of recanting one's status as a homosexual. *Id.* at 69. Further, the dissent concluded that plaintiffs were entitled to argue on remand that the directive "chills individual service members from discussing homosexuality both privately and publicly even when they have no intent to engage in prohibited homosexual conduct." *Id.* at 74. While concluding that the motion to be dismissed should be denied, the dissent also acknowledged that "plaintiffs' burden is a tough one in light of the strong deference owed to Congress and the military seeking to protect unit cohesion." *Id.* at 74.

The Servicemembers Legal Defense Network was created soon after the enactment of "Don't Ask, Don't

Tell." It sought to document the discharges and other adverse effects of this policy on the military. Its 2004 Report documented that discharges ranged from 617 to 1273 during the first ten years of the policy. *See* CONDUCT UNBECOMING: SERVICEMEMBERS LEGAL DEFENSE NETWORK, CONDUCT UNBECOMING: THE TENTH ANNUAL REPORT ON "DON'T ASK, DON'T TELL, DON'T PURSUE, DON'T HARASS (2004). In addition to documenting discharges, the report also documented harassment, and even murder, that occurred because of anti-gay attitudes within the military. The 2004 Report recommended a thirteen-point anti-harassment action plan to counter such problems. *Id.* at 4–5.

§ 6.6 REPEAL OF "DON'T ASK, DON'T TELL"

With the lower courts split on the constitutionality of "Don't Ask, Don't Tell," on December 22, 2010, Congress enacted the Don't Ask, Don't Tell Repeal Act of 2010, Pub. L. No. 111–321, § 2(b), (f)(1)(A), which provided that "Don't Ask, Don't Tell" was repealed effective sixty days after the last requirements and certifications required by subsection (b) of § 2 occurred. On July 22, 2011, President Obama and Defense Secretary Leon Panetta, and Joint Chiefs of Staff Chairman Admiral Mike Mullen certified that the repeal of "Don't Ask, Don't Tell" would not harm United States military readiness, making the law official on September 20, 2011. *See* Elisabeth Bumiller, *Obama Ends 'Don't Ask, Don't Tell' Policy*, N.Y. TIMES, July 22, 2011.

Less than six years later, Eric Fanning, an openly gay man, became Secretary of the Army, suggesting a dramatic change in a relatively brief period of time. *See* The Editorial Board, *An Openly Gay Man Runs the Army*, N.Y. TIMES. May 21, 2016.

§ 6.7 TRANSGENDER SERVICE MEMBERS

Defense Secretary Ashton Carter announced on July 13, 2015, that the Pentagon intended to allow transgender people to serve openly in the military. *See* Press Release, United States Department of Defense, Statement by Secretary of Defense Ash Carter on DOD Transgender Policy, Release No: NR–272–15 (July 13, 2015). He created a working group that would study the matter over the next six months but "start with the presumption that transgender persons can serve openly without adverse impact on military effectiveness and readiness, unless and except where objective, practical impediments are identified." Following the completion of the report of the working group, on June 30, 2016, Defense Secretary Ashton Carter announced: "Effective immediately, transgender Americans may serve openly." *See* Matthew Rosenberg, *Transgender People Will Be Allowed to Serve Openly in Military*, N.Y. TIMES, June 30, 2016.

On July 26, 2017, President Trump announced on his twitter page that transgender individuals would no longer be allowed to serve in any capacity in the U.S. Military. After years of memorandums and changing policies, the Trump administration eventually won a victory in the Supreme Court when

Justices Roberts, Alito, Gorsuch, Kavanaugh and Thomas voted to lift a preliminary injunction against the enforcement of a ban on certain transgender people being able to serve in the military. *See Trump v. Stockman,* 139 S. Ct. 950 (2019). Justices Ginsburg, Breyer, Sotomayor and Kagan stated that they would have denied the application for staying the preliminary injunction.

The restrictions on transgender people serving in the military were lifted on January 25, 2021 when President Biden signed the "Executive Order on Enabling All Qualified Individuals to Serve Their Country in Uniform," available at https://www.federalregister.gov/documents/2021/01/28/2021-02034/enabling-all-qualified-americans-to-serve-their-country-in-uniform. Executive Order 14004. On March 31, 2021, the Pentagon announced that transgender servicemembers would not be at risk of involuntary discharge and can reenlist. They also announced that the military will provide support for gender transitions, including medical care and a procedure to change gender markers. *See* U.S. Dept of Defense, *DOD Announces Policy Updates for Transgender Military Service* (March 31, 2021), available at https://www.defense.gov/Newsroom/Releases/Release/Article/2557220/dod-announces-policy-updates-for-transgender-military-service/.

The day he was inaugurated, President Trump issued Executive Order 14148, revoking E.O. 14183. The policy required the Secretary of Defense to discharge every transgender service member within 60 days. A district court judge preliminarily enjoined the enforcement of that order on March 27, 2025. *See* Shilling v. United States, 773 F. Supp.3d 1069 (W.D. Wash. 2025). The Ninth Circuit denied a stay, but the Supreme Court granted a stay pending an appeal on May 6, 2025. *See United States v. Shilling,* 2025 WL 1300282 (May 6, 2025). Justices Sotomayor, Kagan, and Jackson would have denied the application for a stay.

In a memo to military directors, the Secretary of Defense said that transgender troops have until June 6, 2025, to voluntarily separate. Troops that remain after that date will be subject to "involuntary separation." *See* Memorandum for Senior Pentagon Leadership Commanders of the Combatant Commands Defense Agency and DOD Field Activity Directors from Secretary of Defense, May 8, 2025, https://media.defense.gov/2025/May/08/2003706668/-1/-1/1/IMPLEMENTING-POLICY-ON-PRIORITIZING-MILITARY-EXCELLENCE-AND-READINESS.PDF. From various news reports, it appears that many transgender service members applied for voluntary separation to retain some benefits after discharge. Thus, the denial of the stay pending appeal largely effectuated Trump's intentions to remove all transgender people from the military.

At this time (July 2025), news reports suggest that trans service members subsequently learned they would be terminated if they did not separate from the military. It is unknown if any legal steps are still available to them if they do not resign.

CHAPTER 7

STATE AND LOCAL NONDISCRIMINATION LAWS

Note: To learn about federal laws that protection the LGBTQ+ community, *see Nutshell* Chapter 3.

§ 7.1 LOCAL GOVERNMENT ORDINANCES

Local ordinances often ban discrimination in housing, public accommodations and employment on the basis of sexual orientation, gender identity and gender expression. Their remedies, based on their state constitution, may be limited to a misdemeanor. But they may have some kind of local community reconciliation organization that seeks to remedy violations of the ordinance. There is usually a religion exception such as:

> Nothing in this section shall bar any religious or denominational institution or organization, or any charitable or educational organization, which is operated, supervised, or controlled by or in connection with a religious organization, from giving preference to persons of the same religion or denomination, or from making such selection as is calculated by such organization to promote the religious principles or the aims or purposes for which it is established or maintained.

Columbus, Ohio, Code of Ordinances § 2331.02(B) (codified through Ordinance No. 0249–2016, passed January 25, 2016). In light of the Supreme Court's decision in *Fulton v. City of Philadelphia*, 593 U.S. 522 (2021), (discussed in *Nutshell* § 9.1), one can imagine that such exceptions will eventually be found to be constitutionally required.

There is often a sex discrimination exception for shared rooming situations where there is a single bathroom facility:

> Nothing in this section shall bar any person from refusing to rent, lease, or sublease any room, suite of rooms, or apartment to any person because of sex if such room, suite of rooms, or apartment is located in a building in which the only toilet and bathroom facilities provided for such room, suite of rooms, or apartment are for the common use of all occupants.

Columbus, Ohio, Code of Ordinances § 2331.02(C) (codified through Ordinance No. 0249–2016, passed January 25, 2016).

§ 7.2 TYPICAL STATE STATUTES

Twenty-two states and the District of Columbia ban discrimination on the basis of sexual orientation and gender identity or expression in employment, housing, and public accommodations. An additional five states provide partial nondiscrimination protection. *See* Movement Advancement Project, *Nondiscrimination Laws,* available at https://www.lgbtmap.org/equality-maps/non_discrimination_laws. *See also* ACLU, LGBT Rights Across the Country (updated every Wednesday), available at https://www.aclu.org/legislation-affecting-lgbt-rights-across-country. The Williams Institute also provides excellent information about state statutes.

A. ILLINOIS

Illinois is typical of states that have enacted laws banning sexual orientation discrimination and some aspects of gender identity discrimination. The Illinois Human Rights Act, which became effective on January 1, 2006, bans discrimination in employment and housing on the basis of sexual orientation. Like the Employment Non-Discrimination Act ("ENDA") legislation proposed in Congress, it provides that the statute should not be construed to require "any employer, employment agency, or labor organization to give preferential treatment or special rights based on sexual orientation or to implement affirmative action policies or programs based on sexual orientation." Illinois Human Rights Act, 775 ILCS 5 § 1–101.1 (Ill. 2006).

It also has a somewhat unusual definition of "sexual orientation" to preclude the statute being used for the benefit of those who might be considered pedophiles. The statute provides that sexual orientation "means actual or perceived heterosexuality, homosexuality, bisexuality, or gender-related identity, whether or not traditionally associated with the person's designated sex at birth. 'Sexual orientation' does not include a physical or sexual attraction to a minor by an adult." *Id.* at § 1–103 (O–1).

The language stating that the statute covers "perceived sexual orientation" is an important aspect of many state nondiscrimination statutes. The Williams Institute reports that all but five states with nondiscrimination statutes ban "perceived" orientation.

The Illinois statute, like other state statutes, contains a typical religious exemption specifying that an employer does not include:

> [A]ny religious corporation, association, educational institution, society, or non-profit nursing institution conducted by and for those who rely upon treatment by prayer through spiritual means in accordance with the tenets of a recognized church or religious denomination with respect to the employment of individuals of a particular religion to perform work connected with the carrying on by such corporation, association, educational institution, society or non-profit nursing institution or its activities.

Id. at § 2–101(B)(2).

This religious exemption exempts religious entities from any coverage under the state statute, not merely an exemption from rules that might conflict with their religious beliefs.

In the housing section of the statute, the Illinois statute provides that it is permissible to restrict the rental of rooms in a housing accommodation to persons of one sex. It also provides that the owner of an owner-occupied residential building with four or fewer units is not forbidden to make "decisions regarding whether to rent to a person based upon that person's sexual orientation." *Id.* at § 3–106(H–

1). (That rule only permits sexual orientation discrimination; does not permit the landlord to engage in the other bases of forbidden discrimination.)

Although this *Nutshell* cannot provide a comprehensive review of the cases under the Illinois law, the Illinois Appellate Court, Second District, affirmed a decision in favor of a transgender woman whose employer did not allow her to use the women's bathroom. *See Hobby Lobby Stores, Inc. v. Sommerville,* 2021 Il App.(2d) 190362 (Ill. App. Ct., 2nd District 2021).

B. UTAH

One novel approach to a state nondiscrimination bill became law in Utah in 2015. The law tried to reach a compromise between religious liberty and sexual orientation and gender identity protection. *See* Antidiscrimination and Religious Freedom Amendments, S. 296, 2015 Gen. Sess., (Utah 2015) available at http://le.utah.gov/~2015/bills/static/sb0296.html.

The Utah statute provides for protection against sexual orientation and gender identity discrimination but has a somewhat contradictory definition of "gender identity" for the purpose of the statute's protection. It says:

> "Gender identity" has the meaning provided in the Diagnostic and Statistical Manual (DSM-5). A person's gender identity can be shown by providing evidence, including but not limited to,

> medical history, care or treatment of the gender identity, consistent and uniform assertion of the gender identity, or other evidence that the gender identity is sincerely held, part of a person's core identity, and not being asserted for an improper purpose.

Id. § 34A–5–102(1)(k).

The DSM-5, however, does not define something broadly called "gender identity." It refers to "gender dysphoria." The DSM-5 decided to move away from the term "gender identity disorder" which had been found in DSM-IV. The Utah definition also seems to be a medical definition, not recognizing that some people do not consider their gender identity to be a "disorder" requiring "treatment" even if their identity is inconsistent with the gender they were assigned at birth. It is also not clear what would constitute an "improper purpose."

The Utah statute has four important exceptions.

First, it provides that the statute does not preclude "an employer from adopting reasonable dress and grooming standards not prohibited by other provisions of federal or state law, provided that the employer's dress and grooming standards afford reasonable accommodations based on gender identity to all employees." *Id.* § 34A–5–109.

Second, it provides that the statute "may not be interpreted to prohibit an employer from adopting reasonable rules and policies that designate sex-specific facilities, including restrooms, shower facilities, and dressing facilities, provided that the employer's rules and policies adopted under this section afford reasonable accommodations based on gender identity to all employees." *Id.* § 34A–5–110.

Third, it provides that the statute should not be interpreted to infringe the First Amendment. *Id.* § 34A–5–111.

Fourth, it provides quite specific protections to employees who express their religious beliefs inside or outside the workplace:

> (1) An employee may express the employee's religious or moral beliefs and commitments in the workplace in a reasonable, non-disruptive, and non-harassing way on equal terms with similar types of expression of beliefs or commitments allowed by the employer in the workplace, unless the expression is in direct conflict with the essential business-related interests of the employer.
>
> (2) An employer may not discharge, demote, terminate, or refuse to hire any person, or retaliate against, harass, or discriminate in matters of compensation or in terms, privileges, and conditions of employment against any person otherwise qualified, for lawful expression or expressive activity outside of the workplace regarding the person's religious, political, or personal convictions, including convictions against marriage, family, or sexuality, unless the expression or expressive activity is in direct conflict with the essential business-related interests of the employer.

Id. § 34A–5–112.

Because Utah does not have a general "public accommodation" rule that might prevent discrimination at a bakery or florist that does not want to provide services for a same-sex wedding, these rules about religious expression have no impact on those kinds of situations.

C. BROAD RELIGIOUS EXEMPTION

Although all states exempt religious employers from coverage, Nevada takes an even broader exemption approach. They exempt all tax-exempt entities from having to comply with the sexual orientation and gender identity employment provisions. *See* Nev. Rev. Stat. Ann. § 613.320 (LexisNexis 2012).

§ 7.3 STATE ADMINISTRATIVE RULES OR EXECUTIVE ORDERS

Another option to provide protection to the LGBTQ+ community is the creation of state administrative rules. For example, the Illinois Administrative Code prohibits gender identity discrimination in group health insurance plans. *See* 50 Ill. Admin. Code § 2603.35 (West, Westlaw through rules published in the Illinois Register Vol. 40, Issue 29, July 15, 2016).

Many states that do not have legislation banning sexual orientation discrimination have an executive order banning such discrimination in public employment. *See, e.g.*, Kan. Exec. Order No. 07–24

(Aug. 21, 2007); Ohio Exec. Order No. 2007–10S (May 17, 2007) (banning discrimination in public employment on the basis of sexual orientation or gender identity). The Ohio Executive Order expired at the end of Governor Ted Strickland's term in 2010. Governor John Kasich signed a new executive order on January 22, 2011, which omitted coverage of gender identity. *See* Ohio Exec. Order No. 2011–05K (Jan. 21, 2011). A limitation of executive order coverage is that it can change rapidly without any legislative involvement.

§ 7.4 ENFORCEMENT OF STATE STATUTES

Typically, states require an individual to file a complaint with a state administrative agency to investigate the allegation of discrimination (as the state does for complaints on the basis of race or gender). Individuals cannot file suit in state court until they exhaust the state administrative process. Many complaints are resolved at the administrative level but no state maintains accurate publicly available records of the results achieved under their state statutes. Thus, it is very difficult to assess the effectiveness of these state statutes.

The Williams Institute has published a comprehensive discussion of enforcement under each state's statute. *See generally* The Williams Institute, Chapter 15: Analysis of Scope and Enforcement of State Laws and Executive Orders Prohibiting Employment Discrimination Against LGBT People. Their 2010 report contains comprehensive statistics from some states regarding the number of complaints filed on behalf of sexual orientation or gender identity but does not provide much sense of the range of relief that individuals may have achieved under these state statutes. In most cases, states refused to cooperate with the Williams Institute by providing copies of the actual complaints or dispositions of the cases. Nonetheless, they were able to document that many charges of discrimination have been filed with the appropriate administrative agency in each of these states.

Some of the state administrative decisions are reported in Westlaw. *See, e.g., MCAD v. Town of Reading*, No. 10 BEM 00986, 2016 WL 929630 (Mass. Comm'n Against Discrimination Feb. 26, 2016) (successful complaint by heterosexual man that he was subjected to homophobic names and a sexual assault by his lieutenant); *Melissa Elaine Klein*, Nos. 44–14, 45–14, 2015 WL 4868796 (Or. Bureau of Labor & Indus. July 2, 2015) (awarding complainants $75,000 and $60,000 for emotional and mental suffering from denial of cake baking services).

An unusual administrative complaint was filed against Judge Gary Tabor (State of Washington) after he stated at an administrative meeting that he felt "uncomfortable" performing same-sex marriages and would prefer other judges to perform those marriages in his place. *See The Honorable Gary Tabor*, WA Jud. Disp. Op. 7251–F–158, 2013 WL 5853965 (Wash. Comm'n Judicial Conduct Oct. 4, 2013). The Commission on Judicial Conduct found that, under Washington State's law against discrimination, RCW 49.60, a judge who agrees to solemnize wedding must "make himself available . . . . in a way that does not discriminate or appear to discriminate against a statutorily-protected class of people." *Id.* at *2.

There are some cases on the merits involving state nondiscrimination statutes, although, many of them are not included in official reporters. *Nutshell* § 9.5, discusses *Craig v. Masterpiece Cakeshop, Inc.*, 370 P.3d 272 (Colo. App. 2015) and *Elane Photography v. Willock*, 309 P.3d 53 (N.M. 2013), because they involve arguable conflicts with free exercise of religion. As mentioned above, most sexual orientation discrimination complaints seem to be handled at the administrative level, and those results are not reported. As Title VII is increasingly interpreted to cover LGBTQ+ issues, it may be the case that complaints are increasingly filed under federal law instead of state law. That issue will be one to watch in the future. The discussion below seeks to summarize the available information regarding enforcement of state statutes.

Further, the Supreme Court has permitted a business entity to fail to comply with a state nondiscrimination statute if compliance would compel the business to engage in objectionable expressive activity. *See 303 Creative LLC v. Elenis*, 600 U.S. 570 (2023) (discussed in *Nutshell* § 8.1).

§ 7.5 CALIFORNIA

As early as 1979, the California Supreme Court interpreted Article 1, Section 7, Subdivision(a) of the California Constitution as barring a public utility from engaging in arbitrary employment discrimination, including discrimination on the basis of sexual orientation. *See Gay Law Students Ass'n v. Pac. Tel. & Tel. Co.*, 595 P.2d 592, 597 (Cal. 1979).

Current California law comprehensively bans employment discrimination on the basis of "race, religious creed, color, national origin, ancestry, physical disability, mental disability, medical condition, genetic information, marital status, sex, gender, gender identity, gender expression, age, sexual orientation, or military and veteran status of any person." Cal. Gov't Code § 12940 (West 2011).

§ 7.6 CONNECTICUT

The Connecticut Fair Employment Practices Act provides that it is a discriminatory practice "to refuse to hire or employ or to bar or to discharge from employment any individual or to discriminate against him in compensation or in terms, conditions or privileges of employment because of the individual's sexual orientation or civil union status." Conn. Gen. Stat. Ann. § 46a–81c (West 2016).

Donald Denault sued his employer under the Connecticut law, alleging he was discharged because of his sexual orientation. *See Denault v. Conn. Gen. Life Ins. Co.*, No. CV 950050418S, 1999 WL 549454 (Conn. Super. Ct. June 29, 1999). He alleged that he was subjected to negative comments about his sexual orientation from his supervisor and other sales people. Five months after he complained to his supervisor about these hostile comments, he was suspended and terminated for alleged improprieties related to an expense report. The defendant moved for summary judgment. The trial court granted the motion for summary judgment because there was no evidence that "the people in the defendant company who decided to terminate the plaintiff" had engaged in discriminatory statements or activity. *Id.* at *13.

§ 7.7 DISTRICT OF COLUMBIA

The District of Columbia Human Rights Ordinance states:

> It is the intent of the Council of the District of Columbia, in enacting this chapter, to secure an end in the District of Columbia to discrimination for any reason other than that of individual merit, including, but not limited to, discrimination by reason of race, color, religion, national origin, sex, age, marital status, personal appearance, sexual orientation, gender identity or expression, familial status, family responsibilities, matriculation, political affiliation, genetic information, disability, source of income, status as a victim of an intrafamily offense, and place of residence or business.

D.C. Code Ann. § 2–1401.01 (2012).

One of the earliest cases brought under this ordinance was brought by Michael Sondheimer who claimed that he was the victim of discrimination on the basis of sexual orientation and religion when he was not hired as an area supervisor of a physical plant at Georgetown University "because he is a homosexual Jew." *Sondheimer v. Georgetown Univ.*, No. CIV.A. 87–1052–LFO, 1987 WL 14618, at *1 (D.D.C. Oct. 20, 1987). Sondheimer had written on his employment application:

> The belief that homosexuality is a 'sin' is a religious opinion. I intend to defend my religious human rights to the letter of the laws of the United States of America so help me God. Despite the Catholic Church and the tax free American dollars they spend to deny homosexual Jews the human right to 'dance' as do heterosexual Jews, I WILL DANCE.

Id. at *2.

Sondheimer lost before the District of Columbia Office of Human Rights and the federal district court. They found that the position had already been offered to another, well-qualified applicant before he submitted his application. The Office of Human Rights also noted that his application was "replete with extraneous and combative language which appears to have been calculated to confront Respondent on issues completely unrelated to the position applied for." *Id.* at *2.

Another early case under the D.C. ordinance was *Underwood v. Archer Mgmt. Serv., Inc.*, 857 F. Supp. 96 (D.D.C. 1994). Patricia Underwood brought this claim of discrimination before the D.C. statute was amended to cover "gender identity." She alleged that she was discharged because of her transgender status. At the time she brought this case, the D.C. statute did ban discrimination on the basis of "personal appearance." She alleged that "she is a transsexual and retains some masculine traits." *Id.* at 97. The court allowed that complaint to go forward and dismissed the claim of discrimination on the basis of sex or sexual orientation.

LuEthel Tate Green also brought a case under the District of Columbia Human Rights Act that was decided by the District of Columbia Court of Appeals in 1994. *See Howard Univ. v. Green*, 652 A.2d 41 (D.C. Ct. App. 1994). Green alleged that she was included in a reduction-in-force in retaliation for complaining of sexual orientation discrimination in the Howard University Hospital Division of Nursing. She alleged that lesbians received preferential treatment in her department. The court of appeals overturned the trial court verdict in Green's favor, finding that that there was nothing in the record to suggest that the Director was ever alerted that Green had complained about sexual orientation discrimination. *Id.* at 48. This is an unusual case in that it involves discrimination against someone because of her *heterosexuality*. It was unsuccessful.

§ 7.8 ILLINOIS

The Illinois Human Rights Act provides:

> [F]or all individuals within Illinois the freedom from discrimination against any individual because of his or her race, color, religion, sex, national origin, ancestry, age, order of protection status, marital status, physical or mental disability, military status, sexual orientation, pregnancy, or unfavorable discharge from

> military service in connection with employment, real estate transactions, access to financial credit, and the availability of public accommodations.

775 Ill. Comp. Stat. Ann. 5/1–102 (West 2011 & Supp. 2015).

Tawanna Young filed a claim of discrimination under the Illinois statute with the state's Human Rights Commission, alleging that she faced a lack of overtime, suspension, and discharge because of her sexual orientation. The Human Rights Commission found that her adverse treatment was consistent with workplace policies. The Illinois Appellate Court upheld that determination. *See Young v. Ill. Human Rights Comm'n*, 974 N.E.2d 385 (Ill. App. Ct. 2012).

§ 7.9 IOWA

The Iowa Civil Rights Act provides that it shall be unlawful employment practice "to refuse to hire, accept, register, classify, or refer for employment, to discharge any employee, or to otherwise discriminate in employment against any applicant for employment or any employee because of the .... sexual orientation .... of such applicant or employee, unless based upon the nature of the occupation." Iowa Code Ann. § 216.6(1)(a) (West 2009).

Sharon Marie Robertson sued the Siouxland Community Health Center for alleged harassment and discharge because of her sexual orientation. *See Robertson v. Siouxland Cmty. Health Ctr.*, 938 F. Supp. 2d 831 (N.D. Iowa 2013). Although dismissing her Title VII claim of sexual orientation discrimination, the court allowed her state law claim to go forward. *Id.* at 842.

In 2012, Christopher Godfrey sued Governor Terry Branstad, Branstad's legal counsel and the state government, arguing that he was subjected to an adverse and unlawful employment action on the basis of his sexual orientation under Iowa law and Iowa Constitution. He prevailed at trial with the jury returning a verdict of $500,000 on his state law claim and $1,000,000 for violation of the state's due process clause. *See Godfrey v. State,* 2019 WL 3753974 (Iowa Dist. July 22, 2019). The Iowa Supreme Court reversed. *See Godfrey v. State,* 962 N.W.2d 84 (Iowa 2021). The primary basis for reversal was that the evidence did not indicate that the sole decision maker—the governor—knew Godfrey was gay. The dissent criticized the majority for substituting its evaluation of the evidence for that of the jury.

§ 7.10 MAINE

The Maine Human Rights Act prohibits an employer from failing or refusing to:

> [H]ire or otherwise discriminate against any applicant for employment because of race or color, sex, sexual orientation, physical or mental disability, religion, age, ancestry or national origin . . . . or, because of those reasons, to discharge an employee or discriminate with respect to hire, tenure, promotion, transfer, compensation, terms, conditions, or privileges of

> employment or any other matter directly to indirectly related to employment. . . .

Me. Rev. Stat. Ann. tit. 5, § 4572 (2013).

One case filed under the Maine Human Rights Act reached the First Circuit Court of Appeals. *See Flood v. Bank of Am. Corp.*, 780 F.3d 1 (1st Cir. 2015). Shelly Flood filed discrimination charges with her state human rights commission against her employer, Bank of America, and was issued a right to sue letter. She then sued the bank in the Maine Superior Court alleging employment discrimination and defamation. The case was removed to federal court on the basis of diversity jurisdiction. After discovery, the bank moved for summary judgment. The case was assigned to a magistrate judge who issued a recommendation to grant the defendant's motion for summary judgment and the district court affirmed the recommendation summarily. *See Flood v. Bank of Am. Corp.*, No. 1:12–CV–00105–GZS, 2013 WL 4806863 (D. Me. Sept. 9, 2013), *aff'd in part, vacated in part, remanded*, 780 F.3d 1 (1st Cir. 2015). The First Circuit reversed the dismissal of her discharge and hostile work environment claims.

Flood was arguably subjected to harassment because of her sexual orientation (i.e., bisexual), although, that harassment did not take the form of the use of explicit homophobic statements. The primary antagonist was Diana Castle, who was Flood's immediate supervisor and mentor. Flood had worked at the bank since 2006 with no workplace problems. Starting in April 2010, when Castle saw Flood sit at the LGBT table, with a photograph of

Flood embracing her partner, Castle began to treat Flood adversely. Castle imposed restrictive personal policies on Flood and downgraded her job performance. Castle also retroactively reclassified some of Flood's hours, making her appear less productive. Another supervisor, Michelle Tabbutt, also began treating Flood adversely by overly scrutinizing her personal behavior and downgrading her job performance.

Because Flood was emotionally distraught by this harassment and adverse job action, she did not return to work after September 22, 2010. A supervisor sent a letter to Flood on September 27, 2010, saying that the bank would assume she had voluntarily resigned if she did not communicate with the supervisor within three days. On September 30, 2010, Flood sent a letter to Castle complaining of her mistreatment. Her employment was terminated, effective October 1, 2010, on the grounds that she had abandoned her job.

With respect to the discharge claim, the district court judge treated that claim as if Flood had alleged what is called a "constructive discharge." The legal standard for a constructive discharge is exceptionally difficult. One must meet the "heavy burden" of showing that she had "no reasonable alternative to resignation because of intolerable working conditions." 780 F.3d at 7. By contrast, the burden of proof would be less onerous if Flood were merely alleging that "the Bank used job abandonment as a pretext for improperly terminating her employment." *Id.* at 8. Under the somewhat easier legal theory, to survive a motion to dismiss, Flood would need to demonstrate that a reasonable fact-finder might conclude that the bank knew Flood did not abandon her job and that the bank had discriminatory animus towards Flood. The magistrate judge had explicitly found evidence supporting a finding of discriminatory animus. The First Circuit concluded that a reasonable fact-finder could conclude that Flood's letter to Castle on September 30, 2010, satisfied the requirement to notify the bank she had not abandoned her job.

With respect to the hostile work environment theory, the magistrate judge had found: "Viewed objectively, the evidence in this case does not reasonably support a finding of hostile work environment. The evidence does not divulge severe harassment or pervasive harassment, any physical threats, any humiliating treatment, or any offensive utterances." *Flood v. Bank of Am. Corp.*, No. 1:12–CV–00105–GZS, 2013 WL 4806863, at *10 (D. Me. Sept. 9, 2013), *aff'd in part, vacated in part, remanded*, 780 F.3d 1 (1st Cir. 2015). The First Circuit reversed, finding that a jury could find that a hostile work environment existed. While the bank argued that there was no "blatant vitriol," the First Circuit found that harassment need not be "overt" to be "based on sexual orientation." 780 F.3d at 11. Further, the First Circuit found that a jury could conclude the harassment was sufficiently severe and pervasive to constitute unlawful harassment because the evidence included "atmospheric and job performance-related incidents." *Id.* at 12. Thus, five years after being terminated for job abandonment, the magistrate's dismissal of Flood's case was overturned. This case is considered to be one of the few cases where a plaintiff alleged discrimination on the basis of her bisexuality.

§ 7.11 MASSACHUSETTS

Although there are not a lot of reported state court cases in Massachusetts, there are a lot of successful complaints filed with the Massachusetts Commission Against Discrimination ("MCAD"). Massachusetts law provides that it is an unlawful practice:

> For an employer, by himself or his agent, because of the race, color, religious creed, national origin, sex, gender identity, sexual orientation, which shall not include persons whose sexual orientation involves minor children as the sex object, genetic information, or ancestry of any individual to refuse to hire or employ or to bar or to discharge from employment such individual or to discriminate against such individual in compensation or in terms, conditions or privileges of employment, unless based upon a bona fide occupational qualification.

Mass. Gen. Laws Ann. ch. 151B, § 4 (LexisNexis Supp. 2016).

An early case under Massachusetts law was brought by Sandra LaFleur. *See LaFleur v. Bird-Johnson Co.*, No. 93–703, 1994 WL 878831 (Mass. Super. Ct. Nov. 3, 1994). LaFleur alleged that she was discriminated against on the basis of her perceived sexual orientation. She was actually transgendered, not gay, but argued that she was perceived as homosexual by her co-workers. *Id.* at *4. She claimed that she was subjected to harassment after she transitioned from male to female in the workplace. The court found that the comments were just "casual" and "sporadic" and did not rise to the level of illegal harassment. LaFleur had mentioned two incidents:

> LaFleur first testified that a co-worker, Scott Lowe, called LaFleur a 'faggot' and said he'd kill LaFleur if she ever came near him. . . . LaFleur also testified that she was told that a colleague had written graffiti on the men's room wall suggesting that LaFleur and the male janitor were involved in an affair. LaFleur never saw the graffiti, which the janitor immediately removed.

Id. at *5 n.23.

LaFleur's case is unusual in that it rests on a "perceived sexual orientation" theory. In light of the comments allegedly made at the workplace, it appears to have been a cognizable theory even if the court did not find the comments to be sufficient to constitute illegal harassment.

In a case from 2001, Patricia Weber sued Community Teamwork, Inc. when she was not promoted to the position of executive director, and eventually terminated. *See Weber v. Cmty. Teamwork, Inc.*, 752 N.E.2d 700, 702 (Mass. 2001). The trial court judge had found in favor of Weber on the discharge claim, finding that the organization had a pervasively sexist culture and that the termination was "callous." Although Weber was openly known as a lesbian, there is no discussion of specific anti-lesbian comments made against her. The Massachusetts Supreme Court reversed the trial court decision saying that the trial judge needed to find evidence of "improper discriminatory animus" to rule in Weber's favor. *Id.* at 713.

In a 2007 case, Tammy Walker survived the defendant's motion for summary judgment in a case against the police department for claims of gender, race, and sexual orientation discrimination involving her suspension and termination. *See Walker v. City of Holyoke*, 523 F. Supp. 2d 86 (D. Mass. 2007). Her complaint involved numerous complaints about harassing language such as "you shouldn't go sticking your tongue where it don't belong" and referring to her by the male name "Tyrone" instead of her given name "Tammy." *Id.* at 95.

In another state court case, Matthew Barrett filed a discrimination claim against Fontbonne Academy after his offer of employment as Food Service Director was rescinded when he listed his husband as his emergency contact. *See Barrett v. Fontbonne Acad.*, 33 Mass. L. Rptr. 287, 2015 WL 9682042 (Mass. Superior Ct. 2015). The defendant sought to argue that he was denied the position because he was in a same-sex marriage, not because of his sexual orientation. The court found that the law recognizes no such distinction. By analogy, the court noted: "A tax on wearing yarmulkes is a tax on Jews." *Id.* at *2.

The defendant also argued that, as a Catholic school, they were allowed to insist that Barrett act consistently with the teachings of the Catholic Church. The court rejected that claim as well, saying the issue of what kinds of exemptions to allow in a statute is one for the legislature. The Massachusetts legislature had not included language in their statute to exempt the Catholic school for this type of coverage under the statute. The trial court therefore denied the defendant's motion for summary judgment and granted the plaintiff's motion for summary judgment with respect to liability. It requested the parties to address whether a trial needed to take place on the issue of damages. *Id.* at *11.

§ 7.12 MINNESOTA

In an early case under the Minneapolis Civil Rights Ordinance, the Minnesota Supreme Court reversed the determination of the Minneapolis Commission on Civil Rights that had been rendered in favor of complainant Timothy Campbell. Campbell had applied for the positions of Programs Coordinator and Employment Clearinghouse Coordinator with the Minnesota Chemical Dependency Association. When he was not selected for the position, he filed a complaint with the Minneapolis Commission on Civil Rights, arguing that he had been a victim of discrimination on the basis of "affectional preference." *Minn. Chem. Dependency Ass'n v. Minneapolis Comm'n on Civil Rights*, 310 N.W.2d 497, 498 (Minn. 1981). The basis for his claim of discrimination was that he was asked six questions not asked of the other applicants that indirectly probed into his gay rights activism. Although the Commission had found that those questions "evidenced unequal treatment based on complainant's affectional preference," *Id.* at 500, the Minnesota Supreme Court found that the line of questions were reasonably seeking to determine if he could handle the requirements of the position. "The inquiry into complainant's involvement in several special interest groups, including those promoting gay rights, was limited to a consideration of the effect that the allocation of time and effort to such activities would have on complainant's job performance." *Id.* at 501.

The Minnesota Human Rights Act also prohibits discrimination based on sexual orientation. *See* Minn. Stat. Ann. § 363A.08 (West 2012). Many of the reported cases have been unsuccessful.

Veronica Thomas lost her case under the Minnesota statute in a case that was affirmed by the court of appeals in 2000. *See Thomas v. Coleman Enter.*, No. C6–99–1327, 2000 WL 385479 (Minn. Ct. App. Apr. 18, 2000). Thomas introduced evidence about two anti-lesbian remarks made by her supervisor—one out of the workplace and one in the workplace. The court was not willing to assume that the Minnesota statute even covered "sexual orientation harassment" but, even if it did, found that Thomas had not offered sufficient evidence to give rise to such a claim. *Id.* at *4–5.

In a more recent case, Philip Sieden also lost his case under the Minnesota Human Rights Act. *See Sieden v. Chipotle Mexican Grill, Inc.*, 128 F. Supp.3d

1133 (D. Minn. 2015). He alleged that he was terminated because of his sexual orientation. His primary evidence of discrimination was a greeting by his manager who stated; " 'guten morgen, fraulein,' which means 'good morning, lady' in German." *Id.* at 1144. The court found that although the remark "may have been offensive, it does not support a finding of discrimination or pretext because it is a stray remark remote in time from and unrelated to the adverse employment decision." *Id.* at 1144. Thus, the court granted the defendant's motion for summary judgment.

Sara Thorson lost her case under the Minnesota statute because of its religious exemption. *See Thorson v. Billy Graham Evangelistic Ass'n*, 687 N.W.2d 652 (Minn. Ct. App. 2004). Thorson had worked for the defendant since 1971 as a mailroom employee; she was fired after two employees reported seeing her kiss another woman in the parking lot at work. *Id.* at 655. The Minnesota statute exempted religious associations from coverage except for "secular business activities engaged in by the religious association . . . . which is unrelated to the religious and educational purposes for which [the religious association] is organized." Minn. Stat. Ann. § 363A.26 (2012). Because Thorson worked in the mailroom, she argued that the religious exemption did not apply to the defendant. The Minnesota Court of Appeals, however, ruled that the religious exemption did apply because the defendant's "business activities are exclusively related to its evangelical ministry." *Id.* at 658. Similarly, Randall Egan lost his case against the Hamline United

Methodist Church due to the religious exemption. *See Egan v. Hamline United Methodist Church*, 679 N.W.2d 350 (Minn. Ct. App. 2004).

§ 7.13 NEW JERSEY

The New Jersey Law Against Discrimination provides:

> All persons shall have the opportunity to obtain employment, and to obtain all the accommodations, advantages, facilities, and privileges of any place of public accommodation, publicly assisted housing accommodation, and other real property without discrimination because of race, creed, color, national origin, ancestry, age, marital status, affectional or sexual orientation, familial status, disability, nationality, sex, gender identity or expression or source of lawful income used for rental or mortgage payments, subject only to conditions and limitations applicable alike to all persons. This opportunity is recognized as and declared to be a civil right.

N.J. Stat. Ann. § 10:5–4 (West 2013).

Carla Enriquez sued West Jersey Health Systems after she was terminated from her employment. *See Enriquez v. West Jersey Health Sys.*, 777 A.2d 365 (N.J. Super. Ct. App. Div. 2001). She was terminated from her position as a physician after she began transitioning from male to female. The "gender identity" language had not yet been added to the New Jersey Law Against Discrimination ("LAD"), so she filed suit on the basis of gender, sexual orientation and disability. The trial court found she did not establish a prima facie case of sexual orientation discrimination because the alleged discrimination was not on the basis of " 'affectional, emotional or physical attraction' to others." *Id.* at 371. Further, the trial court found, and the court of appeals agreed, that the term "sex" does not encompass discrimination on the basis of "transsexuality." *Id.* at 372. Nonetheless, the court of appeals concluded that "gender dysphoria" is a recognized disability under the LAD and remanded the case back to the trial court to consider that argument. *Id.* at 377.

§ 7.14 NEW YORK

Many of the reported sexual orientation nondiscrimination cases are under the state of New York's nondiscrimination statute as well as New York City's Human Rights Law.

The New York City Human Rights Law provides that it is an unlawful employment practice for an employer "to refuse to hire or employ or to bar or to discharge from employment such person or to discriminate against such person in compensation or in terms, conditions or privileges of employment" on the basis of gender, marital status, partnership status or sexual orientation. New York City, N.Y., Admin. Code § 8–107, (West, Westlaw through Local Law 113, except L.L. 38, of 2015 and Chapters 1–589 of the Laws of the State of New York for 2015.

Although many city ordinances only provide for relief akin to a minor misdemeanor violation, the

New York City Human Rights Law is a vehicle for quite significant relief. A New York state appellate court upheld a $1.6 million award for Mirella Salemi under New York City Human Rights Law. *See Salemi v. Gloria's Tribeca, Inc.*, 982 N.Y.S.2d 458 (N.Y. App. Div. 2014). Judge Carol Huff denied defendants' motion to set aside or reduce the verdict and entered judgment in favor of Salemi. The defendant appealed the decision and it was affirmed on appeal.

Salemi worked as a chef and manager at a restaurant owned by Gloria's Tribecamex. The owner held mandatory weekly prayer meetings and repeatedly stated that homosexuality is a sin and that gay people are "going to go to hell." Salemi filed suit under New York City law, alleging that he faced discrimination on the basis of religion and sexual orientation. The court of appeals found that the trial court judge correctly instructed the jury that "discrimination on the basis of sexual orientation or religion must be beyond what is considered petty slights and trivial inconveniences." *Id.* at 460. The court of appeals rejected the argument that the jury instruction should have relied on a "severe and pervasive" standard. *Id.* at 460.

The New York State Human Rights Law can also be a vehicle for quite significant relief. In addition to prohibiting discrimination in employment and housing, it also prohibits discrimination by places of public accommodation. It provides that it shall be:

> [A]n unlawful discriminatory practice for any person, being the owner, lessee, proprietor, manager, superintendent, agent or employee of

> any place of public accommodation, resort or amusement, because of the race, creed, color, national origin, sexual orientation, military status, sex, or disability or marital status of any person, directly or indirectly, to refuse, withhold from or deny to such person any of the accommodations, advantages, facilities or privileges thereof, including the extension of credit, or, directly or indirectly, to publish, circulate, issue, display, post or mail any written or printed communication, notice or advertisement, to the effect that any of the accommodations, advantages, facilities and privileges of any such place shall be refused, withheld from or denied to any person on account of race, creed, color, national origin, sexual orientation, military status, sex, or disability or marital status, or that the patronage or custom thereat of any person of or purporting to be of any particular race, creed, color, national origin, sexual orientation, military status, sex or marital status, or having a disability is unwelcome, objectionable or not acceptable, desired or solicited.

N.Y. Exec. Law § 296 (McKinney Supp. 2016).

Melisa McCarthy and Jennifer McCarthy achieved a successful outcome under this statute when they filed a complaint with the New York State Division of Human Rights. Cynthia Gifford had told them that her company, Liberty Ridge Farm, would not be willing to be a venue for the McCarthys' wedding ceremony and reception because Liberty Ridge Farm did "not hold same[-]sex marriages." *Gifford v. McCarthy*, 137 A.D.3d 30, 34 (N.Y. App. Div. 2016). An Administrative Law Judge ("ALJ") recommended that the McCarthys each be awarded $1,500 in compensatory damages and a civil fine be imposed on Liberty Ridge Farm of $10,000. *Id.* at 34. The operators of Liberty Ridge Farm petitioned for judicial review of the State's determination. Judge Karen Peters heard this appeal and affirmed the results below. As in the *Barrett* case, the defendant argued that they were not discriminating on the basis of sexual orientation. They simply objected to their same-sex marriage. *Id.* at 37. The court rejected that argument, finding that "the statute 'does not permit businesses to offer a "limited menu" of goods or services to customers on the basis of a status that fits within one of the protected categories.' " *Id.* at 37–38 (quoting *Elane Photography, LLC. v. Willock*, 309 P.3d at 62). "Thus, petitioners' purported willingness to offer some services to the McCarthys does not cure their refusal to provide a service that was offered to the general public." *Id.* at 38.

Some plaintiffs bring a cause of action under both the City and State Human Rights laws. The New York courts have repeatedly noted that the City's statute is more liberally construed than the State's statute.

Jane Doe brought a claim against the City of New York under the New York State Human Rights Law and New York City Human Rights Law. *See Doe v. City of New York*, 42 Misc.3d 502 (N.Y. Sup. Ct. 2013). Doe was a client of the New York City Human

Resources Administration's HIV/AIDS Service Administration ("HASA"). She requested that HASA update its records to reflect her legal name change and change of gender information. She also requested that she be addressed by her female name with female pronouns. In ruling in favor of the plaintiff, the court noted that the City's Human Rights Law "is more expansive than that of the State's." *Id.* at 505. It also noted that defendant's insistence on calling Jane Doe by her previous male name and using male pronouns caused her to feel demeaned due to "abject discriminatory reasons." *Id.* at 507.

Bryan Waters brought suit under New York's Human Rights Law as well as New York City's Human Rights Law when he was allegedly subjected to homosexual slurs when he used the sauna at the New York Sports Club. He also allegedly was chased from the sauna to the locker room while continuing to be subject to homosexual animus. *See Waters v. Town Sports Int'l Holdings*, 997 N.Y.S.2d 102 (N.Y. Sup. Ct. 2014). Citing *Doe v. City of New York*, the court noted that the New York City Human Rights Law "is intended to be even more expansive" than the State's statute. *Id.* at *9. Defendant's argument to have the claim dismissed was denied. A preliminary conference was scheduled; the outcome is unknown.

§ 7.15 WASHINGTON STATE

The Washington Law Against Discrimination ("WLAD") provides protection against employment protection on the basis of "age, sex, marital status, sexual orientation, race, creed, color, national origin, honorably discharged veteran or military status, or the presence of any sensory, mental, or physical disability or the use of a trained dog guide or service animal by a person with a disability, unless based upon a bona fide occupational qualification." Wash. Rev. Code Ann. § 49.60.180 (West 2008).

In *Davis v. Fred's Appliance, Inc.*, 287 P.3d 51 (Wash. Ct. App. 2012), the court ruled that the state did not protect against discrimination on the basis of *perceived* homosexuality when the plaintiff was actually heterosexual. These kinds of rulings have caused some states to explicitly include "perceived" sexual orientation as a protected category. The Washington court also found that the plaintiff did not allege sufficient facts for a claim of sexual orientation harassment. Namely, three references to employee by the name of television character "Big Gay Al" were insufficient to meet a claim for a hostile work environment. *Id.* at 58. By contrast, a federal district court, interpreting the Washington statute, found that plaintiff survived defendant's motion for summary judgment on a hostile work environment claim with allegations that a co-worker told plaintiff that he "sounded like a queer on the phone," directly addressed him as a "queer" and "faggot" and ultimately refused a work assignment saying "What are you going to do about it faggot"? *Hotchkiss v. CSK Auto,* 918 F. Supp. 2d 1108, 1119 (E.D. Wash. 2013).

The state of Washington was involved in a high-profile case involving a florist who refused to provide flowers for a same-sex wedding. *See State v. Arlene's Flowers,* 441 P.3d 1203 (Wash. 2019). This case involved a denial of services to Robert Ingersoll and Curt Freed when they sought to purchase flowers for their upcoming wedding in 2013, soon after the state of Washington voted to recognize same-sex marriages. The owner of the flower shop told Freed that she was unable to honor his request, even though he had been a customer of her store for many years, because of her religious beliefs. She gave him names of other florists who might be willing to serve him. After the state became aware of this denial of services, it brought an enforcement action against the florist. The state was successful in the enforcement action and the florist sought review in the United States Supreme Court. After deciding *Masterpiece Cakeshop*, the Supreme Court vacated the Washington Supreme Court's original judgment and remanded for consideration in light of *Masterpiece Cakeshop, Ltd. v. Colorado Civil Rights Commission,* 584 U.S. 617 (2018). *See Arlene's Flowers, Inc. v. Washington*, 585 U.S. 1013 (2018) (mem.).

As discussed in *Nutshell* Ch. 9, the Supreme Court held in *Masterpiece Cakeshop* that the adjudicatory body tasked with deciding a particular case must remain neutral; it must give full and fair consideration to the dispute before it and avoid animus toward religion. Disputes "must be resolved with tolerance, without undue disrespect to sincere religious beliefs, and without subjecting gay persons to indignities when they seek goods and services in an open market." *Id.* at 640.

On remand, the Washington Supreme Court concluded that the courts resolved the dispute with tolerance and that the florist's religious liberty rights were not violated. On July 2, 2021, the Supreme Court denied the florist's cert. petition effectively ending the case and allowing the state's enforcement action to be upheld. Only three members of the Court were willing to accept cert. (Justices Gorsuch, Thomas and Alito). At this time, it therefore appears that cities and states can enforce sexual orientation nondiscrimination statutes over objections by private entities that providing those services conflicts with their religious beliefs so long as the adjudicatory authority does not display disrespect to sincere religious beliefs. *But see Chelsey Nelson Photography v. Louisville/Jefferson County Metro Government*, 479 F. Supp.3d 543 (W.D. Ky. 2020) (preliminarily enjoining county government from enforcing sexual orientation nondiscrimination ordinance against wedding photographer on First Amendment grounds). Nonetheless, a free expression is defense is now available in light of the Supreme Court's decision in *303 Creative LLC v. Elenis*, 600 U.S. 570 (2023) (discussed in *Nutshell* § 8.1).

§ 7.16 INFLUENCE OF TITLE VII ON STATE LAW

Every state has a statute banning sex discrimination, often modeled on the language in Title VII. One interesting interpretive question is whether those state statutes that ban sex discrimination, but do not explicitly ban sexual orientation discrimination or gender identity discrimination, will be interpreted liberally to ban such discrimination.

In Virginia, the State Attorney General has been asked to issue an advisory opinion on that issue. Attorney General Mark Herring issued an advisory opinion on May 10, 2016. *See* Applicability of Va. ANTI-Discrimination Statutes, 2016 WL 2940460 (Op. Va. Att'y Gen May 10, 2016). The Virginia Attorney General stated that the Virginia Human Rights Act prohibits all sex-based discrimination prohibited by federal law. Given the trend in the circuit courts and the position of the EEOC, he stated his opinion "that a Virginia court faced with the issue would likely find that discriminatory conduct against gay and lesbian Virginians based on sex-stereotyping or on treating them less favorably on account of their sex violates the Commonwealth's anti-discrimination statutes." *Id.* at *13. Further, he stated that "in an appropriate case a Virginia court could well conclude that discrimination on account of an individual's transgender status is an impermissible form of sex discrimination that violates Virginia's public policy and various anti-discrimination statutes." *Id.* at *12.

By contrast, the Ohio Court of Appeals has ruled that an allegation of discrimination because of sexual orientation is not actionable under Ohio Law, R.C. 4112.01(A) "until the legislature or the Ohio Supreme Court addresses the issue directly." *See Inskeep v. Vukovich*, 30 OPER ¶ 135, 30 Ohio Pub. Employee Rep. ¶ 135, 2013 WL 1214609 (Ohio Ct. App. March 8, 2013).

It is too soon to know how *Bostock* might influence state courts where a claim of sexual orientation or gender identity discrimination is brought in a state that does not have a specific statute banning such conduct but does have a sex discrimination statute. Because some state statutes cover small employers that are not otherwise covered by Title VII or cover public accommodations that are not subject to federal law, there can be strategic reasons to file under a state nondiscrimination statute rather than Title VII.

The Michigan Supreme Court followed *Bostock's* reasoning in concluding that their state statute does ban sexual orientation discrimination. *See Rouch World v. Department of Civil Rights,* 510 Mich. 398 (2022). Because the EEOC appears not to be taking cases involving gender identity or sexual orientation issues, plaintiffs may increasingly want to pursue their options in state court. Of course, the EEOC's failure to bring cases does not preclude plaintiffs from bringing their own cases in federal court.

Many state courts have concluded that their state does not prohibit discrimination on the basis of sexual orientation or gender identity. *See Doe v. Catholic Relief Services,* 484 Md. 640 (2023); *Jones v. Lumberport,* 2024 WL 5201657 (W. Va. Interm. Ct. App. Dec. 23, 2024)(sexual orientation); Gauthreaux v. City of Gretna, 360 So.3d 930 (Ct. App. La. 5th Circuit 2023)(sexual orientation); *Vroegh v. Iowa Department of Corrections,* 972 N.W.2d 686 (Iowa 2022)(gender identity). This is not a comprehensive list but an issue to follow in various state jurisdictions.

CHAPTER 8
FREEDOM OF EXPRESSION AND ASSOCIATION

§ 8.1 FREE SPEECH RIGHTS OF STUDENTS: GENERAL PRINCIPLES

The First Amendment has been a very important source of constitutional protection for the LGBTQ+ community. Before the Supreme Court began to extend privacy and equality rights to the LGBTQ+ community, many lower court decisions had helped protect the LGBTQ+ community from overt forms of freedom of speech violations. Lawyers who represent the LGBTQ+ community often find themselves needing solid knowledge of the First Amendment. One might even argue that the acquisition of First Amendment protections is an important step towards a group attaining other sorts of legal protections through use of the political process.

Many of the cases involving LGBTQ+ free speech issues involve students, where public entities have greater latitude to regulate speech than they would otherwise have under the First Amendment. The general principles regarding content-based restrictions on free speech are governed by the three-part test specified in *United States v. O'Brien*, 391 U.S. 367 (1968): whether "it furthers an important or substantial governmental interest; if the governmental interest is unrelated to the suppression of free expression; and if the incidental restriction on alleged First Amendment freedoms is no greater than is essential to the furtherance of that interest." *Id.* at 377. In a 7–1 decision for the Court, Chief Justice Warren concluded the prohibition against destroying or mutilating selective service certificates met that constitutional standard. Reversing the First Circuit, the Supreme Court upheld the conviction of David O'Brien for burning his draft card as a protest against the Vietnam Conflict. Although the *O'Brien* test sometimes benefits members of the LGBTQ+ community who want to state controversial political positions, it can also be used to strike down measured designed to benefit the LGBTQ+ community. For example, in *Otto v. City of Boca Raton,* 981 F.3d 854 (11th Cir. 2020), the Eleventh Circuit that city and county ordinances prohibiting therapy to minors with the goal of changing their sexual orientation or gender identity violated the First Amendment rights of licensed marriage and family therapists. The Third Circuit found a similar New Jersey statute did not violate the free speech or free exercise rights of licensed counselors. *See King v. Governor of the State of New Jersey,* 767 F.3d 216 (3rd Cir. 2014). But the Supreme Court abrogated some of the reasoning in *King* when it found that professional speech is not a separate category of speech exempt from the rule that content-based regulations of speech are subject to strict scrutiny. *See National Institute of Family and Life Advocates v. Becerra,* 585 U.S. 755 (2018) (overturning California statute that required crisis pregnancy centers to disseminate information about contraception and abortion).

Another important long-standing exception to First Amendment protections is when material is considered to be "obscene." *See Roth v. United States*, 354 U.S. 476 (1957) (upholding federal and state statutes that punished the mailing of material that is obscene, lewd, lascivious or filthy). The legal standard is whether the "average person, applying contemporary community standards" would find that the work, taken as a whole, appeals to the prurient interest. *Id.* at 489. Although the Court was splintered in how it defined obscenity, it sought to add some clarity in *Miller v. California*, 413 U.S. 15 (1973) when Chief Justice Burger's 5–4 opinion re-affirmed the conclusion from *Roth* that obscene material is not protected by the First Amendment, it can restricted without a demonstration that it is "utterly without redeeming social value," and that it can be defined "by applying contemporary community standards." *Id.* at 37.

The Court further extended the ability of government to regulate speech, when it is being broadcasted into the home, when it is "vulgar," "offensive," or "shocking," without necessarily being "obscene" under the *Miller* test. *See F.C.C. v. Pacifica Found.*, 438 U.S. 726, 746 (1978). In upholding the validity of the restriction in *Pacifica Foundation*, the Court emphasized that the broadcast was "uniquely accessible to children," because it was broadcast during the day rather than merely available in print. *Id.* at 749. These holdings are sometimes cited by school districts when they try to limit student access to some forms of overtly sexual speech.

The scope of the free speech rights of students is a contested issue, but it is well-accepted that students do not "shed their constitutional rights to freedom of speech or expression at the schoolhouse gate." *Tinker v. Des Moines Indep. Cmty. Sch. Dist.*, 393 U.S. 503, 506 (1969). One of the earliest cases to consider the scope of students' free speech rights was *West Virginia State Board of Education v. Barnette*, 319 U.S. 624 (1943) in which the Supreme Court found that students have a First Amendment right to refuse to engage in the salute of the flag. Compelling the flag salute "invades the sphere of intellect and spirit which it is the purpose of the First Amendment to our Constitution to reserve from all official control." *Id.* at 642. Such censorship, the Court found, could only be imposed "when the expression presents a clear and present danger of action of a kind the State is empowered to prevent and punish." *Id.* at 633.

Barnette is part of the Court's "compelled speech" doctrine under which it is inappropriate for the government to tell people what they must say. It received further support in *Wooley v. Maynard*, 430 U.S. 705, 717 (1977), in which the Court found it was unconstitutional for New Hampshire motorists to be required to display the state motto "Live Free or Die" on their license plates. The Supreme Court refused to extend the "compelled speech" doctrine to protect universities that did not want to comply with the "Solomon Amendment" under which universities were required to permit military recruiters on campus or lose significant federal financial assistance. *See Rumsfeld v. Forum for Acad. & Inst.*

Rights, Inc., 547 U.S. 47 (2006). A unanimous Court (with Justice Alito not participating) found that a requirement that military recruiters be allowed to use campus resources was nothing like "a Government-mandated pledge or motto that the school must endorse." *Id.* at 62.

In an opinion authored by Chief Justice Roberts, the *Rumsfeld* Court found that the conduct regulated by the Solomon Amendment was not inherently expressive "because the schools are not speaking when they host interviews and recruiting receptions." *Id.* at 64. The Court further noted: "[w]e have held that high school students can appreciate the difference between speech a school sponsors and speech the school permits because legally required to do so, pursuant to an equal access policy. . . . Surely students have not lost that ability by the time they get to law school." *Id.* at 65. Even if the Solomon Amendment were deemed to be a regulation of expressive conduct, the Court found it would pass the *O'Brien* test because "the means chosen by Congress add to the effectiveness of military recruitment." *Id.* at 67. As in *O'Brien* (the draft card burning case), the Court found that the government's military justification served a substantial government interest. Finally, the Court rejected the argument that the Solomon Amendment violated a law school's associational rights. "A military recruiter's mere presence on campus does not violate a law school's right to associate, regardless of how repugnant the law school considers the recruiter's message." *Id.* at 70.

In the most recent case in the "compelled speech" line of cases, the Court held that a website designer could not be compelled to comply with Colorado's sexual orientation nondiscrimination statute by providing services to a same-sex couple. *See 303 Creative LLC v. Elenis*, 600 U.S. 570 (2023). The holding is arguably narrow in that it only applies when the business's product is expressive and customized, and the message is understood to be that of the business. Further, the Court clarified that the business's objection to providing the product must because of the message in the product, not the customer's status. Because the Court did not define "expressive activity," there will be further litigation in other cases clarifying that issue. The state conceded that the website designer engaged in expressive activity in this case.

The freedom of association line of cases will be discussed further in *Nutshell* §§ 8.6 & 8.7, below.

Outside of the forced speech context, the *Barnette* holding was further extended in *Tinker v. Des Moines Independent Community School District*, 393 U.S. 503 (1969), where the Supreme Court, in a 7–2 opinion authored by Justice Fortas, found that it was unconstitutional for a school district to suspend students for wearing "on their sleeve a band of black cloth, not more than two inches wide" to classes in December 1965 to protest the war in Vietnam. *Id.* at 514. The Court stated: "In the absence of a specific showing of constitutionally valid reasons to regulate their speech, students are entitled to freedom of expression of their views." *Id.* at 511. Rather than confine a school district to arguing the student's expression constituted a "clear and present danger," the Court stated that the student may "express his opinions, even on controversial subjects like the conflict in Vietnam, if he does so without 'materially and substantially interfere(ing) with the requirements of appropriate discipline in the operation of the school' and without colliding with the rights of others." *Id.* at 513 (quoting *Burnside v. Byars*, 363 F.2d 744, 749 (1966)). Under that legal standard, *Tinker* was an easy case because the school district had sought to punish the students for a "silent, passive expression of opinion, unaccompanied by any disorder or disturbance on the part of [the students]." There was "no indication that the work of the schools or any class was disrupted." *Id.* at 508. Tinker's expression of his speech did not collide with the rights of others.

The *Tinker* case received further clarification in *Mahanoy Area School District v. B.L.*, 594 U.S. 180 (2021). In an 8–1 decision, the Court ruled that a school district violated a student's First Amendment rights when it suspended her from the cheerleading squad after she posted profanity in a social media post, made off campus and on a Saturday concerning her inability to make the cheerleading varsity squad. This case was novel because the speech was made off-campus using social media.

Both the district court and the Third Circuit had ruled for the student. *See B.L. by and through Levy v. Mahanoy Area School District,* 964 F.3d 170 (3rd Cir. 2020). Because the student's speech took place off campus, the Third Circuit concluded that *Tinker* did not apply, and the school consequently could not discipline the student for engaging in a form of pure speech. The Supreme Court granted cert. on the issue of whether the *Tinker* standard applies to student speech that occurs off campus.

Disagreeing with the Third Circuit, the Supreme Court ruled that the special characteristics that give schools additional license to regulate student speech does not always disappear when a school regulates speech that takes place off campus. While not determining all the features that might diminish a schools' right to regulate off-campus speech, the Court delineated three features that "diminish the strength of the unique educational characteristics that might call for special First Amendment leeway." These features are: (1) off-campus speech rarely places the school *in loco parentis*; (2) regulations of off-campus speech might curtail student speech during the full 24-hour day; and (3) the school has an interest in protecting a student's unpopular expression off campus as part of encouraging students to participate in a democracy.

As applied to the plaintiff in this case, the Court found that the school district did not have a strong interest in punishing the student's utterance. First, because the speech occurred in a private, off-campus establishment, the Court found that the school did not stand *in loco parentis* to try to impart good manners. Second, even under the *Tinker* standard, there was no evidence that the speech caused a "substantial disruption" to a school activity. Third, a vague concern for team morale could not meet the *Tinker* substantial interference or disruption test. Under *Tinker*, a simple "undifferentiated fear or apprehension . . . . is not enough to overcome the right to freedom of expression." *Tinker,* 393 U.S. at 508. Thus, the Court concluded that the school district violated the First Amendment rights of the student. Further, the Court offered some guidance suggesting that schools need to cautious in seeking to regulate off-campus speech merely because of its vulgarity. In the LGBTQ+ context, such a ruling certainly suggests that a school district could not treat a student adversely for participating in off-campus gay pride events or expressing controversial political views about transgender issues, even if the student uses profanity to express those views.

An additional First Amendment issue that the Supreme Court confronted in the public school context was the right of a school board to remove books from high school and junior high school libraries because they were purportedly "anti-American, anti-Christian, anti-Sem[i]tic, and just plain filthy." *Bd. of Educ. v. Pico*, 457 U.S. 853 (1982). In a plurality opinion authored by Justice Brennan, the Court found that the school district did not have "absolute discretion to remove books from their school libraries." *Id.* at 869. While a school district maintains "significant discretion to determine the content of their school libraries," they may not exercise that discretion in a "narrowly partisan or political manner." *Id.* at 870. It would be acceptable, however, for a school district to remove books because they "were pervasively vulgar." *Id.* at 871.

The result of the Court's holding was to remand the case back to the trial court for a determination if the school board had a proper rationale for removing the books. In his dissent, Justice Powell argued that no remand was necessary because it was clear that the censored books were "vulgar or racist." *Id.* at 897 (Powell, J., dissenting). In support of that argument, Justice Powell included an appendix with quotations from many of the censored books: *Soul on Ice* by Eldridge Cleaver; *A Hero Ain't Nothing But a Sandwich* by Alice Childress; *The Fixer* by Bernard Malamud; *Go Ask Alice* by Anonymous; *Slaughterhouse Five* by Kurt Vonnegut, Jr.; *Black Boy* by Richard Wright; *Laughing Boy* by Oliver LaFarge; and *The Naked Ape* by Desmond Morris. Each of these passages contained graphic, sexual scenes and explicit sexual terms. Many of the passages also contained language that made explicit racial references. In Chief Justice Burger's dissent, he describes Justice Brennan's plurality opinion as "a lavish expansion going beyond any prior holding under the First Amendment." *Pico,* 457 U.S. at 885 (Burger, C.J., dissenting).

Next, the Supreme Court ruled in favor of the school district in a student free-speech case in *Bethel School District No. 403 v. Fraser*, 478 U.S. 675 (1986). Chief Justice Burger delivered the 7–2 opinion of the Court, upholding the right of the school district to discipline a high school student, Matthew Fraser, for giving a lewd speech at a school assembly, which was allegedly prohibited by a school district conduct rule.

This is the language the school district found offensive:

> I know a man who is firm—he's firm in his pants, he's firm in his shirt, his character is firm—but most . . . . of all, his belief in you, the students of Bethel, is firm.
>
> Jeff Kuhlman is a man who takes his point and pounds it in. If necessary, he'll take an issue and nail it to the wall. He doesn't attack things in spurts—he drives hard, pushing and pushing until finally—he succeeds.
>
> Jeff is a man who will go to the very end—even the climax, for each and every one of you.
>
> So vote for Jeff for A.S.B. vice-president—he'll never come between you and the best our high school can be.

Id. at 687 (Blackmun, J., concurring). The lower courts had ruled in favor of Fraser, finding that his speech was akin to the black armband in *Tinker* because there was insufficient evidence that it had a disruptive effect on the educational process. The school district's evidence of disruption was that "[s]ome students hooted and yelled; some by gestures graphically simulated the sexual activities pointedly alluded to in respondent's speech. Other students appeared to be bewildered and embarrassed by the speech." *Id.* at 678.

The Supreme Court reversed. It noted that the First Amendment "has acknowledged limitations on the otherwise absolute interest of the speaker in reaching an unlimited audience where the speech is sexually explicit and the audience may include children." *Id.* at 684. The Court also mentioned that a "school board has the authority to remove books that are vulgar." *Id.* at 684. Further, the government has "an interest in protecting minors from exposure to vulgar and offensive spoken language." *Id.* at 684. Applying those principles, the Court concluded that:

> The First Amendment does not prevent the school officials from determining that to permit a vulgar and lewd speech such as respondent's would undermine the school's basic educational mission. A high school assembly or classroom is no place for a sexually explicit monologue directed towards an unsuspecting audience of teenage students.

Id. at 685. It was constitutional for the school to discipline a student for delivering a speech that was legally obscene because the school was entitled to "disassociate itself" from the speech in a manner that would demonstrate to others that such vulgarity is "wholly inconsistent with the 'fundamental values' of public school education." *Id.* at 685–86.

Similarly, the Supreme Court upheld the right of a school district to excise two pages of a school newspaper from publication out of concern that the newspaper article unfairly impinged on the privacy rights of some pregnant students. *See Hazelwood Sch. Dist. v. Kuhlmeier*, 484 U.S. 260 (1988). Building on the *Fraser* decision, the Court emphasized that the "determination of what manner of speech in the classroom or in school assembly is inappropriate properly rests with the school board." *Id.* at 267 (quoting *Bethel Sch. Dist.*, 478 U.S. at 683). The Court also found that a school newspaper is not subject to "traditional public forum[ ]" doctrine under which a public entity would have very limited grounds (under *Tinker*) for restricting speech, because it considered publication of the newspaper as part of a school's educational mission. The Court stated:

> Accordingly, we conclude that the standard articulated in *Tinker* for determining when a school may punish student expression need not also be the standard for determining when a school may refuse to lend its name and resources to the dissemination of student expression. Instead, we hold that educators do not offend the First Amendment by exercising editorial control over the style and content of student speech in school-sponsored expressive activities so long as their actions are reasonably related to legitimate pedagogical concerns.

Id. at 272–73.

Under this lenient standard, the Court found that the high school principal had legitimate pedagogical reasons to delete two pages of the student newspaper. In a strong dissent, Justice Brennan, joined by Justices Marshall and Blackmun, argued that the principal had violated the "First Amendment's prohibitions against censorship of any student expression that neither disrupts classwork nor invades the rights of others, and against any censorship that is not narrowly tailored to serve its purpose." *Id.* at 278 (Brennan, J., dissenting).

Finally, in 2007, the Supreme Court approved the latitude of school officials in a free speech case in *Morse v. Frederick*, 551 U.S. 393 (2007). In *Morse*, a principal had confiscated a student's banner during a school-sponsored field trip and suspended the student responsible for displaying it, because the principal interpreted the banner as promoting illegal drug use. The banner said: "BONG HiTS 4 JESUS." *Id.* at 397. Writing for a divided Court, Chief Justice Roberts concluded that the school district was entitled to restrict the student's speech in light of a school district's " 'important—indeed, perhaps compelling' interest" in deterring drug use. *Id.* at 407.

Justice Thomas concurred separately, stating that he would overturn *Tinker* because "it cannot seriously be suggested that the First Amendment 'freedom of speech' encompasses a student's right to speak in public schools." *Id.* at 419 (Thomas, J., concurring). Justice Alito concurred separately, in an opinion joined by Justice Kennedy. In contrast to Justice Thomas, they re-affirmed *Tinker* and agreed with Justice Stevens (in dissent) that the majority opinion "provides no support for any restriction of speech that can plausibly be interpreted as commenting on any political or social issue, including speech on issues such as 'the wisdom of the war on drugs or of legalizing marijuana for medicinal use.' " *Id.* at 422 (Alito, J., concurring, quoting Steven, J., dissenting). The *Morse* holding may, therefore, be confined to the sensitive topic of illegal, student drug use.

These cases suggest three different approaches to the First Amendment rights of high school students. First, school officials may restrict speech that is "vulgar" even though it is not legally "obscene" without a showing of disruption at school, but that power may not extend to off-campus speech. Second, school officials may restrict speech that is related to a school project when the limitation is reasonably related to legitimate educational concerns. Third, school officials may prohibit speech that is neither vulgar nor related to a school-sponsored activity only if it causes substantial and material disruption of the school's operation or harms the rights of others. We will next consider how these principles have been applied in the LGBTQ+ context.

§ 8.2 FREE SPEECH RIGHTS OF STUDENTS: LGBTQ+ CONTEXT

A. PROM

Lower courts have typically handled cases involving the First Amendment rights of LGBTQ+ students by ruling in favor of the students. In *Fricke v. Lynch*, 491 F. Supp. 381 (D.R.I. 1980), a gay male student, Aaron Fricke, sought a preliminary injunction to prevent the school district from barring him from bringing a male date, Paul Guilbert, to the senior prom. The district court granted the preliminary injunction despite evidence that the school principal had a good faith concern that

Fricke's attendance at the prom could cause a risk of violence. In the previous year, when Guilbert sought to attend the junior prom, he was subject to adverse "widespread community and student reaction" and the school found it necessary to arrange "an escort system" for him to go to classes. *Id.* at 383. After Fricke made his request to bring a male date to the prom, "a student shoved and, the next day, punched [Fricke, necessitating] five stiches under [his] right eye." *Id.* at 384.

Focusing on the fourth factor from *United States v. O'Brien*, 391 U.S. 367 (1968)—whether the incidental restriction on alleged first amendment freedoms is not greater than essential to the furtherance of that interest—the district court ruled in favor of Fricke. The court granted the request for a preliminary injunction because it concluded "meaningful security measures" were possible that would have allowed him to attend the prom and not stifle his freedom of expression. *Fricke*, 491 F. Supp. 381 at 388.

The *Fricke* case was decided before *Fraser* provided additional latitude to school administrators to avoid disruptions at school and *Hazelwood* allowed additional latitude to limit school activities. Given the evidence that two adverse incidents had already occurred on school grounds, and the prom was a school-sponsored event, it is not clear that other courts would agree with the *Fricke* analysis. But *Fricke* is certainly distinguishable from *Morse v. Frederick* in that a school district has no compelling interest in preventing a male student from bringing a male date to prom in light of the recent same-sex marriage cases. *See Obergefell v. Hodges*, 576 U.S. 644 (2015) (discussed in *Nutshell* § 5.6). Further, the argument that two male students dancing together at a school prom would be a disruptive activity is not likely to be given serious weight today.

Other school districts have subsequently tried to ban LGBTQ+ students from prom.

On May 19, 2006, the principal at a high school in Gary, Indiana "stretched her arms across the door of the senior prom, blocking [K.K.] Logan's entrance because Logan was wearing a dress; at the time, Logan identified as a feminine male." Lambda Legal brought a lawsuit on Logan's behalf. The school district settled and issued a public apology at which is promised "to ensure that something like this does not happen again." *See Lambda Legal Reaches Settlement Agreement with Indiana School District After Transgender Student Was Barred from Prom*, Jan. 28, 2011, https://legacy.lambdalegal.org/news/in_20110128_reaches-agreement.

In 2009, the Russell, Alabama school district tried to bar a lesbian from attending the prom. After receiving a demand letter from the ACLU, it reversed its decision. *See Alabama School Reverses Decision to Bar Lesbian Student From Attending Prom With Her Girlfriend*, ACLU, Nov. 20, 2009, https://www.aclu.org/press-releases/alabama-school-reverses-decision-bar-lesbian-student-attending-prom-her-girlfriend. In 2010, school district officials in Fulton, Mississippi sought to bar a lesbian student from wearing a tuxedo and attending prom with her girlfriend. In response to a demand letter, the school board issued a statement that it was canceling prom for all students. The ACLU filed suit and attained relief in the district court where the judge said:

> The record shows Constance has been openly gay since eighth grade and she intended to communicate a message by wearing a tuxedo and to express her identity through attending prom with a same-sex date. The Court finds this expression and communication of her viewpoint is the type of speech that falls squarely within the purview of the First Amendment. The Court is also of the opinion that the motive behind the School Board's cancellation of the prom, or withdrawal of their sponsorship, was Constance's requests and the ACLU's demand letter sent on her behalf.

Court Rules that Mississippi School Violated First Amendment Rights of Lesbian Student, ACLU, March 23, 2010, https://www.aclu.org/press-releases/court-rules-mississippi-school-violated-first-amendment-rights-lesbian-student.

The parents organized a private prom, which was open to all students, so the Court did not insist that the school district reinstate its own prom. *Id.*

Students continue to report instances of discrimination at prom. For an excellent website that collects these stories, see Meredith Nardino, *Prom Discrimination: Student Stories From All 50 States,* DO SOMETHING, April 26, 2019, https://dosomething.org/article/prom-discrimination-stories.

B. DRESS CODES

Similarly, First Amendment case law has been used to protect a high school student who was frequently sent home from school for wearing " 'girls' make-up, shirts, and fashion accessories to school." *Doe v. Yunits*, No. 001060A, 2000 WL 33162199, at *1 (Mass. Super. Ct. Oct. 11, 2000). In ruling in favor of the student, the court admonished the school district for being:

> [U]nable to distinguish between instances of conduct connected to plaintiff's expression of her female gender identity, such as the wearing of a wig or padded bra, and separate from it, such as grabbing a male student's buttocks or blowing kisses to a male student. . . . [E]xpression of gender identity through dress can be divorced from conduct in school that warrants punishment, regardless of the gender or gender identity of the offender.

Id. at *5.

Nonetheless, the Second Circuit ruled in favor of the county in a case outside of the public school and gender identity context, but which also involved a desire to wear certain female clothing. In *Zalewska v. County of Sullivan*, 316 F.3d 314 (2d Cir. 2003), plaintiff Grazyna Zalewska objected to a new county rule, requiring all van drivers to wear pants. She preferred to wear a skirt as "an expression of a deeply held cultural value." *Id.* at 318. The Second Circuit found that her desire to wear a skirt was not sufficiently specific to constitute a particularized or comprehensible message. In contrast to *Yunits*, where the plaintiff's "message was readily understood by others in his [sic] high school context, because it was such a break from the norm . . . . a woman today wearing a dress or a skirt on the job does not automatically signal any particularized message about her culture or beliefs." *Id.* at 320. So, a decision to wear a skirt appeared to only receive First Amendment protection when someone assigned the male sex at birth decided to wear a skirt but not if someone assigned a female sex at birth decided not to wear one.

A more recent district court case suggests that there is First Amendment protection for clothing choices. Tracy Monegain, a former Virginia Department of Motor Vehicles employee sued her employer after it instituted a new dress code that was written specifically to bar her from wearing traditional female attire. *Monegain v. Department of Motor Vehicles,* 491 F. Supp.3d 117, 128 (E.D. Va. 2020). Monegain was fired shortly after she returned to work following gender reassignment surgery. She sued under Title VII and Section 1983 (alleged First Amendment, Equal Protection, and Due Process violations). The court ruled for her on her first amendment claim, finding that "Monegain alleges sufficient facts plausibly stating that her presentation in dress associated with the female gender was speech 'upon a matter of public concern' and just speech 'as an employee about a matter of personal interest.' " *Id.* at 136. There is no record of any appeal in this case.

Dress code rules are also challenged under Title VII. Title VII is discussed in *Nutshell* Chapter 3. For example, Braidwood Management, Inc., which describes itself as a "Christian" business "enforces a sex-specific dress code that disallows gender-non-conforming behavior." *Braidwood Management, Inc. v. EEOC,* 70 F.4th 914, 919 (5th Cir. 2023). The district court had found that the dress code policies did not violate Title VII because they applied equally to both sexes. The district court also ruled for Braidwood on religious freedom grounds. The Fifth Circuit affirmed the district court's religious freedom decisions while assuming that the employer was "breaking EEOC guidance" and were "at risk of being prosecuted." *Id.* at 926. The religious freedom arguments will be considered in *Nutshell* Chapter 9.

C. T-SHIRT CASES

Cases involving student t-shirts are subject to the general case law, discussed above. A school district can restrict a student's t-shirt if it is "vulgar" but not on the grounds that the t-shirt is, itself, a school-sponsored activity. If the t-shirt is not vulgar, then it can only be excluded if it would cause a serious disruption at the school. Because "vulgar" is not the same as "legally obscene," there is some ambiguity about the meaning of that term. And whether a "serious disruption" might occur depends, in part, on the reaction of the audience to the speech itself. Finally, the potential harm to other students is a subjective factor, especially if the speech is suppressed before such harm could occur.

The case law has typically involved schools trying to censor *anti*-LGBTQ+ speech. In *Harper v. Poway Unified School District*, 445 F.3d 1166 (9th Cir. 2006), *judgment vacated on mootness grounds*, 549 U.S. 1262 (2007), Tyler Harper wore a t-shirt to school that said on the front: "BE ASHAMED, OUR SCHOOL EMBRACED WHAT GOD HAS CONDEMNED" and, on the back, read: "HOMOSEXUALITY IS SHAMEFUL." He wore that t-shirt to protest a "Day of Silence" that was held to "teach tolerance of others, particularly those of a different sexual orientation." *Id.* at 1171. Harper was required to remain in the principal's office for most of the school day; he was not suspended. *Id.* at 1173. The justification for forcing him to stay in the principal's office was that there was concern about possible "physical conflict on campus" due to some incidents in a previous year and the response to Tyler's t-shirt that year. *Id.* at 1172.

Tyler brought an action in federal court challenging what he called his "suspension." The district court denied his motion for a preliminary injunction, and he appealed. *Id.* at 1173. The Ninth Circuit analyzed the case under *Tinker*. *Tinker* had recognized that school districts can regulate students even if it is "the very sort of political speech that would be afforded First Amendment protection outside of the public school setting." *Id.* at 1176. The two exceptions recognized by *Tinker* were: (1) speech that would "impinge upon the rights of other students," and (2) speech that would result in "substantial disruption of or material interference with school activities." *Tinker*, 393 U.S. at 509, 514.

With respect to the first exception, the Ninth Circuit found that the speech impinged upon the rights of other students because it was detrimental to the psychological health and well-being of young gay and lesbian students by demeaning them. Citing extensive studies, the Ninth Circuit concluded "it is well established that attacks on students on the basis of their sexual orientation are harmful not only to the students' health and welfare, but also to their educational performance and their ultimate potential for success in life." *Id.* at 1179. In response to a scathing dissent by Judge Kozinski, the majority opinion also offered some qualifications to its conclusion.

> Accordingly, we limit our holding to instances of derogatory and injurious remarks directed at students' minority status such as race, religion, and sexual orientation. Moreover, our decision is based not only on the type and degree of injury the speech involved causes to impressionable young people, but on the locale in which it takes place. . . . Accordingly, we do not condone the use in public colleges or other public institutions of higher learning of restrictions similar to those permitted here.

Id. at 1183. Because the court relied on the first exception, it did not determine whether the substantial disruption factor could be met.

In another t-shirt case, *Nuxoll v. Indian Prairie School District No. 204*, 523 F.3d 668 (7th Cir. 2008), the Seventh Circuit ruled in favor of the high school student. Alexander Nuxoll sought to wear a t-shirt saying "Be Happy, Not Gay" following the day after the school's "Day of Silence." *Id.* at 670. The school district banned the t-shirt, considering it to be a derogatory comment on a particular sexual orientation in conflict with school district policy. The district court judge denied the student's motion for a preliminary injunction.

On appeal, the Seventh Circuit reversed in an opinion written by Judge Posner. He found that, " 'Be Happy, Not Gay' is only tepidly negative; 'derogatory' or 'demeaning' seems too strong a characterization." *Id.* at 676. Further, he found the record too "scanty" to justify banning the t-shirt out of fear of a substantial disruption. *Id.* at 676. After the Seventh Circuit decision, there was a remand to district court. Ultimately, the Seventh Circuit affirmed a permanent injunction to permit the student to wear the t-shirt as well as nominal damages of $25 for each student precluded by the high school from displaying their desired messages on certain days. *See Zamecnik v. Indian Prairie Sch. Dist.*, 636 F.3d 874 (7th Cir. 2011). An earlier case reached a similar result. *See Chambers v. Babbitt,* 145 F. Supp. 2d 1068 (D. Minn. 2001) (school district not permitted to ban sweatshirt that said, "Straight Pride," where there was not a "reasonable belief that such expression could lead to substantial disruption of the school environment or material interference with school activities.")

The First Circuit reached a different result on a similar case involving a seventh-grade student, L.M. L.M. wore a black t-shirt to school that said "There Are Only Two Genders" in black capitalized letters with thick white outlines. *L.M. v. Town of Middleborough, Massachusetts,* 103 F.4th 854 (1st Cir. 2024). The school had a dress code that said, in part:

> Clothing must not state, imply, or depict hate speech or imagery that target[s] groups based on race, ethnicity, gender, sexual orientation, gender identity, religious affiliation, or any other classification.
>
> Any other apparel that the administration determines to be unacceptable to our community standards will not be allowed.

Id. at 861.

It is hard to know if such reasoning will be supported under the Trump administration's policies regarding gender identity. The First Circuit referenced the ability of the school district to enforce "community standards," implying that school districts can support transgender rights as part of their community standards. With the Trump administration aggressively requiring school districts not to endorse when it calls "gender ideology," (*See Nutshell* Chapter 3) it may not be permissible for school districts that receive federal funds from enforcing that kind of community standard. The reader should follow current developments in this area.

The cases discussed above concerned students who want to wear t-shirts that might be offensive to the LGBTQ+ community. There are also cases involving t-shirts worn by students who are supportive of the rights of LGBTQ+ people. For example, in *Young v. Giles County Board of Education,* 181 F. Supp.3d 459 (M.D. Tenn. 2015), Rebecca Young obtained a preliminary injunction to protect her free speech interests. She had worn a t-shirt to school on her first day of her senior year that said: "Some People Are Gay, Get Over It." *Id.* at 461. The principal summoned Young to the front of the school cafeteria and said that she could wear that t-shirt to school or "any other shirt referencing LGBT rights." *Id.* at 462. In ruling for Young, the court emphasized that it was problematic that the principal only prohibited messages "*supporting* the LGBT community." *Id.* at 464 (emphasis in original). The *Young* decision is consistent with an earlier case involving the disclosure of a student's sexual orientation although not through a t-shirt. *See Henkle v. Gregory,* 150 F. Supp. 2d 1067 (D. Nev. 2001) (student had First Amendment right to be able to disclose his sexual orientation without experiencing retaliation).

§ 8.3 FREE SPEECH RIGHTS OF FACULTY AND STAFF TO ADVOCATE FOR OR CRITICIZE LGBTQ+ RIGHTS

Another area of the law that has raised First Amendment principles is the right of faculty, administrators and students to express their political views without fear of sanctions or discrimination from public officials. The leading case on this issue is *Pickering v. Board of Education*, 391 U.S. 563 (1968). Marvin Pickering, a school teacher, had written a letter to the local newspaper criticizing how the school board had spent previous tax increases, and urging voters to vote against a proposed tax increase. At the disciplinary hearing, at which he was dismissed, the School Board found that some of his statements were false, including statements about how much was expended on athletics. *Id.* at 572. The Illinois Supreme Court upheld his dismissal, concluding that publication of the letter was detrimental to the best interests of the school. *Id.* at 567.

The Supreme Court reversed. In an opinion authored by Justice Marshall, the Court found that "in a case such as this, absent proof of false statements knowingly or recklessly made by him, a teacher's exercise of his right to speak on issues of public importance may not furnish the basis for his dismissal from public employment." *Id.* at 574. This "knowingly or recklessly made" test stemmed from the landmark case, *New York Times Co. v. Sullivan*, 376 U.S. 254 (1964).

The *Pickering* test does not give public employees complete freedom to criticize their employer but does give them significant legal protection when "the fact of employment is only tangentially and insubstantially involved in the subject matter of the public communication made by a teacher." *Id.* at 574. In this case, the teacher made no statements that would appear to have stemmed from his special knowledge as a teacher; anyone could have commented on the publicly-available school budget figures. The *Pickering* test can provide useful protection when public school teachers want to comment on controversial LGBTQ+ issues in a public forum.

While not citing *Pickering* specifically, a Maine district court considered similar principles in resolving whether a teacher could claim retaliation for asserting her First Amendment rights. *See MacDonald v. Brewer School Department,* 651 F. Supp.3d 243 (D. Maine 2023). Plaintiff Michelle MacDonald was a high school English teacher who was well known for her LGBTQ+ advocacy. She alleged that she faced retaliation because of her support for LGBTQ+ rights at the school. The court found that she met the advocacy for matters of public concern requirement even if her advocacy only occurred internally at the school. It concluded that "Statements made only inside the workplace may support a claim for First Amendment retaliation even though they are not shared with the general public." *Id.* at 268. It rejected the school principal's motion to dismiss because he had chosen not to rehire plaintiff as curriculum leader and had moved her to a small classroom. *Id.* at 268. There is no record of an appeal in this case, so it presumably settled after this district court decision.

A different First Amendment issue involving faculty that has begun to emerge is whether a public university can require a faculty member to address a transgender student by their preferred pronoun. That issue was raised in *Meriwether v. Hartop,* 992 F.3d 492 (6th Cir. 2021). The Sixth Circuit applied the *Pickering* framework and concluded that the professor's refusal to use the student's preferred pronoun involved a matter of public concern. Applying the *Pickering* balancing test, the court concluded that his refusal to use particular gender-identity-based pronouns during political philosophy classes outweighed the state's interest. The professor also made a free exercise of religion claim. Because of the hostility that some university officials exhibited towards the professor's religious beliefs, the Sixth Circuit found that the government may not refuse to extend exemptions to cases of religious hardship without a compelling reason. Although the Sixth Circuit decided this case before the Supreme Court decided *Fulton v. City of Philadelphia,* 594 U.S. 180 (2021) (discussed in *Nutshell* § 9.1), its reasoning parallels the *Fulton* analysis. And, as discussed above, it is hard to know what policies may emerge from the Trump education department. Will schools be required to gender children by reference to the sex assigned at birth in order to receive federal funds? Again, this is an area of emerging policy that the reader should update.

Finally, an additional First Amendment issue concerns the rights of student organizations to receive university or public school funds on a nondiscriminatory basis. Some of those cases are now resolved under a federal statute, discussed in *Nutshell* § 8.2. But they can also involve constitutional principles. In *Rosenberger v. Rector and Visitors of the University of Virginia*, 515 U.S. 819 (1995), the Supreme Court held in a 5–4 decision that a university's decision to deny funding to a newspaper published with a Christian editorial viewpoint violated the First Amendment. The dispute between the majority and the dissent involved the issue of whether government funding of this speech would constitute a violation of the Establishment Clause. Everyone agreed that the decision was a content-based decision that otherwise would violate the First Amendment. Justice Kennedy's opinion for the Court concluded there was no Establishment Clause problem because the university is facilitating the speech of others rather than expressing the speech itself. *Id.* at 834. Justice Souter's dissent (which was joined by Justices Stevens, Ginsburg and Breyer) emphasized that the Court's decision was permitting the "direct funding of core religious activities by an arm of the State" in violation of the Establishment Clause. *Id.* at 863 (Souter, J., dissenting).

Despite the *Rosenberger* decision, a university may refuse to fund student organizations if they refuse to abide by university nondiscrimination policies. That kind of refusal is not considered to be an unconstitutional viewpoint discrimination under *Rosenberger*. In *Christian Legal Society Chapter of the University of California v. Martinez*, 561 U.S. 661 (2010), the Supreme Court, in a 5–4 opinion authored by Justice Ginsburg, upheld the ability of a law school to deny funding to a student organization that refused to open eligibility for membership and leadership to all students, including the LGBTQ+ community. Drawing on a long line of cases concerning "limited public forums," the Court found that it was constitutional for the law school to apply "only indirect pressure" on the student group's membership policies because the only impact of the law school's rule was a denial of official law school recognition. *Id.* at 682. Unlike the freedom of association cases, discussed in *Nutshell* § 8.7, the organization was not compelled to include unwanted members in its group. *Id.* at 682. In a sharply worded dissent, Justice Alito argued that the law school's policy was explicitly content-based and constituted discrimination indistinguishable from the discrimination disallowed in *Rosenberger*.

Subsequent cases draw into question the implications of the *Christian Legal Society* precedent. For example, in *Business Leaders in Christ v. University of Iowa*, 991 F.3d 969 (8th Cir. 2021), the Eighth Circuit concluded that the university could not use its nondiscrimination policy to bar university recognition for a Christian group in the business school, that would bar participation by lesbians or gay men, because it had not consistently applied that nondiscrimination policy to other student groups. *Id.* at 973–74. *See also Intervarsity Christian Fellowship/USA v. The University of Iowa*, 408 F. Supp.3d 960 (S.D. Iowa 2019) (granting summary judgment to national student religious organization that did not want to comply with university's nondiscrimination policy; applying strict scrutiny because policy was not content neutral); *Intervarsity Christian Fellowship/USA v. Board of Governors of Wayne State University*, 5 F.4th 855 8th Cir. 2021 (affirming grant of summary judgment to plaintiffs).

§ 8.4 FREE SPEECH RIGHTS OF TEACHERS: LGBTQ+ CONTEXT

A. TEACHERS WHO ARE OPEN ABOUT THEIR SEXUAL ORIENTATION

The rights of the LGBTQ+ community to be open about their sexual orientation received modest support in *Acanfora v. Board of Education*, 491 F.2d 498 (4th Cir. 1974). Joseph Acanfora had failed to list his membership in "Homophiles of Penn State" in response to a question on a teaching application asking him to list all of his extracurricular activities. He failed to list this information because he "believed disclosure would foreclose his opportunity to be considered for employment on an equal basis with other applicants." *Id.* at 501. After he was employed as a junior high school teacher, Acanfora "appeared with his parents on a program designed to help parents and homosexual children cope with the problems that confront them. Acanfora also consented to other television, radio, and press interviews." *Id.* at 500. His teaching position was rescinded; he challenged that action as a violation of his First Amendment rights. The school district successfully argued in the district court that the television programs tended to "spark controversy," included an element of "sensationalism" and "exhibited an indifference to the bounds of propriety governing the behavior of teachers." *Id.* at 500. The school district also acknowledged that it would not have hired him if he had disclosed his membership in the "Homophiles of Penn State" organization. *Id.* at 503 n.3.

On appeal, the Fourth Circuit found that his public statements were protected by the *Pickering* standard. The issue was one of public interest and there was "no evidence that the interviews disrupted the school, substantially impaired his capacity as a teacher, or gave the school officials reasonable grounds to forecast that these results would flow from what he said." *Id.* at 500–01. Nonetheless, in an opinion authored by former Supreme Court Justice Tom Clark (who was retired and sitting by designation on the Fourth Circuit), the Fourth Circuit upheld the adverse employment action as a result of Acanfora's deliberate omission of information in the employment application. "Acanfora purposely misled the school officials so he could circumvent, not challenge, what he considers to be their unconstitutional employment practices. He cannot now invoke the process of the court to obtain a ruling on an issue that he practiced deception to avoid." *Id.* at 504.

The Fourth Circuit's decision, therefore, provided some protection to LGBTQ+ school teachers who wish to speak openly about their sexual orientation, after being hired, but did nothing to prevent a school district from failing to hire an applicant due to that person's status as a member of the LGBTQ+ community. This decision, however, is consistent with the trend that members of the LGBTQ+ community received some protection under the First Amendment before receiving privacy or equality protections.

The contrast between protection under the First and Fourteenth Amendments for public school teachers became even clearer in the Tenth Circuit's decision in *National Gay Task Force v. Board of Education*, 729 F.2d 1270 (10th Cir. 1984), *aff'd by an equally divided Court*, 470 U.S. 903 (1985). An Oklahoma statute provided that a teacher could be refused employment, dismissed, or suspended for engaging in "public homosexual conduct or activity." *Id.* at 1272. "Public homosexual activity" was defined as engaging in the "crime against nature" with a person of the same sex in a manner that is "indiscreet and not practiced in private." *Id.* at 1272. "Public homosexual conduct" was defined as including "advocating, soliciting, imposing, encouraging or promoting public or private homosexual activity in a manner that creates a substantial risk that such conduct will come to the attention of school children or school employees." *Id.* at 1272.

The National Gay Task Force challenged the constitutional validity of this statute. The district court found both the ban on conduct and activity to be constitutional. *Id.* at 1272. On appeal, the Tenth Circuit found that the ban on homosexual activity did not violate the Equal Protection Clause of the Fourteenth Amendment, but found that the homosexual conduct provision did not satisfy the *Pickering* test, because there was not a requirement that the "expression results in a material or substantial interference or disruption in the normal activities of the school." *Id.* at 1274. The dissenting judge would have affirmed the district court decision, upholding the validity of the broad ban on "homosexual conduct." *Id.* at 1275 (Barrett, C.J., dissenting). Given the constitutionality of statutes, such as Oklahoma's "crimes against nature," before the Supreme Court's decision in *Lawrence v. Texas*, 539 U.S. 558 (2003), the plaintiffs could only receive protection under the First Amendment for speaking publicly about their sexual orientation but could not receive protection under the Fourteenth Amendment to protect their right to engage in sexual activity.

First Amendment protections, however, are not always available for public school employees. Guidance counselor Marjorie Rowland was fired after she told various school personnel that she was bisexual and had a female lover. *Rowland v. Mad River Local Sch. Dist.*, 730 F.2d 444, 445 (6th Cir. 1984). She challenged that termination in federal court and obtained a successful jury verdict. *Id.* at 448. In a 2–1 decision, the Sixth Circuit reversed. Rather than rely on the *Pickering* test to determine if the termination were constitutional, the Sixth Circuit relied on the following passage from the Supreme Court's decision in *Connick v. Myers*, 461 U.S. 138, 146 (1983):

> When a public employee speaks not as a citizen upon matters of public concern, but instead as an employee upon matters of personal interest, absent the most unusual circumstances, a federal court is not the appropriate forum in which to review the wisdom of a personnel decision taken by a public agency allegedly in reaction to the employee's behavior.

Because Rowland limited her discussion of her sexual orientation to others at the workplace, rather than in a broader, public forum, the Sixth Circuit found that her "own treatment of the issue of her sexual preference indicates that she recognized that the matter was not one of public concern." 730 F.2d at 449.

The dissent recognized that Rowland had not deliberately thrust her speech into a public context but the public nature of her speech was what ultimately led to her discharge:

> [T]he speech may not have had its origin in an overt attempt to exercise freedom of speech. But speech it was. It revealed plaintiff's status as a homosexual in what at the outset she may have presumed to be a confidential relationship. When, however, that speech was spread to school authorities and the community, plaintiff's adherence to her right both to be what she was and to state the fact brought down on her head the wrath of some parents and termination of her job by the ruling authorities of her school.

Id. at 453 (Edwards, C.J., dissenting).

With respect to the jury's Equal Protection verdict in her favor, the Sixth Circuit found that there "was absolutely no evidence to support the finding that Ms. Rowland was treated differently from other similarly situated employees. There was no evidence of how other employees with different sexual preferences were treated." *Id.* at 450. In other words, the majority did not believe there was sufficient evidence to conclude that a male employee, who confessed to being in love with a woman, would not have been treated adversely. In a scathing dissent, Judge Edwards said: "My colleague's opinion seems to me to treat this case, *sub silento*, as if it involved only a single person and a sick one at that—in short, that plaintiff's admission of homosexual status was sufficient in itself to justify her termination." *Id.* at 454 (Edwards, C.J., dissenting). (Both the majority and dissent described Rowland as a "homosexual" although she described herself as bisexual.)

Rowland sought certiorari in the United States Supreme Court. In a 6–2 decision, issued eleven years after Rowland was suspended from her position, the Court denied her petition. *See Rowland v. Mad River Local School District,* 470 U.S. 1009 (1985) (Justice Powell did not participate in the petition). In an unusually strong opinion, Justice Brennan, joined by Justice Marshall, argued that the Court should have heard the case. With respect to the free speech claim, Brennan noted that prior cases adverse to the interests of employees involved statements that "arguably had some disruptive effects in the workplace." *Id.* at 1013. This case, by contrast, involved "no critical statements, but rather an entirely harmless mention of a fact about petitioner that apparently triggered certain prejudices held by her supervisors." *Id.* Brennan argued that the Court should therefore have accepted certiorari to decide "the open question whether nondisruptive speech . . . . can constitutionally serve as the basis for termination under the First Amendment." *Id.* at 1014.

Justice Brennan's equal protection argument, however, stands as one of the strongest statements about the constitutional rights of the LGBTQ+ community. He concluded that "homosexuals" are a significant and insular minority that has faced "immediate and severe opprobrium" and are "particularly powerless to pursue their rights openly in the political arena." *Id.* at 1014. Thus, he concluded that actions taken against this group should receive "strict, or at least heightened, scrutiny by this Court." *Id.* at 1014. Although the Court has subsequently voted in favor of plaintiffs in cases raising issues of sexual orientation, equal protection violations, a majority of the Court has never concluded that strict or heightened scrutiny should attach to those cases. For a discussion of the Rowland case and its relationship to current struggles for the rights of LGBTQ+ teachers, *see* MARGARET A. NASH & KAREN L. GRAVES, MAD RIVER, MARJORIE ROWLAND, AND THE QUEST FOR LGBTQ TEACHERS' RIGHTS (2022).

The question of the scope of teachers' rights to mention their own sexual orientation is an ongoing issue. Florida's "Parental Rights in Education" law, which opponents called the "Don't Say Gay" bill, raised this question. The Florida legislature passed this law, HB 1557, on March 28, 2022. The bill prohibits classroom instruction on sexual orientation or gender identity before the fourth grade and requires such instruction to be "age-appropriate or developmentally appropriate" thereafter.

In 2024, Florida education officials and civil rights attorneys reached a settlement in this case. Students and teachers can discuss sexual orientation and gender identity so long as it is not part of instruction. Similar bills have been passed in Alabama, Arkansas, Indiana, Iowa, Kentucky, and North Carolina. *See Florida teachers can discuss LGBTQ topics under "Don't Say Gay" law, settlement says*, March 11, 2024, https://www.npr.org/2024/03/11/1237730819/florida-dont-say-gay-law-settlement-lgbtq.

B. CURRICULUM CONTENT

Courts have struggled with the extension of the *Pico* line of cases to issues involving censorship of gay rights themes in the curriculum. The school board for Madison High School cancelled a proposed Tolerance Day program when the program organizer insisted that a lesbian would be one of the speakers who would help lead some classroom discussions after a mandatory assembly. *See Solmitz v. Me. Sch. Admin. Dist. No. 59*, 495 A.2d 812, 815 (Me. 1985). Rather than view this action as censorship of a controversial point of view, as in *Pico*, the Maine Supreme Court, in a unanimous opinion, emphasized that "the Board cancelled the *entire* program in the face of threats of disruptive activity by some members of the community." *Id.* at 820. Teachers were free to talk about homosexuality in their regular classrooms. The Maine Supreme Court also refused to follow *Pico* because it did not consider the individual classrooms to be a "limited public forum." *Id.* at 820.

Similarly, the Fourth Circuit found that Margaret Boring, a public high school teacher, did not have a First Amendment right to determine what play was produced by her theatre students. The Fourth Circuit found that her decision to choose a play with an explicit lesbian theme was governed by *Connick* because a teacher's selection of a reading list is not a matter of public concern. *Boring v. Buncombe Cty. Bd. of Educ.*, 136 F.3d 364, 369 (4th Cir. 1998) (en banc). The en banc panel concluded that the teacher did not have a constitutionally protected right to select a particular play because (1) play was part of school's curriculum, (2) the selection of the play did not involve a matter of public concern that would give it constitutional protection, and (3) school officials had a legitimate pedagogical interest in regulating that speech.

The issue of how much control states and school districts can exert on teachers' pedagogical decisions will be further considered in the challenges to Florida's "Don't Say Gay" bill. The Florida law, which took effect on July 1, 2022, provides: "Classroom instruction by school personnel or third parties on sexual orientation or gender identity may not occur in kindergarten through grade 3 or in a manner that is not age-appropriate or developmentally appropriate for students in accordance with state standards." Educators who violate this law can be disciplined or terminated. Aside from constitutional issues raised by this law, educators are also entitled to protection under Title VII and Title IX. In light of the *Bostock* decision, (discussed in *Nutshell* § 3). LGBTQ+ educators and staff should not be subject to sexual orientation discrimination if they, for example, are subjected to harassment or differential treatment because of this law. As discussed above, *Nutshell* § 8.4(A), a settlement, was reached in Florida. Students and teachers can now discuss sexual orientation and gender identity issues in the classroom so long as it is not part of formal instruction. However, the law was not repealed, and Florida Governor Ron DeSantis has called it a major win, because it forbids classroom curriculum dealing with LGBTQ+ topics. *See What Florida's "Don't Say Gay' settlement changes and what restrictions remain,* March 14, 2004, PBS NEWS HOUR, https://www.pbs.org/newshour/show/what-floridas-dont-say-gay-settlement-changes-and-what-restrictions-remain.

Relying on *Pico,* courts have sometimes rebuffed school district efforts to move books from their library. *See Case v. Unified Sch. Dist. No. 233*, 908 F. Supp. 864 (D. Kan. 1995) (attempted censorship of books involving same-sex relationships; injunction granted to plaintiffs). In recent years, however, school districts have successfully challenged allegations that they are unconstitutionally banning books when they remove them from their library. *See, e.g., C.K.-W by and through T.K. v. Wentzille R-IV School District*, 619 F. Supp.3d 906 (E.D. Mo. 2022), a court criticized Justice Brennan's opinion in *Pico* and upheld a school district's authority to remove books based on "educational suitability" or "pervasive[ ] vulgar[ity]." *Id.* at 915. Similarly, the Fifth Circuit has ruled that the right to receive information does not apply to challenge a library's decisions about which books to buy, keep, or remove. *See Little v. Llano County,* 138 F.4th 834 (5th Cir. 2025). Because of the fractured nature of the *Pico* precedent, the Fifth Circuit said that "*Pico* is of no precedential value as to the application of the First Amendment to these issues." *Id.* at 844.

The Supreme Court has also strengthened the right of parents to complain about public school curriculum. In *Mahmoud v. Taylor,* 145 S. Ct. 2332 (2025), the Supreme Court held that parents had a First Amendment, free exercise of religion right to object to certain instruction. Parents had a right to request their children not be exposed to certain storybooks. This case will be discussed further in *Nutshell* Chapter 9, but it may be a harbinger of increased authority of parents to object to curriculum that is supportive of the LGBTQ+ community.

§ 8.5 STATUTORY PROTECTIONS FOR LGBTQ+ PUBLIC SCHOOL GROUPS

Congress enacted the Equal Access Act ("EAA") to prohibit public secondary schools which receive federal financial assistance from "deny[ing] equal access or a fair opportunity to, or discriminat[ing] against, any students who wish to conduct a meeting within that limited open forum on the basis of the religious, political, philosophical, or other content of the speech at such meetings." 20 U.S.C. § 4071(a) (2003). Nonetheless, the Act also provides that it shall not be "construed to limit the authority of the school, its agent or employees, to maintain order and discipline on school premises, to protect the well-being of students and faculty, and to assure that attendance of students at meetings is voluntary." 20 U.S.C. § 4071(f) (2003).

Although Congress may have enacted the EAA primarily to protect the rights of voluntary student religious groups, it has been used extensively to require school districts to allow students to form various gay-straight student organizations. *See, e.g.*, *Straights & Gays for Equal. (SAGE) v. Osseo Area Sch. Dist. No. 279*, 471 F.3d 908 (8th Cir. 2006); *Boyd Cty. High Sch. Gay Straight All. v. Bd. of Educ.*, 258 F. Supp. 2d 667 (E.D. Ky. 2003); *Colin v. Orange Unified Sch. Dist.*, 83 F. Supp. 2d 1135 (C.D. Cal. 2000); *E. High Gay/Straight All. v. Bd. of Educ.*, 81 F. Supp. 2d 1166 (D. Utah 1999).

Some school districts have tried to use the *Fraser* "lewd" exception to bar LGBTQ+ student organizations on the ground that schools can restrict sexually explicit material. *Compare Gay-Straight All. of Okeechobee High Sch. v. Sch. Bd. of Okeechobee Cty.*, 483 F. Supp. 2d 1224 (S.D. Fla. 2007) (granting preliminary injunction to high school student association) with *Caudillo v. Lubbock Indep. Sch. Dist.*, 311 F. Supp. 2d 550 (N.D. Tex. 2004) (granting summary judgment for school district under EAA where gay-straight student association had a website with sexually explicit content and school district had a policy against discussion of sexual activity and conduct as well as birth control methods other than abstinence).

§ 8.6 OTHER RESTRICTIONS ON FREE SPEECH

Although schools have been the locus of most of the free speech cases involving the LGBTQ+ community, other state restrictions have also generated First Amendment considerations. Bans on drag shows have been the most recent foray into free speech restrictions.

A Tennessee restriction on drag shows has generated a legal challenge. The Tennessee law made it an offense to "perform adult cabaret entertainment: (A) On public property; or (B) In a location where the adult cabaret entertainment could be viewed by a person who is not an adult." Tenn. Code Ann. § 7–51–1407(c)(1)(2023). In a pre-enforcement challenge, the district court entered judgment in favor of the plaintiff theater organization. *See Friends of Georges, Inc. v. Mulroy,* 675 F. Supp.3d 831 (W.D. Tenn. 2023). On appeal, the Sixth Circuit reversed on standing grounds, concluding that the plaintiff had no pre-enforcement injury and thereby lacked standing. *See Friends of George's Inc. v. Mulroy,* 108 F.4th 431 (6th Cir. 2024). The Sixth Circuit interpreted the statute to be limited to those situations where children could be viewing the performances.

By contrast, the Eleventh Circuit affirmed a district court case that enjoined enforcement of a Florida statute that prohibited exposure of children to "adult live performance." *See HM Florida-ORL, LLC v. Governor of Florida,* 137 F.4th 1207 (11th Cir. 2025). The Eleventh Circuit concluded that the statute's use of "lewd conduct" was impermissibly overbroad and that the statute's age-variable standard was impermissibly overbroad. To determine whether conduct was illegal, it must be "without serious literary, artistic, political, or scientific value for the age of the child present." *Id.* at 1213. The court found this test to "impossible vague" and noted that the state's lawyer could not offer guidance for how to determine what is acceptable for a twelve-year-old but not an eight-year-old." *Id.* at 1241. In a 5–4 vote, the Supreme Court rejected an application for a stay of the district court's decision for plaintiff at an earlier stage of the litigation. *See Griffin v. HM Florida-ORL, LLC,* 144 S. Ct. 1 (Mem) (2023).

Drag show litigation continues around the country. *See, e.g., Woodlands Pride, Inc. v. Paxton,* 694 F. Supp.3d 820 (S.D. Tex. 2023) (granting injunction in pre-enforcement challenge to Texas drag show law); *Texas A&M Queer Empowerment Council v. Mahomes,* 772 F. Supp.3d 792 (S.D. Tex. 2025) (granting preliminary injunction to enjoin enforcement of university's decision to ban drag shows); *Southern Utah Drag Stars v. City of St. George,* 677 F. Supp.3d 1252 (D. Utah 2023) (granting preliminary injunction to enjoin enforcement of ordinance that banned drag shows); *Naples Pride, Inc. v. City of Naples,* 2025 WL 1370174 (M.D. Fla. May 12, 2025) (granting preliminary injunction in an as-applied challenge to city's permitting rules for a "family friendly" drag performance); *Imperial Sovereign Court of Montana v. Knudsen,* 684 F. Supp.3d 1095 (D. Montana 2023) (granting preliminary injunction against enforcement of Montana law banning "drag story hours" and prohibiting minors from attending "sexually oriented performances." *But see Spectrum WT v. Wendler*, 693 F. Supp.3d 689 (N.D. Tex. 2023) (denying request for injunction in case involving university's ban on drag shows).

§ 8.7 FREEDOM OF ASSOCIATION CASES: RIGHTS OF LGBTQ+ COMMUNITY

Another right that has been found to be protected by the First Amendment is called the "freedom of association." Sometimes, the LGBTQ+ community asserts this right when it wants to form an organization at a school or university and their request to associate is denied. Other times, groups who are opposed to LGBTQ+ rights assert this right in order to avoid being forced to associate with the LGBTQ+ community.

An early case recognizing the rights of LGBTQ+ students to associate by forming a student organization was protected in *Gay Lib v. University of Missouri*, 558 F.2d 848 (8th Cir. 1977). The University had refused to recognize "Gay Lib" as an official student organization because they argued that recognition of the group would "likely result in imminent violations of Missouri sodomy laws." *Id.* at 853. In a 2–1 decision, the Eighth Circuit ruled in favor of the student organization. It noted that it "is difficult to singularly ascribe evil connotations to the group simply because they are homosexuals. . . . An interesting fact is that not all members of the group are homosexuals." *Id.* at 856. The court found in favor of the students' right to associate even if it accepted the medical testimony of the state's experts "that homosexual behavior is compulsive." *Id.* at 854.

Following a refusal to re-hear the case en banc (in a tied vote), the Supreme Court refused to accept certiorari to hear the *Gay Lib* case. *See Ratchford v. Gay Lib*, 434 U.S. 1080 (1978). In a somewhat unusual move, Justice Rehnquist wrote a dissent from the denial of certiorari petition, which was joined by Justice Blackmun. Chief Justice Burger also wrote a dissent from the denial of certiorari. Justices Rehnquist and Blackmun suggested that more weight should be given to the university's argument that recognition of the student organization would cause increased violations of the state's sodomy statute. Similarly, Chief Justice Burger emphasized that the university was merely refusing "to recognize an organization whose activities were found to be likely to incite a violation of a valid state criminal statute." *Id.* at 1082 (Burger, C.J., dissenting).

LGBTQ+ organizations have consistently prevailed under the First Amendment when state universities have sought to limit their right to associate. *See, e.g., Gay & Lesbian Students Ass'n v. Gohn*, 850 F.2d 361 (8th Cir. 1988); *Gay Student Servs. v. Texas A & M Univ.*, 737 F.2d 1317 (5th Cir. 1984). These assertions have been more difficult when made against private universities, especially private universities controlled by religious entities. The case that reflected tension between a human rights law that prohibited sexual orientation discrimination and the religious rights of a university occurred in the context of Georgetown University. *See Gay Rights Coal. of Georgetown Univ. Law Ctr. v. Georgetown Univ.*, 536 A.2d 1 (D.C. 1987). Although Congress used its plenary authority over the District of Columbia to amend its human rights law so as to exempt religiously-affiliated institutions from coverage, Georgetown University agreed to voluntarily comply with the court's order that it grant equal benefits to the LGBT group.

§ 8.8 RIGHTS OF OTHERS NOT TO ASSOCIATE WITH LGBTQ+ COMMUNITY

In *Roberts v. United States Jaycees*, 468 U.S. 609 (1984), the Supreme Court established the basic framework that dictates how courts should resolve the tension between state public accommodation statutes and the freedom of association. In that case, a Minnesota statute provided that a nonprofit entity, like the United States Jaycees, could not limit full voting membership to men. *Id.* at 612–13. The Jaycees argued that the state statute violated their freedom of association because their membership selection policy affected their advocacy of political and public causes. The district court ruled for the state, but the Eighth Circuit found that:

> [T]he State's interest in eradicating discrimination is not sufficiently compelling to outweigh this interference with the Jaycees' constitutional rights, because the organization

> is not wholly 'public', the state interest had been asserted selectively, and the anti-discrimination policy could be served in a number of ways less intrusive of First Amendment freedoms."

Id. at 617.

In a unanimous decision, reversing the Eighth Circuit, the opinion by Justice Brennan explained the broad principles that apply to these types of cases. In the first category of cases, "choices to enter into and maintain certain intimate human relationships must be secured against undue intrusion by the State because of the role of such relationships in safeguarding the individual freedom that is central to our constitutional scheme." *Id.* at 617–18. In the second category of cases, "the Court has recognized a right to associate for the purpose of engaging in those activities protected by the First Amendment—speech, assembly, petition for the redress of grievances, and the exercise of religion." *Id.* at 618. The Court called the first kind of freedom as one of "intimate association." It called the second type of freedom as one of "expressive association." *Id.* at 618.

The Court found that the first type of associative freedom did not apply to Jaycees because they were neither small nor selective. "Moreover, much of the activity central to the formation and maintenance of the association involves the participation of strangers to that relationship." *Id.* at 621. Therefore, the association could not seek to argue that they had a right to intimate association, such as those involved with marriage, childbirth, or the raising of one's children.

As to the right to expressive association, the Court found that it was plainly implicated by the statute's attempt to "interfere with the internal organization or affairs of the group." *Id.* at 623. Nonetheless, the Court found that the right of expressive association is not absolute. "Infringements on that right may be justified by regulations adopted to serve compelling state interests, unrelated to the suppression of ideas, that cannot be achieved through means significantly less restrictive of associational freedoms." *Id.* at 623. Further, the Court found that "eradicating discrimination against its female citizens" constituted a compelling state interest. *Id.* at 623. It also explained that government has a compelling state interest in preventing "invidious discrimination in the distribution of publicly available good, services, and other advantages." *Id.* at 628. It analogized the Jaycees' policies of exclusion as akin to "potentially expressive activities that produce special harms distinct from their communicative impact." *Id.* at 628. It also found that the state statute barring such discrimination was sufficiently narrow because it infringed the Jaycees' speech in a way that is "no greater than is necessary to accomplish the State's legitimate purposes." *Id.* at 628.

The Jaycees' argument of infringement was likely weakened by their practice of permitting women to share in nearly all the group's activities. Women were simply not permitted to be full voting members. As we will see, public accommodation nondiscrimination laws do not always withstand constitutional challenge when the LGBTQ+

community seeks to take advantage of their nondiscrimination requirements.

The Irish-American Gay, Lesbian and Bisexual Group of Boston was unsuccessful in obtaining relief under the Massachusetts public accommodation law, when they were excluded from the St. Patrick's Day parade. *See Hurley v. Irish-Am. Gay, Lesbian and Bisexual Grp. of Bos., Inc.*, 515 U.S. 557 (1995).

Massachusetts' public accommodation law prohibited "any distinction, discrimination or restriction on account of . . . . sexual orientation . . . . relative to the admission of any person to, or treatment in any place of public accommodation, resort or amusement." *Id.* at 561. The state trial court found that the St. Patrick's Day parade fell within the statutory definition of a public accommodation, and that, therefore, the parade organizers could not exclude the LGBT group that sought to march in the parade, carrying its own banner. The Massachusetts Supreme Court affirmed, concluding that the parade organizers could not seek to use the First Amendment to overturn the state statute because the Court could not "discern any specific expressive purpose entitling the Parade to protection under the First Amendment." *Id.* at 564.

The United States Supreme Court granted certiorari "to determine whether the requirement to admit a parade contingent expressing a message not of the private organizers' own choosing violates the First Amendment." *Id.* at 566. In a unanimous decision authored by Justice Souter, the Supreme Court reversed the Massachusetts Supreme Court, concluding that the application of the state statute to the parade organizers violated the First Amendment.

The Supreme Court emphasized that the parade organizers did not seek to ban all members of the LGBT community from marching in the parade. Rather, the organizers insisted that they did not want the LGBT group to carry "its own banner" in the parade. *Id.* at 572. By focusing on the communication that the group intended to express along the parade route, the Supreme Court could distinguish this case from the pure membership aspects of the *Jaycees* case. Instead, this case became about the right of the parade organizers to control their own speech and not be compelled to accept the speech of another participant. The parade was deemed an "expressive parade." *Id.* at 577.

The next freedom of association claim brought by a member of the LGBTQ+ community produced a more splintered reception in the Supreme Court. *See Boy Scouts of Am. v. Dale*, 530 U.S. 640 (2000). The Boy Scouts of America had revoked the adult membership of James Dale, a former Eagle Scout, when it learned he was an "avowed homosexual." *Id.* at 644. James brought suit under New Jersey's public accommodation law, which prohibits discrimination on the basis of sexual orientation in places of public accommodation. Although James lost at the state trial court, he prevailed on appeal, and before the New Jersey Supreme Court. The New Jersey Supreme Court considered his claim to be covered by New Jersey's public accommodation law; further, it found that the Boy Scouts did not have a valid First

Amendment defense under *Hurley* because the Boy Scouts' membership policies were nonselective and the reinstatement of Dale did not "compel Boy Scouts to express any message." *Id.* at 647.

In a 5–4 opinion, authored by Chief Justice Rehnquist, the Supreme Court reversed, finding that the requirement to readmit Dale to the Boy Scouts violated the Boy Scouts' First Amendment right of expressive association. First, the Court found that the Boy Scouts engaged in expressive association, specifically on the topic of homosexuality. *Id.* at 648–49. Second, it found that the forced inclusion of Dale as an assistant scoutmaster would significantly affect the Boy Scouts' ability to advocate public or private viewpoints. Making a comparison to *Hurley*, the Court concluded:

> As the presence of [the LGBT Group] in Boston's St. Patrick's Day parade would have interfered with the parade organizers' choice not to propound a particular point of view, the presence of Dale as an assistant scoutmaster would just as surely interfere with the Boy Scouts' choice not to propound a point of view contrary to its beliefs.

Id. at 654. In *Jaycees*, by contrast, the Supreme Court observed that the enforcement of the public accommodation law did "not materially interfere with the ideas that the organization sought to express." *Id.* at 657.

The dissent, authored by Justice Stevens, argued this case should be governed by *Jaycees* and does not involve an infringement of the Boy Scouts' freedom of expression. Further, the dissent distinguished *Hurley* because, unlike the banner in *Hurley*, Dale's inclusion in the Boy Scouts made no cognizable message. "Unlike [the LGBT in Boston's St. Patrick's Day parade], Dale did not carry a banner or a sign; he did not distribute any factsheet; and he expressed no intent to send any message." *Id.* at 694–95 (Stevens, J., dissenting).

Nonetheless, the Supreme Court permitted application of a university rule, akin to a public accommodation law, in *Christian Legal Society v. Martinez*, 561 U.S. 661 (2010). Justice Kennedy was the only member of the Court who was in the majority in both *Dale* and *Christian Legal Society*. Justice Ginsburg delivered the opinion of the Court in which she distinguished *Dale* from the *Christian Legal Society* context. The key difference, she argued, was that Hastings Law School merely dangled "the carrot of subsidy" rather than the "stick of prohibition." *Id.* at 683. Later, she emphasized the narrow nature of the Hastings policy because it offered access to university resources to "conduct meetings and the use of chalkboards and generally available bulletin boards to advertise events." *Id.* at 690. She sharply criticized the dissent for treating this case as if Hastings prohibited the members of Christian Legal Society from speaking. *Id.* at 691.

Thus, it appears that public accommodation laws cannot be used to force groups with restrictive admissions practices to permit members of the LGBTQ+ community to become members or participate fully in their activities, especially if the LGBTQ+ member seeks to make an express statement in conflict with the long-established views of the organization. But public universities retain the right to have an "all-comers" policy under which student organizations cannot engage in restrictive practices and still receive full university financial support.

§ 8.9 FIRST AMENDMENT CHALLENGES TO TRUMP EXECUTIVE ORDERS

On January 20, 2025, President Trump signed Executive Order 14168, 90 Fed. Reg. 8650 (Jan. 2025), entitled "Defending Women From Gender Ideology Extremism and Restoring Biological Truth to the Federal Government." He also signed Executive Order 14151, 90 Fed. Reg. 8339 (Jan. 20, 2025), entitled "Ending Radical and Wasteful Government DEI." Finally, on the next day, he signed Executive Order 14173, 90 Fed. Reg. 8663 (Jan. 21, 2025), entitled "Ending Illegal Discrimination and Restoring Merit-Based Opportunity."

Various organizations challenged one or more of these Executive Orders as violating the First Amendment. These challenges are ongoing at this time (July 2025) but are summarized below.

In *National Association of Diversity Officers in Higher Education v. Trump,* 767 F. Supp.3d 243 (D. Md. 2025), the district court granted a nationwide preliminary injunction to prevent enforcement of an anti-DEI executive order as void for vagueness. The Fourth Circuit unanimously granted the government's emergency request to stay that injunction pending appeal, finding that the Executive Orders, as written on their face, does not violate the Constitution. *See National Association of Diversity Officers in Higher Education v. Trump,* No. 25–1189 (4th Cir. March 14, 2025), https://storage.courtlistener.com/recap/gov.uscourts.ca4.177868/gov.uscourts.ca4.177868.29.0.pdf.

In *Chicago Women in Trades v. Trump,* 778 F. Supp.3d 959 (N.D. Ill. April 14, 2025), the district court found that the certification provision for entities that receive federal funds likely violates the First Amendment because it "does not define the term 'DEI' itself, and it does not refer to any other source indicating what the term means as used in the Order—let alone what might make any given 'DEI' program violate federal anti-discrimination laws." *Id.* at 983. The certification rule requires organizations to certify that they do "not operate any programs promoting DEI that violate any applicable Federal anti-discrimination laws." But a D.C. district court disagreed, finding that the "government need not subsidize the exercise of constitutional rights to avoid infringing them." National Urban League v. Trump, 2025 WL 1275613, at *1 (D.D.C. May 2, 2025).

In a case brought by the San Francisco AIDS Foundation, the district court found that the plaintiffs are likely to prevail on their First Amendment challenges to the Gender Termination, Gender Promotion, and Equity Termination Provisions, as well as the Certification Provision. *See*

San Francisco AIDS Foundation v. Trump, 2025 WL 1621636, at *18, 19 (N.D. Calif. June 9, 2025). These cases are in an early stage of litigation and the reader should check for updates.

CHAPTER 9
RELIGIOUS FREEDOM

§ 9.1 FREE EXERCISE CLAUSE

The First Amendment to the United States Constitution states: "Congress shall make no law respecting an establishment of religion, or prohibiting the free exercise thereof." U.S. CONST. amend. I. The first clause is called the "Establishment Clause" and the second clause is called the "Free Exercise Clause." Although this rule only applies directly to the federal government, the courts have applied the same concepts under the Due Process Clause of the Fourteenth Amendment. *See, e.g.*, *Wisconsin v. Yoder*, 406 U.S. 205 (1972) (upholding free exercise claim of Amish parents against the state of Wisconsin). Thus, states, like the federal government, must comply with the Establishment Clause and free exercise rules.

The scope of the Free Exercise Clause is an issue that has divided the courts. Because individuals who want to resist cooperating with LGBTQ+ nondiscrimination principles often make free exercise arguments, it is worth close attention. The basic issue that has divided the courts is whether strict scrutiny should be triggered because a law has a disparate impact against certain religious practitioners or whether strict scrutiny should only be applied when the state has a discriminatory intent to harm religious practitioners. *Compare Sherbert v. Verner*, 374 U.S. 398 (1963) (government actions that substantially burden a religious practice must be justified by a compelling governmental interest), *with Emp't Div. v. Smith*, 494 U.S. 872 (1990) (only applying strict scrutiny test if law of general applicability was passed with an invidious intent).

In *Employment Division v. Smith*, in an opinion authored by Justice Scalia, the Court found in a 6–3 opinion that Alfred Smith and Galen Black could not find protection under the First Amendment's Free Exercise Clause when they were deemed ineligible for unemployment compensation benefits. Oregon law prohibited the knowing or intentional possession of a controlled substance unless a doctor prescribed it. Smith and Black had ingested peyote for sacramental purposes at a ceremony of the Native American Church. They were fired from their jobs with a private drug rehabilitation organization because they had engaged in what their employer deemed "misconduct." After losing their jobs, they sought unemployment compensation but were found ineligible because they had been fired for engaging in work-related misconduct. *Id.* at 874. When they appealed that determination to the Oregon Court of Appeals, their denial of benefits was reversed because the state court found that the denial violated their free exercise rights under the First Amendment. *Id.* at 874. The Oregon Supreme Court affirmed the conclusion that they were entitled to unemployment compensation benefits. *Id.* at 875.

In a splintered decision, the United States Supreme Court reversed the Oregon Supreme Court, concluding, "the right of free exercise does not relieve an individual of the obligation to comply with a 'valid and neutral law of general applicability on the ground that the law proscribes (or prescribes) conduct that his religion prescribes (or proscribes).' " *Id.* at 879 (quoting *United States v. Lee,* 455 U.S. 252, 263 n.3 (1982)). Because Smith and Black violated an Oregon law of general applicability, which banned ingestion of peyote, it was permissible for Oregon to deny their unemployment compensation claim without violating the Free Exercise Clause. *Id.* at 890. Although four members of the Court agreed with Justice O'Connor that the state should have to asserting a "compelling interest" to burden religious exercise, even under generally applicable laws, the Scalia opinion reflected the views of five members of the Court. *See Id.* at 891 (O'Connor, J., concurring). Thus, the Free Exercise Clause does not provide protection from the application of generally applicable laws (i.e., laws not passed for the purpose or burdening religious exercise).

The Free Exercise Clause continues to receive judicial attention with disagreements about what constitutes a law of general applicability. One of the most recent cases involving this issue occurred in Washington State. *See Stormans, Inc. v. Wiesman,* 794 F.3d 1064 (9th Cir. 2015). The Washington Administrative Code does not require an individual pharmacist to dispense medication "if the pharmacist has a religious, moral, philosophical, or personal objection to delivery." *Id.* at 1072. Nonetheless, another provision in the Administrative Code requires pharmacies to deliver all lawfully obtained prescriptions with no exception for religious objections. *Id.* at 1072. "An objecting pharmacy must deliver the drug or device and may not refer a patient to another pharmacy." *Id.* at 1072–73. Both owners of pharmacies and pharmacists challenged these rules as violating their free exercise rights. The district court ruled in their favor and the government appealed to the Ninth Circuit.

The plaintiffs argued that the state could have permitted "facilitated referrals," which would allow a patient to receive the drug at another pharmacy, as occurs when a drug is unavailable at a particular pharmacy. *Id.* at 1078. The plaintiffs argued that failure to provide that accommodation reflects discriminatory intent, thereby triggering more heightened scrutiny under the Free Exercise Clause. The Ninth Circuit, however, concluded there was no evidence of discriminatory intent because the rule is consistent with the "stated goal of ensuring timely and safe delivery of prescription medications." *Id.* at 1078. The Ninth Circuit also reversed the district court's findings that the state selectively enforced these rules against Catholic-affiliated pharmacies. *Id.* at 1084. Having concluded that the challenged rule was one of general applicability, the court applied the rational basis test and upheld the rule. The Supreme Court denied cert. *See Stormans, Inc. v. Wiesman*, 579 U.S. 942 (2016).

In a closely watched case, the Supreme Court applied the *Smith* test in *Fulton v. City of Philadelphia,* 593 U.S. 522 (2021). The case arose when the city of Philadelphia informed a state-licensed foster care agency affiliated with the Roman Catholic Archdiocese that it would not continue to contract with them for foster care services unless they agreed to certify same-sex couples as foster parents. The foster care agencies challenged this action as a violation of their free exercise and free speech rights under the First Amendment. The district court denied their request for a temporary restraining order or a preliminary injunction. The Third Circuit affirmed. In a unanimous decision, the Supreme Court reversed on free exercise grounds. It did not reach the free speech issue. Chief Justice Roberts delivered the opinion of the Court, which was joined by Justices Breyer, Sotomayor, Kagan, Kavanaugh, and Barrett. Justices Alito, Thomas and Gorsuch concurred separately and did not join the majority opinion.

Like the Supreme Court's decision in *Masterpiece Cakeshop, Ltd. v. Colorado Civil Rights Commission*, 584 U.S. 617 (2018) (discussed in *Nutshell* § 9.5), the holding was quite narrow. Chief Justice Roberts concluded in *Fulton* that the Court did not need to reconsider *Smith* because the city's policies "do not meet the requirement of being neutral and generally applicable." *Id.* at 533. The basis for the conclusion that the law was not generally applicable was the exception clause contained in the rule requiring nondiscrimination on the basis of sexual orientation. The rule applied "unless an exception is granted by the Commissioner or the Commissioner's designee, in his/her sole discretion." *Id.* at 535. Citing *Smith*, the Court said that the city "may not refuse to extend that [exemption] system to cases of 'religious hardship' without compelling reason." *Id.* at 535. The Court then explained that it was requiring the city to justify its refusal under strict scrutiny. "A government policy can survive strict scrutiny only if it advances 'interests of the highest order' and is narrowly tailored to achieve those interests . . . . Put another way, so long as the government can achieve its interests in a manner that does not burden religion, it must do so." *Id.* at 1881. Although the Court did not emphasize application of this aspect of the test, it did note that CCS would direct same-sex couples to another agency, which accepted such applications, if one were made to them. *Id.* at 541.

The Court did not remand the question of whether the city could meet the strict scrutiny test. It resolved that issue itself. While the Court acknowledged that the city had a "weighty" interest in ensuring that "gay person and gay couples" are not "treated as social outcasts or as inferior in dignity and worth," that interest could not justify denying the foster care agencies an exception for their religious exercise. Although the city contended that it had *never* granted an exception to its sexual orientation nondiscrimination policy, the Court found that the city offered "no compelling reason why it has a particular interest in denying an exception to CSS while making them available to others." *Id.* at 542. The court found that it was "irrelevant" whether the Commissioner had ever granted an exception. "The creation of a formal mechanism for granting exceptions renders a policy not generally applicable." *Id.* at 537. Once the policy is found not to be "generally applicable" then its application to a religious entity must meet the strict scrutiny standard.

The Court does not speculate what justifications could meet a strict scrutiny standard but an interest in imposing a sexual orientation nondiscrimination policy, where the covered entity is willing to make a referral to another entity which would provide the requested service, does not meet that standard. Hypothetically, one could imagine a covered entity that refused to make referrals to "mixed-race" couples but offered discretionary exceptions. Because the Court has found that states have a compelling interest in eliminating race discrimination, a state entity might be able to enforce that rule. Elimination of sexual orientation nondiscrimination is considered a "weighty interest" but not a "compelling interest."

Justice Barrett concurred separately and was joined by Justices Kavanaugh and Breyer to note that replacing *Smith* is a complicated issue. They noted skepticism for replacing "*Smith's* categorical antidiscrimination approach for an equally categorical strict scrutiny regime, particularly when this Court's resolution of conflicts between generally applicable laws and other First Amendment rights—like speech and assembly—has been much more nuanced." *Id.* at 1883 (Barrett, J., concurring with Kavanaugh and Breyer (who joined all but the first paragraph). In a paragraph not joined by Justice Breyer, Justices Barrett and Kavanaugh also conclude that "As a matter of text and structure, it is difficult to see why the Free Exercise Clause—lone among the First Amendment freedoms—offers nothing more than protection from discrimination." *Id.* at 543. Justices Alito, Thomas and Gorsuch concurred separately to make it clear that *Smith* should be overruled. While not definitively stating what the new test should be, they say: "The answer that comes most readily to mind is the standard that *Smith* replaced: A law that imposes a substantial burden on religious exercise can be sustained only if it is narrowly tailored to serve a compelling interest." *Id.* at 614. (Alito, J., concurring with Thomas and Gorsuch).

Thus, there appear to be five votes (Alito, Thomas, Gorsuch, Barrett and Kavanaugh) to overturn *Smith* but no clear consensus on what would replace *Smith*. There are also six members of the Court who agree that a state has a "weighty" interest in eliminating sexual orientation nondiscrimination. It seems pretty clear that if the city of Philadelphia amended its ordinance so as to offer no exemptions from its sexual orientation nondiscrimination policy, that it would find itself before the Supreme Court again in a case that more directly requires the Court to consider overturning *Smith* in a way that is likely to protect the free exercise of religion over a city's interest in providing sexual orientation nondiscrimination protection. This may be particularly true when the covered entity says it will make a referral to another foster care or adoption agency.

As discussed above, the Supreme Court refused to grant cert. in the pharmacy case from the state of Washington. *See Stormans, Inc. v. Wiesman,* 579 U.S. 942 (2016). On July 2, 2021, after deciding *Fulton,* the Supreme Court also declined to accept cert. in *State v. Arlene's Flowers,* 441 P.3d 1203 (Wash. 2019). That case involved the enforcement of

Washington's nondiscrimination statute against a florist who refused to sell wedding flowers to a same-sex couple on religious grounds. Justices Thomas, Alito and Gorsuch would have granted the petition for a writ of cert. Other cases involving denial of services on religious liberty cases are in the pipeline but the Supreme Court avoided reconsidering *Smith* by ruling in *303 Creative LLC v. Elenis*, 600 U.S. 570 (2023) that the First Amendment free exercise clause provided protection to a web designer who did not want to provide her services to weddings between two people of the same sex. *See Nutshell* § 8.1.

The latest arena for legal challenges involving the free exercise clause concern the right of parents to insist that the free exercise clause gives them an opportunity to choose to have their children opt out of instruction that is inconsistent with the parents' religious beliefs. In *Mahmoud v. Taylor,* parents of public elementary school students brought an action against a public school board, alleging that the board's refusal to provide notice when "LGBTQ+ inclusive" storybooks would be taught and an opportunity to opt out of such instruction violated their First Amendment right to the free exercise of religion. *See Mahmoud v. Taylor,* 145 S. Ct. 2332 (2025). The lower courts had denied the parents' request for a preliminary injunction. The Supreme Court reversed.

The school district had argued that allowing students to opt out of such instruction would serve a compelling interest in having undisrupted school sessions conducive to learning. Citing other states that permit broad opt outs from discrete aspects of the public school curriculum without widespread consequences, the Court rejected the school district's argument. *Id.* at 2363. The Court rejected the argument that providing this kind of opt out would allow parents to "micromanage the public school curriculum." *Id* at 2263. In dissent, Justices Sotomayor, Kagan and Jackson argued that "the result will be chaos for this Nation's public schools." *Id.* at 2381. The reader should watch for the ripple effects of this decision.

By contrast (but not decided on religious freedom grounds), the Eleventh Circuit affirmed a district court decision in favor of a school board when the middle school chose not to notify a parent about their child's desire to use self-identified name and pronouns at school. *See Littlejohn v. School Board of Leon County,* 132 F.4th 1232 (11th Cir. 2025). The parents had unsuccessfully sought to use a substantive due process argument. In light of *Mahmoud,* it is possible that other parents could pursue a freedom of religion argument, rather than a substantive due process argument to press the notification argument.

§ 9.2 FEDERAL RELIGIOUS FREEDOM RESTORATION ACT: BACKGROUND

The Religious Freedom Restoration Act ("RFRA"), 42 U.S.C. § 2000bb *et seq*. (2012) was enacted in 1993. The Supreme Court found it to be unconstitutional as applied to state and local government in *City of Boerne v. Flores*, 521 U.S. 507 (1997). As will be discussed below, RFRA still applies to *federal statutes* but no longer places a direct restriction on state and local laws. After the decision in *City of Boerne,* many states passed their own versions of RFRA, which are not impacted by the *City of Boerne* decision. Further, Congress enacted the Religious Land Use and Institutionalized Persons Act of 2000 (RLUIPA) on September 22, 2000, which provides a more limited form of religious protection against state and local government than found in the parts of RFRA struck down by *City of Boerne.* Thus, when we talk about the *current* protections found in RFRA, we are talking about protections against religious discrimination by the *federal government.* In order for people to invoke legislative protections against religious discrimination at the state level, they typically rely on state religious freedom protection acts or the narrower RLUIPA.

This topic is relevant to the LGBTQ+ community because individuals or entities sometimes invoke religious arguments to justify their unwillingness to abide by sexual orientation nondiscrimination legislation. While much of the case law does not directly relate to the LGBTQ+ community, one needs to understand the general concepts in this area to understand the implications for the LGBTQ+ community.

§ 9.3 PASSAGE OF RFRA

On November 16, 1993, President Bill Clinton signed RFRA into law after Congress enacted it by an overwhelming majority. *See* Religious Freedom

Restoration Act, Pub. L. No. 103–141, 107 Stat. 1488 (1993) (codified at 42 U.S.C. §§ 2000bb—2000bb–4 (2012)), available at https://www.justice.gov/sites/default/files/jmd/legacy/2014/07/24/act-pl103-141.pdf. Congress passed RFRA because it disagreed with the Court's reasoning in *Employment Division v. Smith*, 494 U.S. 872 (1990). Congress preferred the test outlined by Justice O'Connor in her *Smith* concurrence, but that test was not accepted by a majority of the Supreme Court. RFRA provided that:

> Government may substantially burden a person's exercise of religion only if it demonstrates that application of the burden to the person—
>
> (1) is in furtherance of a compelling governmental interest; and
>
> (2) is the least restrictive means of furthering that compelling governmental interest.

42 U.S.C.A. § 2000bb–1 (2012).

RFRA, as enacted in 1993, applied to both the federal government, and state and local government. In 1997, the Supreme Court ruled in a 6–3 decision, authored by Justice Kennedy, that RFRA was unconstitutional as applied to state and local government. *See City of Boerne v. Flores*, 521 U.S. 507 (1997). As a branch of limited powers, Congress must always have a constitutional basis for enacting legislation. In this instance, Congress justified RFRA as permissible under its Section 5 powers under the Fourteenth Amendment, which allow it to enact measures to enforce Section 1 of the Fourteenth

Amendment. The Supreme Court, however, ruled that Congress did not have the authority under Section 5 of the Fourteenth Amendment to reverse the Supreme Court's decision in *Employment Division v. Smith*. If Congress was not satisfied with the Supreme Court's interpretation of the Constitution, as applied to state and local government, then it needed to seek to amend the Constitution. It could not use the pretext of enforcing the Fourteenth Amendment as a means of overturning a Supreme Court interpretation of the Constitution.

The *City of Boerne* decision, however, had no impact on the ability of Congress to decide that the *federal government* could choose to accommodate religious exercise more than was required by the Constitution (so long as it did not go too far and violate the Establishment Clause by overly-preferencing religious exercise). If Congress has the constitutional authority to enact a statute that regulates the federal government, then it can voluntarily choose to provide more religious freedom than required under the First Amendment. Because *City of Boerne* did not invalidate RFRA as applied to the federal government, many cases have occurred interpreting the meaning of the statute as applied to the federal government. What does it mean for a federal law to "substantially burden" the exercise of religion? When has the government met the "least restrictive means" test?

§ 9.4 INTERPRETATION OF RFRA

In order for RFRA to be relevant, a statute must arguably burden an individual's religious exercise. One way such an arguable burden could take place would be if a public accommodation, such as florist or baker, wanted to exclude the LGBTQ+ community from accessing its services and a statute existed that banned such exclusion. At this time, however, there are no federal statutes requiring entities to engage in nondiscrimination on the basis of sexual orientation or gender identity with respect to public accommodations, like bakeries or florists. The only federal public accommodation laws concern race discrimination and disability discrimination. Thus, there have been no RFRA cases directly impacting the LGBTQ+ community. As we will discuss below, however, some *states* have passed their own version of RFRA. State courts may borrow from the federal case law under RFRA to guide them in interpreting their state statutes. Further, one might imagine that Congress will *some day* pass public accommodation statutes that apply to the LGBTQ+ community. At that time, the federal court interpretations of RFRA could become relevant to the LGBTQ+ community.

The leading Supreme Court case on the interpretation of RFRA is *Burwell v. Hobby Lobby Stores, Inc.*, 573 U.S. 682 (2014). In this case, plaintiffs were for-profit closely held corporations who objected to regulations issued under the Affordable Care Act ("ACA"), which required them to provide coverage for certain contraceptives. They argued that the regulation burdened their exercise of religion and that the government had not chosen the least restrictive means possible to achieve its goal. The Supreme Court accepted certiorari to hear this case after the circuits split on it. Justice Alito authored the 5–4 opinion for the Supreme Court, concluding that the contraceptive mandate did burden the plaintiffs' exercise of religion and the government could have achieved its compelling state interest through a less burdensome alternative.

The first issue the Court resolved was whether the activities of a for-profit closely held corporation are protected by RFRA. Drawing on a long line of cases that consider corporations to be "persons" and to be capable of having religious views, the Court held the plaintiffs were covered by RFRA. *Id.* at 719.

The second issue the Court resolved was whether the contraceptive mandate "substantially burdened" the plaintiffs' exercise of religion. The ACA required the plaintiffs to purchase health insurance for their employees, which included contraceptive coverage, or pay a penalty for failing to provide insurance coverage. The Court decided this question in the affirmative, concluding that the contraceptive mandate imposed a substantial burden on the ability of the plaintiffs to conduct business in accordance with their religious beliefs, even if not one of their employees destroyed an embryo as a result of receiving health care coverage. The Court examined the sincerity of their religious beliefs, not whether those beliefs were reasonable or even plausible. *Id.* at 724–26.

The third issue addressed by the Court was whether the government could satisfy the least restrictive means test, which would allow them to maintain the regulation despite its burden on religious exercise. To satisfy that test, the government must demonstrate that its rule "(1) is in furtherance of a compelling governmental interest; and (2) is the least restrictive means of furthering that compelling governmental interest." *Id.* at 726. The Court assumed, without deciding, that the contraceptive mandate served a compelling state interest but found that the government could not meet the least restrictive means test. Because the government had already created an accommodation for *nonprofit* organizations with religious objections, the Court found that it could create a similar accommodation for the plaintiffs. *Id.* at 730. Under this accommodation, an organization would make a certification that it wants to exclude contraceptive coverage from the group health plan. The insurance carrier would then provide separate payments for any contraceptive services required to be covered without imposing any cost-sharing requirements on the covered entity or plan beneficiaries. *Id.* at 2781.

The majority opinion offered some limitations on its holding. These are some of those limitations:

> We do not decide today whether an approach of this type complies with RFRA for purposes of all religious claims. At a minimum, however, it does not impinge on the plaintiffs' religious belief that providing insurance coverage for the contraceptives at issue here violates their

> religion, and it serves HHS's stated interests equally well.

Id. at 731.

> Our decision should not be understood to hold that an insurance-coverage mandate must necessarily fall if it conflicts with an employer's religious beliefs. Other coverage requirements, such as immunizations, may be supported by different interests (for example, the need to combat the spread of infectious diseases) and may involve different arguments about the least restrictive means of providing them.

Id. at 733.

> [The decision could not be applied to the context of race-based hiring decisions, which] might be cloaked as religious practice to escape legal sanction. . . . The Government has a compelling interest in providing an equal opportunity to participate in the workforce without regard to race, and prohibitions on racial discrimination are precisely tailored to achieve that critical goal.

Id. at 733.

For the LGBTQ+ community, the last limitation may be of the most interest, because the EEOC has begun to interpret Title VII as banning discrimination on the basis of sexual orientation and gender identity. In theory, a religiously-based employer could seek to use RFRA to avoid those requirements. Although banning race discrimination has been found to be a "compelling state interest," the same conclusion has not yet been drawn about banning sexual orientation or gender identity discrimination. It is not clear if courts will use the third point to avoid religious exceptions to nondiscrimination rules on behalf of the LGBTQ+ community.

The fifth vote in *Hobby Lobby* was cast by Justice Kennedy who concurred separately to comment that other cases might exist in which "it is more difficult and expensive to accommodate a governmental program to countless religious claims based on an alleged statutory right of free exercise." *Id.* at 739. Justice Ginsburg wrote a blistering dissent, which disagreed with the majority opinion with respect to every issue. Justices Breyer and Kagan joined that dissent, except with respect to the argument that for-profit corporations should not even be covered by RFRA. *Id.* at 772 (Breyer, J., dissenting). Justice Ginsburg described the majority opinion as having "startling breadth." *Id.* at 739 (Ginsburg, J., dissenting).

The *Hobby Lobby* opinion did not end the controversy concerning requests for religious exemptions under the ACA. In *Hobby Lobby,* the plaintiffs did not challenge the validity under RFRA of allowing them to use the accommodation process available to religiously-affiliated nonprofits—certifying to a third-party administrator that they will not provide contraceptive coverage as part of their regular health care plan. In a dozen or so cases filed under RFRA, religious non-profits challenged the certification process as constituting a substantial burden on their religious exercise. In seven of those cases, they were successful at the district court, although each of these cases was overturned at the court of appeals. *See Catholic Diocese of Beaumont v. Sebelius*, 10 F. Supp.3d 725 (E.D. Tex. 2015); *E. Tex. Baptist Univ. v. Sebelius*, 988 F. Supp. 2d 743 (S.D. Tex. 2013); *S. Nazarene Univ. v. Sebelius*, No. CIV–13–1015–F, 2013 WL 6804265 (W.D. Okla. Dec. 23, 2013); *Geneva Coll. v. Sebelius*, 988 F. Supp. 2d 511 (W.D. Pa. 2013); *Reaching Souls Int'l v. Sebelius*, No. CIV–13–1092–D, 2013 WL 6804259 (W.D. Okla. Dec. 20, 2013); *Persico v. Sebelius*, No. 1:13–00303, 2:13–cv–001459, 2013 WL 6922024 (W.D. Pa. Dec. 20, 2013); *Zubik v. Sebelius*, 983 F. Supp. 2d 576 (W.D. Pa. 2013). The circuit court decisions ruled in favor of the government and included *Priests for Life v. HHS*, 772 F.3d 229 (D.C. Cir. 2014), *Geneva College v. HHS*, 778 F.3d 422 (3d Cir. 2015), *East Texas Baptist University v. Burwell*, 793 F.3d 449 (5th Cir. 2015), and, *Little Sisters of the Poor Home for the Aged v. Burwell*, 794 F.3d 1151 (10th Cir. 2015).

Even though there was no circuit split, the Supreme Court accepted certiorari to hear these consolidated cases on November 6, 2015. *See Zubik v. Burwell*, 577 U.S. 971 (2015). The Court heard oral argument on March 23, 2016, after Justice Scalia had unexpectedly died on February 13, 2016. Then, on March 29, 2016, the Court ordered the parties to submit supplemental briefs addressing the question of: "Whether and how contraceptive coverage may be obtained by petitioners' employees through petitioner's insurance companies, but in a way that does not require any involvement of petitioners beyond their own decision to provide health insurance without contraceptive coverage to their employees."

In an unusual decision, the Supreme Court entered a *per curiam* opinion on May 16, 2016, vacating and remanding each of the court of appeal decisions in response to the order for supplemental briefing:

> Given the gravity of the dispute and the substantial clarification and refinement in the positions of the parties, the parties on remand should be afforded an opportunity to arrive at an approach going forward that accommodates petitioners' religious exercise while at the same time ensuring that women covered by petitioners' health plans "receive full and equal health coverage, including contraceptive coverage."

Zubik v. Burwell, 578 U.S. 403, 408 (2016).

Because of the number of parties involved in the case, it seemed unlikely that a voluntary resolution would be found in each circuit. But the remand gave the Court an opportunity to re-hear the case when it had a full slate of nine Justices.

Despite the uncertainty created by *Zubik*, it does appear that the federal RFRA is an important basis for arguments by entities that they do not want to comply with federal laws that are inconsistent with their religious beliefs. Given the religious objections that have been made at the state level, as will be discussed below, one can imagine these arguments will be further pursued if Congress enacts broader legislative protections for the LGBTQ+ community. Such arguments could also be used, conceivably, to avoid compliance with the new rules and regulations issued by EEOC and HUD, discussed in *Nutshell* §§ 7.17 & 7.19. It was not immediately clear if the Supreme Court's statement that RFRA cannot be used to undermine Title VII's race-based employment protections would also apply to sexual orientation and gender identity protections.

On December 9, 2022, the Eighth Circuit ruled that Catholic plaintiffs demonstrated *per se* irreparable harm from enforcement of ACA's and Title VII's prohibition against discrimination on the basis of sex and were entitled to a permanent injunction. It found that their rights were violated under the First Amendment and the Religious Freedom Restoration Act. *See also Religious Sisters of Mercy v. Becerra,* 55 F.4th 583 (8th Cir. 2022). *See also Christian Employers Alliance v. United States Equal Opportunity Commission,* 719 F. Supp.3d 912 (D. N.D. 2024) (granting injunction to religious employers from enforcement of gender identity rules under ACA and Title VII); *Catholic Benefits Association v. Burrow,* 732 F. Supp.3d 1014 (D. N.D. 2024) (granting motion for preliminary injunction under RFRA to avoid enforcement of EEOC's final rule for the Pregnant Workers Fairness Act and Title VII). Those are only a few of the cases applying RFRA to avoid enforcement of various gender identity rules under Title VII and the ACA. The reader should check for further updates from other circuits.

§ 9.5 STATE RELIGIOUS FREEDOM RESTORATION LAWS

Following the Supreme Court's decision in *City of Boerne v. Flores* in 1993 that the federal RFRA could not be constitutionally applied to state and local government, twenty-nine states have passed their own religious freedom restoration acts, typically parallel to the language used in RFRA. *See* Beckett Fund, *Federal and State RFRA Map*, https://becketfund.org/research-central/rfra-info-central/map/. Most of these laws were passed before gay rights was a politically hot topic.

Although many states already had religious restoration laws, the enactment of such a law in Indiana on March 26, 2015, produced a firestorm of protest, because of its possible implication in the gay rights context. *See* S. 101, 119th Gen. Assemb., 1st Reg., Sess. (Ind. 2015). A legal clarification was enacted less than a week later to clarify that the law "does not authorize a provider to refuse to offer or provide services, facilities, use of public accommodations, goods, employment, or housing to any member or members of the general public." *See* S. 50, 119th Gen. Assemb., 1st Reg. Sess. (Ind. 2015).

Despite the political uproar over the passage of Senate Bill 101 in Indiana, the law would have had little impact on the LGBTQ+ community because Indiana has no state-wide protections for discrimination on the basis of sexual orientation or gender identity. A baker, who does not wish to sell a wedding cake to a gay couple in Indiana, does not need to take advantage of a religious restoration act to do so. The baker can simply decide not to serve a customer on the basis of sexual orientation or gender identity and be unconcerned about potential legal ramifications.

Because few states have *both* sexual orientation nondiscrimination legislation *and* a religious restoration act, there is not a lot of case law on the impact of state religious restoration acts on the implementation of these statutes. Two states have had cases involving the tension between nondiscrimination statutes and religious free exercise—New Mexico and Colorado. In both cases, the company seeking religious liberty protection was unsuccessful. These unsuccessful attempts helped spawn the more comprehensive statute that was passed in Indiana. But, then due to political pressure, that broader impact was curtailed.

The New Mexico case was *Elane Photography v. Willock*, 309 P.3d 53 (N.M. 2013). Vanessa Willock contacted Elane Photography by email to inquire about procuring their services to photograph her commitment ceremony to another woman. The studio owner responded that they do not photograph same-sex weddings. Willock filed a discrimination complaint against Elane Photography with the New Mexico Human Rights Commission. New Mexico law prohibits discrimination by public accommodations on the basis of sexual orientation. *Id.* at 60. The Commission ruled in favor of Willock. Elane Photography appealed the Commission's ruling for a trial de novo in the state trial court. The state court affirmed the Commission's determination. Elane

Photography argued that the Commission's enforcement of the state statute violated the New Mexico Religious Freedom Restoration Act ("NMRFRA").

> The NMRFRA provides:
>
> A government agency shall not restrict a person's free exercise of religion unless:
>
> > A. the restriction is in the form of a rule of general applicability and does not directly discriminate against religion or among religions; and
> >
> > B. the application of the restriction to the person is essential to further a compelling governmental interest and is the least restrictive means of furthering that compelling governmental interest.
>
> Section 28–22–3. "Free exercise of religion" is defined as "an act or a refusal to act that is substantially motivated by religious belief." Section 28–22–2(A).

Elane Photography, LLC v. Willock, 309 P.3d 53, 76 (N.M. 2013).

In a unanimous decision, the New Mexico Supreme Court ruled that the NMRFRA was not applicable to this action because the statute requires that a "government agency" is the one restricting an individual's free exercise of religion. The Court ruled that the statute was not applicable in a dispute between two private parties. Because the New Mexico Human Rights Commission was not a party to the case, and its order no longer has any legal effect, the Court ruled that its "adjudication of disputes between private parties does not constitute government restriction of a party's free exercise rights for purposes of NMRFRA." *Id.* at 77. The Court, therefore, did not have to resolve the "compelling state interest" or "least restrictive means" part of the test.

In response to the *Willock* decision, the Indiana legislature enacted a Religious Freedom Restoration Act that would go further than the New Mexico law to prevent laws of general applicability from being used to force a florist or bakery to provide services to a same-sex couple. The Indiana statute made clear that it could apply even if the state or other governmental entity is not a party to the proceeding. It applied broadly to "all governmental entity statutes, ordinances, resolutions, executive or administrative orders, regulations, customs, and usages, including the implementation thereof, regardless of whether they were enacted, adopted or initiated before, on, or after July 1, 2015." S. 101, 1st Reg. Sess., 119th Gen. Assemb., ch. 9, § 1 (Ind. 2015). Arkansas passed a similar law about the same time, but Arkansas Governor Asa Hutchinson vetoed it.

Unlike New Mexico, Indiana does not have any state-wide laws that ban sexual orientation discrimination so passage of the Indiana statute would have had minimal, if any, effect on the rights of florists or bakers to not provide services to the LGBTQ+ community. (Some cities in Indiana may have nondiscrimination ordinances that apply locally.)

Nonetheless, passage of the Indiana law produced an enormous backlash with many entities threatening to boycott Indiana if it were not repealed. After about a week, the Indiana legislature enacted a new statute that made it clear that the statute would not override the application of sexual orientation nondiscrimination statutes. This new language said that the state's religious freedom act did not:

> (1) authorize a provider to refuse to offer or provide services, facilities, use of public accommodations, goods, employment, or housing to any member or members of the general public on the basis of race, color, religion, ancestry, age, national origin, disability, sex, sexual orientation, gender identity, or United States military service;
>
> (2) establish a defense to a civil action or criminal prosecution for refusal by a provider to offer or provide services, facilities, use of public accommodations, goods, employment, or housing to any member or members of the general public on the basis of race, color, religion, ancestry, age, national origin, disability, sex, sexual orientation, gender identity, or United States military service.

S. 50, 1st Reg. Sess., 119th Gen. Assemb., § .07 (Ind. 2015).

Despite the veto of the Arkansas bill and the clarification of the Indiana law, there are twenty or so states with religious restoration acts and one might expect more cases, similar to *Willock*, in which the courts might find that the plaintiff is covered by the religious restoration statute. In that case, we might see case law parallel to the federal case law under RFRA, which might provide some exemptions for religious entities that do not wish to comply with state law.

The other case that has received a lot of media attention—*Craig v. Masterpiece Cakeshop, Inc.*, 370 P.3d 272 (Col. Ct. App. 2015)—involved a state that has a sexual orientation nondiscrimination statute but no religious restoration act. The defendants tried to use the state constitution's free exercise clause as a way to attain further protection than is available under the United States Constitution's Free Exercise Clause. That attempt was unsuccessful.

This case arose when Charlie Craig and David Mullins visited a bakery in Colorado and requested that the shop create a cake to celebrate their same-sex wedding in 2012. They were planning to get married in Massachusetts and later celebrate with their friends in Colorado (which did not yet recognize same-sex marriages). After the cakeshop denied their request, they filed a charge of discrimination with the Colorado Civil Rights Division ("ALJ"). The shop agreed to sell them baked goods but would not design a wedding cake for them, due to the shop owner's religious beliefs. The ALJ found probable cause and they filed a formal complaint with the Office of Administrative Courts ("the Commission"). The Commission affirmed the ALJ decision.

On appeal, the Colorado Court of Appeals affirmed. It found that Craig and Mullens were discriminated against "because of" their sexual orientation even though the bakery was willing to sell them other products. It also rejected the argument that the denial was not due to their sexual orientation because two men who identity as heterosexual could seek to get married. The court of appeals said: "An isolated example of two heterosexual men marrying does not persuade us that same-sex marriage is not predominantly, and almost exclusively, engaged in by gays, lesbians, and bisexuals." *Id.* at 283.

The Colorado Court also rejected the various First Amendment arguments made by the cake shop. With respect to the free exercise argument, it applied the *Smith* test for neutral laws of general applicability. Such laws only need to be "rationally related to a legitimate governmental interest in order to survive a constitutional challenge." *Id.* at 289. It also rejected the argument that the free exercise protection under its state constitution is different than the analysis required under the United States Constitution. *Id.* at 293. It readily found that the state's nondiscrimination statute met the rational relationship test and affirmed the lower court. The Colorado Supreme Court declined to accept certiorari to hear the case on appeal. *See Masterpiece Cakeshop, Inc. v. Colo. Civil Rights Comm'n*, No. 15SC738, 2016 WL 1645027 (Col. April 25, 2016). Nonetheless, the United States Supreme Court granted a petition for certiorari to hear the case.

In a 7–2 decision authored by Justice Kennedy, the Court found that the Colorado Civil Rights Commission's actions violated the Free Exercise Clause because the "Civil Rights Commission's treatment of his case has some elements of a clear and impermissible hostility toward the sincere religious beliefs that motivated his objection." *Masterpiece Cakeshop, Ltd. v. Colorado Civil Rights Commission,* 584 U.S. 617, 634 (2018). The Court found that Phillips was "entitled to the neutral and respectful consideration of his claims in all the circumstances of the case." *Id.* at 634. It emphasized one comment by one commissioner who said that using religion to justify discrimination "is one of the most despicable pieces of rhetoric that people can use to—to use their religion to hurt others." *Id.* at 635. Because no other Commissioner ever objected to that statement, and the state never disavowed that view in any of their briefs, the Supreme Court found it was an "indication of hostility" toward religion that is impermissible about the Free Exercise clause, especially when articulated by a member of an adjudicatory body deciding a particular case.

The majority opinion did not overturn all public accommodation laws that applied to bakeries or other entities that might be asked to provide goods for members of the LGBTQ+ community. It simply counseled that all "disputes must be resolved with tolerance, without undue disrespect to sincere religious beliefs, and without subjecting gay persons to indignities when they seek goods and services in an open market." *Id.* at 640. Justices Kagan and Breyer concurred separately to emphasize that they agreed with the majority because of the evidence that the state actors showed hostility to religious views rather than offering a neutral and respectful consideration. Justices Ginsburg and Sotomayor dissented, finding insufficient evidence of religious hostility to support the majority decision.

As discussed in *Nutshell* § 9.1, the Supreme Court used a similar analysis to overturn the City of Philadelphia's attempt to enforce its sexual orientation nondiscrimination policy against Catholic Social Services. *See Fulton v. City of Philadelphia,* 593 U.S. 522 (2021). It found that the city policy was not a neutral policy of general applicability because it permitted exceptions at the sole discretion of the Commissioner. Therefore, the city policy was subject to the most rigorous Constitutional level of scrutiny, which it could not meet. The Court did not consider whether the nondiscrimination policy could have withstood Constitutional scrutiny if there had been no discretion in its application.

The impact of *Fulton* on the enforcement of nondiscrimination statutes and ordinances is unclear. As discussed in *Nutshell* § 9.1, the Supreme Court declined to accept cert. in a case challenging the application of a sexual orientation nondiscrimination statute against a florist who objected to providing services on First Amendment grounds.

§ 9.6 RELIGIOUS REFUSAL CASE LAW: KIM DAVIS

Even though a state does not have a nondiscrimination law, it must still abide by the United States Constitution, including the right to marry. That fact has been causing a collision between arguments under state religious protection statutes and implementation of the right to marry. In light of *Obergefell*, some states have also tried to enhance the rights of state employees to refuse to participate in facilitating same-sex marriages.

This issue received a lot of publicity when Kim Davis sought to avoid issuing marriage licenses to same-sex couples in Kentucky. Kentucky has a Religious Restoration Act, enacted in 2013, so she was pursuing that argument, in part, under her state's statute. *See* Ky. Rev. Stat. Ann. § 446.350 (LexisNexis Supp. 2015).

Kim Davis, who identifies as a devout Christian, was elected county clerk for Rowan, Kentucky on November 4, 2014, and took office on January 1, 2015, for a four-year term. Two days after she was elected county clerk, the Sixth Circuit overturned the lower court decision that invalidated Kentucky's ban on same-sex marriage. *See DeBoer v. Snyder*, 772 F.3d 388 (6th Cir. 2014). In January 2015, shortly after Davis took office, the United States Supreme Court announced that it would accept certiorari in *Obergefell v. Hodges*, which included an appeal from the Kentucky marriage equality case. One week later, concerned that she would soon be required to issue marriage licenses and certificates in conflict with her religious beliefs, Davis unsuccessfully requested that the state legislature pass a marriage refusal statute to protect state employees. After the Supreme Court overturned the Sixth Circuit's marriage equality decision on June 26, 2015, in *Obergefell v. Hodges,* 576 U.S. 644 (2015) (discussed in *Nutshell* § 5.6), Davis announced that her office would discontinue issuing marriage licenses in Rowan County to all couples. Four couples filed suit against Davis, arguing she was violating their constitutional rights. Davis filed a third-party complaint in federal court against state officials seeking a religious exemption from authorizing the issuance of Kentucky marriage licenses. Davis was found in contempt of court and jailed until her office began issuing marriage licenses. Her attempt to attain protection from the state's religious freedom restoration act was unsuccessful. *See Miller v. Davis,* 123 F. Supp.3d 924 (E.D. Ky. 2015), *stay denied pending appeal. See also Miller v. Davis,* No. 15–5880, 2015 WL 10692640 (6th Cir. Aug. 26, 2015); *Miller v. Davis,* Nos. 15–5880, 15–5961, 15–5978, 2015 WL 10692638 (6th Cir. Nov. 5, 2015). Her legal challenges ended on October 5, 2020, when the Supreme Court denied cert. in her case. *See Davis v. Ermold,* 141 S. Ct. 3 (Mem) (2020). Although Justices Thomas and Alito joined the decision to deny certiorari, they also concurred separately to say: "By choosing to privilege a novel constitutional right over the religious liberty interests explicitly protected in the First Amendment, and by doing so undemocratically, the Court has created a problem that only it can fix. Until then, *Obergefell* will continue to have 'ruinous consequences for religious liberty.' " *Id.*

In light of the publicity regarding Kim Davis's efforts, other states have sought to pass laws that would specifically allow certain religious officials from refusing to engage in certain duties based on their religious beliefs. Georgia passed such a law, but their Governor vetoed it on March 28, 2016. At a news conference explaining his veto, the Governor said: "I do not think we have to discriminate against anyone to protect the faith-based community in Georgia." *See* Sandya Samashekhar, *Georgia Governor Vetoes Religious Freedom Bill Criticized as ANTI-Gay*, WASH. POST March 28, 2016, available at https://www.washingtonpost.com/news/post-nation/wp/2016/03/28/georgia-governor-to-veto-religious-freedom-bill-criticized-as-anti-gay/?utm_term=.d0cd66fb8ab4. The Georgia bill, if it had become law, would only apply to "ministers of the gospel or clerics or religious practitioners ordained or authorized to solemnize marriages. . . ." It would not have provided protection to a state employee, like Kim Davis.

Title VII already contains a "ministerial exception" which the Supreme Court has interpreted to allow religious institutions absolute freedom to decide whom to employ as ministers without judicial oversight. In a 2012 decision under Title VII, the Supreme Court ruled that the ministerial exception applies to school teachers employed by a religious institution. *See Hosanna-Tabor Evangelical Lutheran School v. EEOC,* 565 U.S. 171 (2012). On July 9, 2021, by a vote of 7 to 3, the Seventh Circuit ruled that the ministerial exception gives churches total immunity from hostile environment claims by their ministerial employees. *See Demkovich v. St. Andrew the Apostle Parish,* 3 F.4th 968 (7th Cir. 2021). The *en banc* decision had overturned a lower court decision in favor of plaintiff Sandor Demkovich, who was the Music and Choir Director and Organist at St. Andrew the Apostle Parish. She was fired after informing his employer that he planned to marry his male partner.

§ 9.7 RELIGIOUS REFUSAL LAWS: NORTH CAROLINA AND UTAH

North Carolina, Utah and Mississippi have passed religious refusal laws. In North Carolina, the assistant register of deeds and deputy register of deeds have the right to recuse themselves from issuing marriage licenses but the register of deeds has the responsibility to ensure that licenses are still issued. N.C. Gen. Stat. Ann. § 51–5.5(b) (LexisNexis 2015). In Utah, the county clerk must name a designee if he or she is unwilling to solemnize a legal marriage. Utah Code Ann. § 17–20–4(2) (LexisNexis Supp. 2016). On April 5, 2016, Mississippi enacted House Bill 1523, the "Protecting Freedom of Conscience from Government Discrimination Act." It was supposed to go into effect on July 1, 2016.

Section 3(8)(a) of House Bill 1523 states:

> Any person employed or acting on behalf of the state government who has authority to authorize or license marriages, including, but not limited to, clerks, registers of deeds or their

> deputies, may seek recusal from authorizing or licensing lawful marriages based upon or in a manner consistent with a sincerely held religious belief or moral conviction described in Section 2 of this act. Any person making such recusal shall provide prior written notice to the State Registrar of Vital Records who shall keep a record of such recusal, and the state government shall not take any discriminatory action against that person wholly or partially on the basis of such recusal. The person who is recusing himself or herself shall take all necessary steps to ensure that the authorization and licensing of any legally valid marriage is not impeded or delayed as a result of any recusal.

H.R. 1523, 2016 Reg. Sess., § 3(8)(a) (Miss. 2016).

§ 9.8 RELIGIOUS REFUSAL LAWS: MISSISSIPPI

In the wake of the *Obergefell* decision, *see Obergefell v. Hodges*, 576 U.S. 644 (2015) (discussed in *Nutshell* § 5.6), the Mississippi legislature enacted House Bill 1523, called the "Protecting Freedom of Conscience from Government Discrimination Act." The Governor signed it into law on April 5, 2016; it was scheduled to go into effect on July 1, 2016.

This law was very broad-reaching and protected private individuals and state employees from a variety of adverse actions that could stem from them acting consistently with what they claim to be their "sincerely held religious belief or moral conviction."

The passage of this law resulted in two lawsuits, which were decided within days of each other.

The first lawsuit contested one section of the law (§ 3(8))—the right of clerks not to issue marriage certificates to same-sex couples. *See Campaign for S. Equal. v. Bryant*, 197 F. Supp.3d 905 (S.D. Miss. 2016). The judge overseeing this case (Judge Carlton Reeves) is the judge who was already responsible for enforcing the *Obergefell* decision in Mississippi. *See generally Campaign for S. Equal. v. Bryant*, 791 F.3d 625, 627 (5th Cir. 2015) (returning case to district court with instructions for the judge to "act expeditiously on remand and .... enter final judgment"). After House Bill 1523 became law, the plaintiffs sought an amended permanent injunction to ensure that compliance with House Bill 1523 would not violate their right to marry under *Obergefell*. They requested that the state's registrar provide them with (1) copies of recusal requests, (2) post recusal requests prominently on the state's website, and (3) require recusing individuals to cease issuing marriage licenses to opposite-sex couples as well. *Id.* at 911. While not immediately granting the specific relief requested by the plaintiffs, the judge did agree to reopen the permanent injunction so that the parties can confer to make sure that House Bill 1523 does not result in circumventing the *Obergefell* injunction. *Id.* at 917.

The second legal challenge, which was consolidated into a case also before Judge Reeves, constituted a broader challenge to House Bill 1523. *See Barber v. Bryant*, 193 F. Supp.3d 677 (S.D. Miss.

2016). This lawsuit challenged many other provisions of the statute, which included:

- Protection from discrimination from the state due to a refusal of a *religious organization* to solemnize a wedding, fail to hire, fail to sell or rent housing, or failure to provide adoptive or foster care services due to a sincerely held religious belief or moral conviction
- Protection from discrimination from the state to a person who is an adoptive or foster parent who seeks to raise a child in a manner consistent with the person's sincerely held religious belief or moral conviction
- Protection from discrimination from the state to a person who declines to participate in the provision of medical treatment or counseling regarding gender identity on the basis of religious belief or moral conviction except this provision "shall not be construed to allow any person to deny visitation, recognition of a designated representative for health care decision-making, or emergency medical treatment necessary to cure an illness or injury was required by law
- Protection from discrimination for a private person's refusal to provide marriage-related services, accommodations, facilities or goods such as photography, floral arrangements or cake or pastry artistry on the basis of sincerely held religious belief or moral conviction

- Protection from discrimination for a private person's establishment of sex-specific standards of policies regarding "employee or student dress or grooming, or concerning access to restrooms, spas, baths, showers, dressing rooms, locker rooms, or other intimate facilities or settings, based upon or in a manner consistent with a sincerely held religious belief or moral conviction"
- Protection from discrimination for a state employee who expresses his or her religion belief or moral conviction, including workplace speech that "is consistent with the time, place, manner and frequency of any other expression of a religious, political, or moral belief or conviction allowed"
- Provides government employees to authority to recuse themselves from issuing marriage licenses if doing so would conflict their religious belief or moral conviction.

In this case, the LGBTQ+ plaintiffs argued that the state statute constituted an unconstitutional establishment of religion and denial of equal protection in violation of the Fourteenth Amendment.

Although the state of Mississippi does not have an LGBTQ+ anti-discrimination statute, some cities and universities have such policies. The plaintiffs, therefore, argued that they would lose their protection from certain anti-discrimination policies if this law were to go into effect. Citing *Romer v. Evans*,

517 U.S. 620 (1996), the court found that this statute was enacted in direct response to *Obergefell* and "condones discrimination against the LGBT community, but in its simplest terms it denies LGBT citizens equal protection under the law." *Id.* at 700.

With respect to the Establishment Clause, the court found that House Bill 1523 "establishes an official preference for certain religious beliefs over others." *Id.* at 716. It drew that conclusion because House Bill 1523 specifically said it was seeking to protect three particular religious beliefs or moral convictions: "(a) Marriage is or should be recognized as the union of one man and one woman; (b) Sexual relations are properly reserved to such a marriage; and (c) Male (man) or female (woman) refer to an individual's immutable biological sex as objectively determined by anatomy and genetics at time of birth." *Id.* at 694 (citing H.R. 1523, 2016 Reg. Sess., § 2 (Miss. 2016)). Because the district court found that the law favored certain denominations, it was subject to strict scrutiny and found not to pass muster under that rigorous test.

Further, the district court found that the statute violated the Establishment Clause because "its broad religious exemption comes at the expense of other citizens." *Id.* at 721. "The bill gives persons with § 2 beliefs an absolute right to refuse service to LGBT citizens without regard for the impact on their employer, coworkers, or those being denied service." *Id.* at 721.

After examining the legal principles for consideration of a preliminary injunction, the district court judge enjoined the enforcement of House Bill 1523. The decision was entered on June 30, 2016, the day before the statute was to go into effect on July 1, 2016.

The state appealed this decision to the Fifth Circuit. The Fifth Circuit reversed the injunction and dismissed the case, finding that the plaintiffs failed to demonstrate standing and an injury-in-fact. *See Barber v. Bryant,* 860 F.3d 345 (5th Cir. 2017). On January 18, 2018, the Supreme Court denied a petition for certiorari, leaving House Bill 1523 in effect. *See Barber v. Bryant,* 583 U.S. 1054 (2018).

INDEX

References are to Sections